HOW
TO
BUY
YOUR
HOME

...and do it right

SUE BECK

Real Estate
Education Company
a division of Dearborn Financial Publishing, Inc.

While a great deal of care has been taken to provide accurate and current information, the ideas, suggestions, general principles and conclusions presented in this text are subject to local, state and federal laws and regulations, court cases and any revisions of the same. The reader is thus urged to consult legal counsel regarding any points of law—this publication should not be used as a substitute for competent legal advice.

Published by Dearborn Financial Publishing, Inc.

Kathleen A. Welton, Publisher
Patrick J. Hogan, Acquisitions Editor
Karen A. Christensen, Associate Editor
Jack L. Kiburz, Senior Project Editor

Printed in the United States of America
94 95 10 9 8 7 6 5 4

Library of Congress Cataloging-in-Publication Data

Beck, Sue.
    How to buy your home--and do it right / by Sue Beck.
        256p.   cm.
    ISBN 0-79310-494-7 (pbk.) : $14.95
    1. House buying.   I. Title.
HD1379.B385   1993
643'.12--dc20   92-31420
                                            CIP

TO MY HUSBAND AND CHILDREN

Dil, Barb, Bev, Jean, John and Andy

and the success of all our home-buying experiences

Table of Contents

III
MONEY LENDERS AND THEIR LOANS

IV
HOME-BUYING STRATEGIES

V
THE SUCCESSFUL HOME HUNT

VI
FROM CONTRACT TO CLOSING

VII
MOVING AND SETTLING IN

Introduction

Your home is the most important purchase you can make. Unfortunately, finding and buying that home is often a bewildering and frustrating experience. From the moment you first consider buying your home until the day you move in, you will have to make many decisions: What features do you want in a home? Which location should you choose? How much can you afford to pay? Which home will be a wise investment? How will you finance your home? What should be included in the contract? What about appraisals, title insurance and warranties? What is involved in closing?

This book was written to simplify the entire home-buying process—to offer first-time and repeat homebuyers the help they need. Buying your home is time-consuming and complicated, but it also can be an enjoyable and rewarding experience if you know what to expect and what your options are *before* you search for the perfect home.

The book is divided into seven parts, each dealing with a particular phase of the home-buying process. The first part will help you define the life-style you want and determine which features in a home will complement that life-style. It will also help you decide how much you should spend for your home. (You must be able to afford your home—and continue to afford it as long as you own it.) If you neglect this essential part of the home-buying process, you may find yourself the owner of a home that dictates, rather than enhances, your life-style.

The many choices you have when selecting a home are pointed out in Part II. The advantages, disadvantages and special concerns of each type of home—house, condominium, townhouse, and duplex—are discussed. Part III acquaints you with the various lenders and types of loans. Even though buying a home is expensive, you can avoid excessive costs. The Loan Profile provides an easy and practical method for understanding and comparing the many financing options.

Next, it is necessary to plan a home-buying strategy that will fit your unique situation and assure you the most benefits both now and in the future. Your immediate and long-range goals, the money you have to spend, your tax situation and the length of time you plan to own the property are just some of the considerations. Information and suggestions for solving many special home-buying problems are in Part IV.

Part V will help you locate that "just right" home. The key to finding the right home is to first find the right REALTOR® and understand what you can expect from the buyer-REALTOR® relationship. Guidelines are given for inspecting the property, writing the purchase offer and negotiating a favorable contract.

Part VI deals with all the concerns from the time the contract is finalized until you take title to your new home. Once you become familiar with each document and its purpose, the real estate transaction will seem less complex; you may look forward with confidence to a successful closing.

The last part of the book will help you move and settle into your new home. Moving really can be easier if you plan ahead and begin to take care of the many details as soon as you select the home. The best ideas, tips and suggestions from many others who have moved are presented to you here. Setting up a simple, effective filing system is the final step in the home-buying process. Information concerning tax deductions and credits, capital improvements and capital gains will help you take advantage of all the tax benefits you are entitled to when you purchase your home, while you own it, and later, when you sell it.

It is recommended that you read through the entire book rather quickly the first time, skipping only those chapters that do not apply to you. This will give you an overview of the entire home-buying process. Then, reread the book more slowly, applying the information and suggestions to your particular situation. While you are buying your home you can refer back to the book for specific information. Amortization factors and a glossary of real estate terms appear at the end of the book for easy reference.

I hope this book will help you find the right home and buy it in the right way. Your comments and suggestions are most welcome.

I
A WINNING BEGINNING

1. Owning Your Home Can Be Good for You

It will be your home; always keep this in mind when you look for a home to buy. Your home will affect your life daily. Your home will be the place where you live, spend time, leave from for work or school or shopping and return to at the end of the day. If you have a family, you will be together in your home. If you have children, they will grow up in your home. For each of us, our home really is "where the heart is."

Perhaps the greatest advantage to home ownership is the tremendous satisfaction that comes from saying, "This is mine. I own it." Pride of ownership is a real benefit. The home you choose, plus the way you decorate it, improve it and care for it, reflects your personality. For many people, feelings of security, contentment and well-being are associated with home ownership. When you own your home, no one can tell you to move. Instead, you can live in your home as long as you want and then you may decide what to do with your home—rent it, sell it or even give it away.

Owning your home gives you clout, both economic and political. As soon as you own your home, you have credit, even if you had no credit rating before. At times, community issues are decided only by homeowner vote. Home ownership is also good business. Your home provides you and your family with shelter, a basic necessity. If you do not own your home, you must pay for some other type of shelter and do not receive the tax and investment benefits that come with home ownership.

As an investment, your own home is at the top of the list. You can buy a home worth many thousands of dollars for a small initial amount of money and stretch out the payments over many years. Your home may also appreciate in value. In the 1970s, homes increased in value at a greater rate than almost any other investment. While home prices may never go up that fast again, it is reasonable to expect that appreciation of a well-cared-for home in a good location will at least keep up with inflation. In some areas of the country, where the demand for housing is much greater than the available supply, prices may increase much faster.

To understand the benefits of appreciation, remember that appreciation is based on the original purchase price, not the small investment made for the down payment and closing costs. For instance, if you make a down payment of $10,000 to buy a $100,000 home, and a year later your home is worth $105,000, you have a 5 percent appreciation in the value of your home. However, you have a 50 percent return on your investment because your $10,000 has increased to $15,000 equity.

Homeowners receive substantial tax benefits. The interest portion of each monthly payment, as well as the property tax you pay each year, are deductible on your federal income tax return. They also may be deductible on your state income tax return. When you sell your home, the tax on the profit you realize may be postponed and perhaps avoided entirely if you follow certain IRS guidelines. Even more benefits may be available in the future. Future laws may allow wage earners to save money, tax-free, when the money will be used for the down payment or for equity payments on their homes. All of these tax benefits actually lower the cost of owning your home.

2. Choose Your Own Life-Style

Few things have a greater effect on your day-to-day living than your home, so it is important that you find a home that is "just right." Don't let the many home-buying choices frighten you away from buying a home and don't be forced into a situation that is not in your best interest. Remember, it is you who will live in the home you buy, so don't let someone else make the decision for you. Don't buy the house your parents, friends or boss think you should have. Decide which features you want in a home and then shop around to find a home that will satisfy your needs and desires.

Some people believe they will never be able to afford their dream home, so they buy any home that is cheap. Although it is better to buy a less expensive home than none at all, even inexpensive homes offer many features and many options, enabling you to buy a home that will enhance your life-style instead of determining it.

Making the right home-buying decision won't be as difficult if you follow a tried-and-true formula: Start at the beginning and take it one step at a time. First, decide what kind of life-style you want. To find the home that will enhance your life-style, you must be able to define your life-style. How do you want to live? How do you want to spend your time and money? What things do you want to do? If you have never made lists before, now is a good time to start.

What Do You Like To Do?

Begin the home-buying process by thinking about all the things you like to do and making a list of these things. Write down everything you like to do. This list is very important! Put down as many things as you can think of now, then add to the list as more ideas occur to you. List the things you like to do outdoors and the things you like to do indoors. List the everyday things you like to do around the house. List the activities you like to do by yourself, with others, after work, on weekends, even when you are on vacation. Make your list as long as necessary. I suggest that you also add a special "someday" section to your list—the special things you dream about doing "someday."

Now go back over the list and make notations describing the features in a home that are needed so you can enjoy each activity. Some of the things on your list, such as playing golf, going skiing or taking a vacation, you will do away from home. These things will require time and money. Estimate the amount of time and money you will need and note it after the item.

What Don't You Want To Do?

Now, make a second list of the chores and tasks you do not like to do. Put a big "X" next to everything on this list you really dislike—even hate—to do. When you have finished, examine the second list and look for ways to eliminate the items marked with an "X." For example, if mowing the yard and shoveling snow are "Xed," you may want to consider a home without a yard to maintain, such as a condominium or townhouse. Or you could decide to budget enough money to hire a neighbor's youngster or a lawn service to do the yard work and shovel the snow. A third choice might be a house with a small, easy-to-maintain yard and a short driveway so snow shoveling is less of a concern. As you can see, there is usually more than one solution to every problem.

Think carefully about how you want to live and how you want to spend your time and money. Both lists—the things you like to do and the things you dislike doing—are very important. If you can picture the life-style you want, it will help you make the right home-buying decisions.

Your "Just Right" Home

Finally, make a third list. If you are buying a family home, this list should be prepared by the whole family. Divide the sheet of paper in half so you have two columns. In the first column, list each feature you would like in your new home. List each room, the garage or carport, and then such things as a dishwasher, fireplace, pantry, air conditioning, wet bar, patio, fenced yard, etc. Also put down such things as size of yard, type of neighborhood, preferred architectural style and proximity to work, schools and recreational facilities. List everything that is important to you.

Next, after each item in the first column, write in the second column a comment about why this feature is wanted or needed, as well as any special requirements. Now go one step further and prioritize the features you want. At the very least, note all the features that are absolutely necessary; these could be marked "A." Other very desirable, but not absolutely essential, features could be marked "B." The remaining features on the list would be appreciated, but are not nearly as crucial as the others. Of course, the list can always be added to and changed. This list will be invaluable later when you discuss your home requirements with your REALTOR®.

Buying a new home gives you the opportunity to have the life-style you want. With your comprehensive lists, you will be better prepared to find the home that will allow you to live the way you choose. Determine what is important to you, and then consider financial matters. You may not be able to afford your ideal home, or you may choose to spend some of your money on things other than your home. Your lists will help you determine what decisions to make so that you get what you want, or at least make the trade-offs that are best for you.

A wide variety of housing choices awaits you. You will have the opportunity to shop around and consider the many options. Even if you seem to have conflicting needs, it may be possible to find a home that satisfies most of them. For example, one couple really loved older neighborhoods, but thought they had to buy in a suburban area where prices were lower. Instead, they found an elegant old mansion that had been remodeled into lovely and affordable condominiums.

Here are a few creative housing choices that have worked for others. Maybe they will give you some ideas:

- An easy-care townhouse with community recreational facilities for a large, active family

- A close-in building site with a south exposure for a new solar house

- A Victorian duplex, just right for treasured antiques, provides extra income and tax shelter

- An older bungalow in need of tender loving care for a young couple with more time, energy and enthusiasm than money

3. Bring Your Financial Picture into Focus

Since buying a home involves a large monetary commitment, it is necessary to have a clear and complete picture of your financial situation. Now, before you choose your home, is the time for a money-planning session. If you have a family, involve each member in the discussion.

Your Financial Picture

The first step is to determine your financial net worth. This requires an inventory of what you own (your assets) and what you owe (your liabilities).

Assets. Everything you own that has either monetary or exchange value is an asset and should be listed. Put a dollar amount after each item, using present value (what it could be sold for today). Estimate if necessary. Your assets include:

- *Cash.* Cash on hand, bank accounts, money market funds

- *Liquid investments.* Investments that can be readily converted to cash, such as stocks, bonds, mutual funds, treasury securities, cash value of life insurance policies, etc.

- *Nonliquid assets.* Investments that cannot be converted to cash immediately, or that will require paying a penalty or accepting less than face value. These include long-term CDs, IRAs, Keoghs, some employee retirement and/or savings plans, shares in limited partnerships, long-term loans to others, etc.

- *Personal property.* Cars, recreational vehicles and equipment, household furnishings, tools, clothing, furs, jewelry, art, antiques, collections, etc.

- *Real property.* Your home, rental property, other real estate

Liabilities. Your debts are liabilities. List all your debts and the amount owed. The total is the amount of money you would need to completely pay off all your debts, except monthly expenses, such as utilities and food costs. Liabilities are:

- *Loans.* Car, boat and camper loans, furniture and appliance loans, education loans, vacation loans, other installment loans, loans against life insurance policies, margin accounts

- *Unpaid bills.* Taxes, charge account and credit card balances, past due alimony and/or child support payments, doctor and dentist bills, all other unpaid bills

- *Mortgages.* Home, rental property, other mortgage loans

Subtract your total liabilities from your total assets and you will have your financial net worth, a picture of your financial situation today. Use this financial statement to plan for next year, five years from now and ten years from now. Take into account all your strengths and resources. Also consider your responsibilities, expectations and wishes. Set financial goals and develop a program to attain them. Achieving your goals may mean making some changes in your shopping patterns, buying habits, use of credit and/or choice of investments. It may mean changing your entire atittude toward money.

Take Charge of Your Spending

Often we give little thought to where our money goes or what we really get for it. When our money won't buy all the things we need or want, we feel very frustrated. The trick is to make money work for *you*. Think of money in simple terms: it is just a medium of exchange—something to trade for something else you want. Money's importance and value can be measured only by what you can exchange it for. Money will give you the greatest benefits if you exchange it for the things you really want.

The most practical way of assuring that you will get the greatest value from your money is to work out a money spending plan, a budget. Developing a good budget takes time and thought. You must review all your sources of income and plan how you want to spend your money. The budget will help you set priorities and allocate funds, not only for necessities, but for those special extras you would like to have. More importantly, it will help you determine how much of your money you want to spend for your home initially and how large a payment you wish to make each month.

Income. Begin by listing each source of income, how often it is received and what the gross and net amounts are. (Budget forms are available at office supply stores, or you can make up your own.) The total annual gross income tells how much money is expected for the entire year before anything is taken out. The monthly net income tells how much is actually available after deductions each month. In addition to salaries and wages, include as income commissions: bonuses and tips; interest payments, dividends and royalties; alimony, separate maintenance and child support payments; disability, retirement, annuity, pension and social security payments; and educational benefits. Even the extra money received from an occasional special job may be included. (The income figures used in your budget will not necessarily be the same as those used on your tax statement or for loan qualifying.)

Expenses. The second part of your budget is an estimate of expenses and purchases, which should be figured on a monthly basis. A review of all receipts, cancelled checks and charge card statements for the past year will help you determine how you have been spending your money. However, if you have used cash for many purchases and you can't recall the items or amounts, you may need to keep close track of all your spending for the next few weeks. Otherwise, you won't be able to set up a realistic budget.

Start by separating expenses and purchases into large categories, and use as many subheadings as necessary. Some categories that may fit your special situation are:

- *Savings and investments*

- *Taxes.* Federal, state, local, FICA

- *Housing.* Mortgage payment, taxes, insurance, maintenance fee (if your home is part of a complex), utilities, maintenance and repair

- *Food.* Supermarket purchases, meals away from home, school lunches

- *Medical and dental.* Insurance premium(s), doctor bills, dentist bills, medication

- *Life insurance*

- *Transportation.* Car payment(s), car insurance, taxes and license, gas, maintenance and repair, public transportation

- *Clothing*

- *Home furnishings*

- *Education.* Tuition, books and supplies, preschool and/or day care, magazine subscriptions

- *Recreation, entertainment, vacation*

- *Alimony, separate maintenance, child support*

- *Personal accounts, allowances*

- *Miscellaneous spending*

Many expenses, such as utilities, vary each month. But by adding up all the bills for a year and including something extra for inflation, then dividing the amount by 12, you should be able to allocate enough money for each month's bill even though the bill amounts are uneven.

Some expenses are paid every three months, every six months or once a year, such as insurance premiums. If you allocate an amount each month for these expenses, you should have enough money to pay the bills when they are due.

If in the past you have overspent and are faced with monthly payments for charge accounts, credit cards, loans, etc., make arrangements in your budget to repay these debts as soon as possible.

The first and most important item in your budget should be a savings account or an investment. As you pay people each month, don't forget to pay yourself. Invest the money you pay yourself to help you become financially secure. If you have a hard time saving money, ask your bank to automatically transfer an amount out of your checking account and into a savings account each month. Don't spend this money. Don't consider these savings as a fund from which to purchase luxury items. Instead, establish a second savings account for big purchases. As your savings grow, invest the money so that it will grow even faster. Remember that a large portion of your savings may be needed for the initial investment in your new home—one of the best investments you can make! But even after you buy your home, you should continue to set aside a certain amount each month for investment purposes.

As you plan your budget, add up the amount you are now paying for income tax—federal, state and local. Depending on how you buy your home, you should be able to reduce your total income taxes. Estimate the tax savings you expect (work through Form 1040, if necessary), and after closing, adjust your budget using the actual figures. Calculate what is being taken for FICA (social security) and how many months it will be deducted from your paycheck. If you "contribute" the maximum amount before the end of the year, you can allocate this money for another purpose.

Finally, review each expense item in your budget to determine if you are getting top value for your dollar. Pay particular attention to areas where substantial savings can be realized, such as insurance. Review each policy (medical insurance, auto insurance, homeowner's insurance, condominium insurance, life insurance, etc.) before the renewal date. Will another company give you the same risk protection at a lower rate? Is it practical to increase the deductible amount and pay a lower premium? Could your life insurance be a renewable term policy rather than a more expensive whole life policy? After you have shopped and compared, act. It takes only a few minutes to change a policy and save a substantial amount of money.

Food is another category where you might be able to save some money. A little advance planning—reading the weekly ads for specials, using coupons, choosing generic or store brands over nationally advertised brands when practical—can cut your food bill considerably. When eating away from home, money can be saved by making less expensive choices some of the time.

Before you purchase your new home, housing expenses will present a big budgeting question mark. Without accurate figures for monthly payments, utilities and upkeep, you should allocate one large amount or an approximate range that you can live with for housing expenses. Remember to stay within this amount when you work with your REALTOR® to choose a home.

Your budget should provide each family member with a personal account or an allowance, money each one is free to spend as he or she chooses. Your budget is your own special plan for setting priorities and allocating funds. Use the budget as a guide and tool to help you attain your goals. Change it when necessary to fit your needs. After you have purchased your home, adjust your budget as necessary to fit your new life-style.

II

AN ARRAY OF OPTIONS

4. Home Ownership:
Rights and Restrictions

Now it's time to take a good look at a variety of housing choices. Try to be creative and open-minded as you match your life-style and budget with such an array of housing options. You may be pleasantly surprised to find that your "just right" home is quite different from what you originally expected to buy.

Fee Simple Title

Whichever home you decide on, you will receive full rights of ownership, known as fee simple absolute title. (The exception to this is if you buy a cooperative apartment. Cooperative ownership is explained in Chapter 6.) Fee simple is the highest estate in real property and includes the rights of possession, control, enjoyment and disposition. As the owner, you may use your home yourself, let someone else use it or rent it. You may sell or trade your property, give it away or will it to your heir(s). As the owner, you have an absolute right in the property, subject only to limitations recorded against the property or imposed by government.

Restrictions/Protections

Almost every property has some limitations or restrictions; a better word might be *protections*. For instance, if you are restricted from parking a large dump truck in your driveway, you are also protected from the possibility that your neighbor will do the same.

Restrictions/protections are intended to enhance property and protect value; they are not a problem until you want to do something that is not allowed. If you are planning to use or improve your property in a manner that might be restricted, add this to your list of features (see Chapter 2). It will help your REALTOR® help you find the right home.

Restrictions/protections can take several forms. Zoning regulations, easements, covenants and deed restrictions are some of the most common. The declaration and bylaws for condominium and townhouse complexes also contain restrictions. These will be discussed in Chapter 6.

Be aware of possible restrictions/protections. Will they add to the value of the property or make it unsuitable for your needs?

Zoning Regulations. The local governing authority has a right to make and enforce zoning ordinances. These laws are intended to provide for the orderly growth of a community. They vary greatly from community to community and include a number of rules and regulations. Typical residential zoning allows for one single-family house on one lot. You may not be able to rent out your basement or a portion of your home to an unrelated person while your family is living there. If in the future you want to rent your home, it may have to be rented as a one-family unit.

Zoning laws may also specify where and how you can build on your lot. There are usually setback requirements for buildings. The height and placement of fences are sometimes regulated so they won't detract from the neighborhood. Duplexes, triplexes and fourplexes may be built only on land zoned for this purpose.

You may or may not be able to operate a pre-school, beauty shop, car repair business, cooking school, bookkeeping service or other business out of your home. You will need to find out whether businesses are allowed, and, if so, which types.

The kinds and number of animals you may keep may also be restricted. Horses are allowed only in certain areas. A large number of dogs or cats can be a nuisance for the neighborhood and may not be allowed. Often, typical farm animals are not allowed, either.

If you have a special need, zoning becomes an important factor in selecting your home. Visit the city or county zoning department, ask specific questions and find out exactly what is or is not allowed before you make an offer on a home.

Easements. Most properties have a utility easement, that is, a strip of property that has been made available to utility companies so they can provide water and sewer, gas, electrical, telephone and cable TV service. Because this area may have to be dug up for repairs, you are not allowed to build over it. This may be an important consideration if you are planning to add a garage or a swimming pool. The property survey will show where the utility easement is located.

Sometimes an easement allows others to cross your property or use a part of the property, such as the driveway. The title search will show all recorded easements. If part of the property you are considering has been used by nonowners on a regular basis for a long period of time, but this part does not show as a recorded easement, discuss the situation with your attorney. Find out about potential problems *before* you buy.

Covenants. Covenants most often are additional protections or restrictions placed on properties by the subdivider or developer. They are intended to enhance the appearance and livability of the area and thereby increase the value of the properties. Some things covenants may prohibit or regulate are:

1. Parking trucks, campers, motor homes, trailers, vans, boats, etc., in driveways or on streets of the subdivision

2. Using outdoor clotheslines

3. Keeping animals on the property. The kinds and numbers of animals are often regulated

4. Building certain types of fences

5. Building additions to or changing the appearance of your property without the approval of an architectural committee

When lots in a subdivision are offered for sale, the size and style of the house to be built, and the materials that may be used, are often regulated by covenants. In some areas, covenants are used to protect owners' access to sunlight when the house uses solar energy.

Not all properties have covenants, and sometimes covenants expire after a stated period of time. Since covenants are recorded documents, the title search can determine what covenants are on the property you are considering.

Deed Restrictions. Sometimes restrictions are written into a deed by a previous owner. If these restrictions are not discriminatory, they must be honored. Often they have to do with dividing up a large portion of land or how the land may be used. Deed restrictions will show up in a title search.

5. The Single-Family House: Still the Favorite

"The house I grew up in." "Grandpa's house in the country." "My best friend's house." "Summers at the beach house." "The house on Westwood Drive." "The old farm house." "Our first house." "Our cabin in the mountains." "The house my Dad and Mom helped build."

So many treasured memories include a home. No wonder the single-family house with its own yard is expected to remain the favorite of homebuyers. How fortunate it is that the single-family house comes in such a variety of styles and sizes and locations with every combination of floor plans and features.

If you decide to purchase a single-family house, it is important that you take your time and find one on a lot that is just right for you. You can choose a house with character or one to which you can give character. You can paint, remodel, decorate and fix up your own house the way you want. You can plant trees and shrubbery and flowers around your house. You can put up a fence or tear one down. You can have a playhouse or swimming pool or tennis court or patio deck or all of these. Being able to choose your own special house and then individualize it to meet your needs is a real benefit of home ownership.

The single-family house also gives you security and privacy. A yard surrounding the house adds a place for outdoor enjoyment and a feeling of spaciousness. It also forms a buffer zone between you and your neighbors and makes it easier to have dogs, cats and other pets.

Most homebuyers decide on an attractive, well-cared-for house in an established neighborhood. The look and feel of the neighborhood, as well as the availability of parks, recreational facilities, schools, places of worship, shopping centers, etc., influence their decision. While these resale homes make up the largest share of the housing market, there are alternatives.

Homes in Need of Tender Loving Care

There is a large group of single-family houses that are older and have not been updated recently. Some do not meet building code requirements. Often they are in declining or transitional neighborhoods. The potential livability of these "forgotten" houses can be very great. Many offer the advantages of more living space, a convenient city location and a reasonable cost. Many people now consider these older houses when they look for a home to buy.

Rehabilitation (or rehab) is the word used to describe the remodeling of older properties. The idea is to bring the house up to present standards and still respect the original craftsmanship and design. Some properties have been well cared for and need only minimal work. Other properties need extensive renovation—almost everything short of building a new structural frame. Parts of the old interior often must be removed to replace the worn-out or inadequate plumbing, heating and electrical systems. Many times unexpected treasures are found when a home is renovated. Layers of paint might hide beautiful old woodwork and flooring. A unique fireplace may have been walled off. Built-in cupboards, archways and interesting architectural details become apparent only after the rehab work is under way.

Rehabilitation, however, has its costs as well as its benefits. Consider one of these older houses only if you have the energy, dedication, commitment and financial backing to follow through with the repairs. It may be difficult and expensive to hire competent people to do this type of work for you. You may need to do much of the work yourself.

If you decide to buy a home that needs renovation, do your homework first. Learn about remodeling techniques and the unique problems you may encounter. Talk with other rehabbers, visit neighborhood groups, check with city planning and zoning departments and find a competent REALTOR®. You will need a REALTOR® who knows and appreciates the older neighborhoods you are considering and understands the property values. Choose the neighborhood you want to live in first. Then find a house that is well located within that neighborhood and fits your requirements. Learn everything you can about the property before you commit yourself.

Arranging financing for an older house may be very difficult, but usually is not impossible. There is a nationwide movement to rehabilitate older houses and rescue and revitalize older neighborhoods. Various programs at the local, state and federal levels provide special monies to make financing available. In some areas, local lenders are pooling their resources. For eligible veterans, VA loans are available for properties that need fixing up. FHA 203(k) purchase and rehabilitation loans may be another financing option. REALTORS® who are familiar with older neighborhoods and involved in rehab projects are your best sources of information. City planning offices should also be able to help.

It may take some time and ingenuity to find the right rehab property. You will want one that is well located, in need of repairs that you can manage, but structurally sound. Make a thorough inspection and get complete estimates for the costs of materials and supplies, as well as the time and energy it will take. Use this information when making your offer on the property.

Small Towns and Rural Areas

Small towns all across America are being rediscovered. There is no big city pollution and congestion. Open spaces and a slower pace may give more joy to living. Neighbors often have more time for one another; the small town atmosphere can be much friendlier. A big advantage to a small town is a sense of belonging and being able to help make your community a better place for you and your family to live.

A major consideration of rural living is the availability of water and sanitation disposal systems. A municipal water and sewer system is a real benefit. If you must depend on a well for your water, have the well inspected. The purity of the water (that is, the lack of harmful bacteria) is only one consideration. You will want a complete water analysis to reveal the presence of any harmful chemicals. Also, the depth and capacity of the well, the size of the storage tank, the condition of the pump, etc., should be checked to see that they are satisfactory.

Septic systems are used in many rural areas. If these systems are not properly maintained, they become unusable and must be replaced in another location. Septic systems may also contaminate the water supply. Be sure the septic systems on your property and the land near you will not harm your water supply. A complete septic inspection is advisable. It is best to have a property large enough to install a new septic system if it ever becomes necessary.

Many real estate horror stories are about access problems. Often a building lot, acreage or a lovely home in a rural area or small town is set back from the main road. Access to the property is by a lane or private road across someone else's property. Don't assume you can always use this access.

Also, has anyone else been cutting across the property you are considering? What rights do these people have? A new survey of the property will show recorded easements both for utilities and access to other people. However, if others have been crossing the property for a period of time, they may have certain rights, although unrecorded, because of continued use. Discuss this with the seller but *don't rely* on the word of the seller. *Have your attorney investigate this.*

Does the purchase price of the property you are considering include permanent access rights, giving you a recorded easement? Be sure to purchase title insurance on your property and be sure that the title policy includes title work for and a guarantee of the access rights to your property. See Chapter 41.

Pay special attention to this matter. Because institutional lenders are reluctant to make loans on properties that are not adjacent to a public road, many of these properties are purchased with cash or private financing. The buyer does not have the benefit of an institutional lender looking out for both of their interests.

Financing a home in a small town or rural area may be more difficult than financing a home in a metropolitan area. Smaller banks are sometimes very conservative and lack the resources to meet the needs of a growing area. Big city lenders, on the other hand, are often prevented from financing in rural areas by distance and population requirements. Farmers Home Administration (FmHA) and The Federal Land Bank both provide financing for rural properties. VA loans are available for eligible veterans.

Brand New Homes

Moving into a brand new home is exciting. It's so fresh and clean! Buying a brand new house can also be a very practical and financially sound decision. You may be able to choose your own carpet, countertops and fixtures. Everything—the furnace, the water heater, the roof—is new. Nothing that will cost you extra money should go wrong immediately. New houses, like appliances, also come with warranties.

A new house may also be very energy efficient, no small consideration since utility bills can claim a good portion of your budget. Look for double-glazed or triple-glazed windows, well-insulated ceilings and walls and new appliances designed for lower operating costs. Many houses will have solar features (some may qualify for tax advantages) that may make your home a more pleasant place to live while saving on utilities.

Some special precautions are necessary if you are buying a house that is not yet built or is not completed. First, check the reputation and financial stability of the builder/developer. Is the builder a member of the local and state chapters of the National Association of Home Builders? Look at other homes built by the company and talk to the owners to see if they are satisfied. Were problems taken care of promptly? Would they buy another home built by the same builder?

Use the show homes to determine whether the floor plan, room sizes and special features fit your needs. However, realize that the decorating in the show models is a sales tool. Ask to see the plan you choose in a plain, undecorated version so you can more easily judge the quality of workmanship and materials used in the house you are considering.

If you cannot actually see a house like the one you are going to have built, be sure you understand the blueprints. Sit down with the builder and go over the details of the house; know exactly what is included in the agreed-upon price. In every instance, you should have a list of the features and the make and model number of the furnace, hot water heater, kitchen appliances, etc. You should also know the type and/or grade of carpet, quality of floor coverings, countertops, kitchen cabinets, windows and doors, etc. All of this information should be in writing and should be made part of the purchase contract. The builder should not be allowed to make substitutions without your permission. At the time you sign the contract, schedule a series of meetings with the builder so that he or she can keep you informed of the progress of your house and you will have the opportunity to discuss any necessary revisions or substitutions.

A final inspection of every new house should take place before closing. Don't be pushed into closing before the home is finished. Give the builder time to complete all the work and make any necessary changes or repairs before you close and take possession. It will be less of an inconvenience for you, and the builder will be more motivated to complete the job if he or she doesn't get paid until it is finished.

If only minor problems remain and you feel you must close and move into your new home, be sure you make a list of the work to be completed and have the builder sign it. If you suspect the builder might not immediately complete the work to your satisfaction, discuss with your REALTOR® and/or attorney the possibility of placing a sum of money in escrow until the work is completed.

Most new houses are in developments of either one or more builders. How will the area look when you take possession of your new home? Sometimes the fences and sprinkling systems are in place, the sod is laid and the whole neighborhood looks almost lived in before the first home is occupied. In other areas, the builder will grade the lot area but it is the new owner's responsibility to put in the yard, landscaping and fences. By doing much of the work themselves, the new homeowners can add to the value of the property immediately. However, if you want to fence your yard, but your neighbor does not want to spend the money for his or her share of the fence, you must pay for it all yourself or wait until the neighbor is ready. If one homeowner in the area does not choose to put in a yard right away, it can detract from the appearance of the entire neighborhood.

Sometimes lots are sold in an area and the owners make arrangements to have the homes built at a later date. If you are among the first homeowners in an area, be prepared to put up with weedy vacant lots and blowing dirt. It may be months or even years before all the houses are finished.

Attractive financing is often available for new houses in developments. As part of the marketing plan, the builder may offer loans at below-market interest rates and/or pay a large portion of the closing costs. Other loans offered by builders are designed to look great in the Sunday newspaper advertisements, but when the full story is revealed in the mortgage documents, the financing plans may not be in the buyer's best interest. Be sure you do a complete Loan Profile of the loans being offered so you know exactly what you are getting (see Chapter 10).

Build-It-Yourself Homes

The build-your-own-home movement is growing every year as many people realize they can beat the rising cost of home construction by being their own builder. For those who choose this method of acquiring a new home, many kinds of help are available—books and instruction manuals, adult education classes in the building trades, building supply businesses with consulting departments and a wide range of companies that provide precut house packages. Even with all this assistance, building your own home is not easy or possible for everyone. It is not a particularly good way to save money, even if you are competent and have worked in the home building trades. For the great majority of homebuyers, the purchase of an existing house or one from a builder is a much better choice.

If you are sure you can build your own house, do your homework first so you realize what you are getting into. To start with, you need a lot with the proper zoning. In most areas your building plans must be approved by the local building authority, and you will need a building permit or series of permits. You must arrange for water, waste disposal, electricity, heating fuel and telephone service. Don't just assume you can connect into a water and sewer system or drill your own well and install a septic system. Be sure you have the necessary permissions and reliable cost estimates. A competent attorney can help you avoid legal problems.

Many times the homeowner/builder acts as the general contractor and does only the jobs at which he or she is competent, contracting out the other work. The value of the finished home depends to a great extent on the quality of the workmanship. Unless you can do the work in a professional manner, hire someone who can and allow ample time to complete your home.

Financing a build-it-yourself house may take some ingenuity. It is best if you own your lot free and clear before you start to build. If this is not possible, perhaps you can get the owner of the lot you want to buy to carry the financing for you. Be sure you have a subordination clause in your contract to purchase the lot; this clause will subordinate the interest of the investor holding the note on the lot to the interest of the investor providing the financing for the improvements.

Many building supply companies and companies that sell precut home packages will finance the building materials and supplies for you.

Or you may prefer to obtain a construction loan from a bank. These are usually short-term loans that cover the cost of materials and subcontractors' labor charges. In either case, you probably will be unable to finance materials and/or labor charges unless the loan for these can be a first mortgage.

When the house is completed, it may be possible to have it appraised in order to obtain long-term, permanent financing. The money from this loan may be used to pay off the construction loan and lot loan. You might even end up with some money in your pocket. Be sure to look into the possibility of permanent financing *before* you start your project. Find out which regulations you must meet. Both VA and FHA will want to see your plans and make inspections during the construction. If necessary, buy a loan commitment as protection against a changing money market.

Despite all the hard work, drawbacks and problems, many families have built their own houses—lovely homes that complement their lifestyles and have a value far greater than the actual dollar cost.

Factory-Built Houses

Another alternative available to homebuyers in many areas is a house built in a factory and then moved to a permanent site. Unlike some of the prefabs of the 1950s, many of today's factory-built houses are constructed with top-quality materials and workmanship. The increased use of factory-built housing is one of the most exciting trends in the housing industry today.

Often the homes are built inside a factory in large sections. Each section is then transported by truck to the housing site and placed on a basement or foundation. The sections are joined together and final hookups for heating/air conditioning, electrical and plumbing systems are completed. A wide variety of home styles, floor plans, features (fireplaces are common) and materials are available. You can order a completely finished house or complete some of the work yourself.

Building a house inside a factory has many advantages:

1. Weather does not delay construction and the factory can operate around the clock, if necessary.

2. A permanent construction crew can be employed and work can be scheduled more efficiently.

3. Materials can be ordered in quantity and are available when needed.

4. Quality of materials and workmanship can be controlled more effectively.

5. Losses due to theft and vandalism are minimal.

6. Because most houses are sold before they are built and the construction time is shorter, construction finance charges are kept to a minimum.

All these advantages often add up to a quality home, available sooner, and at a lower price than a house built entirely at the housing site. These advantages more than offset the transportation and setup costs.

Factory-built houses are often purchased by individual homebuyers, then permanently placed on their own lots. Sometimes entire subdivisions of houses are built in a factory and then trucked to the site.

Many financing options are available for high-quality, factory-built houses that are permanently affixed to land owned by the borrower.

6. Condominiums and Cooperatives: Work-Free, Worry-Free Living

Millions of homeowners are enjoying the many advantages of living in a condominium or a cooperative. It's a work-free, worry-free life-style: no big yard to take care of, no snow to shovel, no outside painting and no other maintenance chores. Often many amenities are available, such as a swimming pool, tennis courts, a clubhouse or even a golf course. More living space at a lower cost is an attractive advantage. Also, many complexes offer special security provisions so owners can take long trips or stay at home alone without being concerned about intruders. A condominium or a cooperative could be just the home for you.

Condominiums and cooperatives are alike in most ways with one important difference: The way title to the property is taken. Ownership of a cooperative will be discussed after the section on condominium ownership.

Condominium Ownership

What are you buying when you buy a condominium? You are buying with fee simple title your apartment home and a part of the entire condominium complex. You receive a deed, a title insurance policy, the tax advantages and all the other benefits of home ownership, just as if you bought a single-family house.

A condominium is a certain described amount of **air space** that constitutes a living unit. Everything within the outside walls and the floor and ceiling of your unit is yours. This includes the interior walls and partitions, the carpet and wall coverings and all fixtures within your air space.

Condominium ownership also includes an undivided interest in all the common elements, that is, the building or buildings that make up the complex (except for the air spaces that make up the individual units), the condominium grounds, the parking areas, the swimming pool, clubhouse, tennis courts and everything else that may be part of the condominium complex.

Because each home is part of a large complex, special condominium documents are necessary and usually required by law. These documents—the declaration, the bylaws and the budget—will give you important information concerning rights and responsibilities of condominium ownership.

The **declaration**, or master deed, is the main condominium document that creates the terms and conditions of ownership. The "decs," as it is often called, defines the legal rights and obligations of the owners, describes the entire complex and each unit in it, designates areas of general use and areas of limited use and provides for the homeowners' association. In some states, the declaration is known as the condominium covenants, conditions and restrictions, or CC&Rs.

Each declaration is unique; it is written to fit the special needs of the condominium complex and it is often more than thirty pages in length. Some of the things you will find described in the declaration are:

- Your share of ownership of the common elements

- Your nonoptional membership in the homeowners' association

- Your voting rights

- Procedures for determining fees

- Procedures invoked if the maintenance fee is not paid

- Permissible occupants and uses of the unit

- Any restrictions on renting or selling your unit

- Ownership limitations (i.e., whether the condominium owners hold fee simple title to the entire complex or if some of the land or amenities are leased)

The **bylaws of the homeowners' association** are the written rules and regulations that govern the activities of the members. They also provide for the administration and maintenance of the entire complex. The bylaws may be amended and restrictions may be added or dropped by a vote of the entire association.

Every homeowners' association also has a **budget** that gives an estimate of expenses and required revenue. The monthly maintenance fee is assessed according to the method set forth in the declaration so that each homeowner pays his or her share of the expenses.

Cooperative Ownership

When you buy a cooperative you receive a stock certificate issued by a corporation rather than fee simple title to your own unit. A corporation actually owns the cooperative housing complex. As a stockholder you have the right to occupy an apartment and participate in the operation of the corporation as an elected member of the governing board or as a voter. The corporation itself holds title to the complex and is directly responsible for the mortgage, taxes and operating and maintenance expenses. Your responsibilities and benefits depend on how the corporation is set up, the terms of your proprietary lease with the corporation and the laws of the state in which the cooperative is located.

Financing for a cooperative is different from that for a condominium because you cannot mortgage your individual unit. However, in many cases you may use your stock certificate as collateral for a loan to finance the stock purchase. If you plan to buy a cooperative apartment, you will need an experienced sales agent who is qualified to handle the purchase. Be sure you understand exactly what you are buying and the benefits and risks involved.

The rest of this chapter has information that applies to buying a home in a complex, whether the complex is a cooperative or a condominium. While the word condominium is used throughout, everything that is said may also apply to cooperatives.

Find the Right Condominium Complex for You

Condominiums come in an almost infinite variety. When describing them, however, they can be grouped into three categories: High-rise, low-rise and townhouse-style. High-rise condominiums are homes in tall buildings that require elevators. Several hundred living units may be in a single building. Low-rise condominiums are in buildings of one, two or three stories. Sometimes main entrances in each building serve a number of individual homes; each condominium has its own private entrance off a hall or stairway. In other complexes, each condominium has its own private outside entrance with outside stairways serving the homes that are not on ground level.

Townhouse-style condominiums most closely resemble the single-family house. They are built in rows or clusters and share common walls, but the homes are not stacked on top of each other. Each has a private ground-level entrance and many have attached garages or carports. Many homes have basements and/or second floors.

The **condominium conversion** is a rental apartment complex that has become a condominium complex. The conversion process is essentially a change of ownership. Originally the owner of the entire apartment complex rented units to many tenants. During the conversion each apartment became a condominium and was sold as a separate home; the complex now has many owners. The converted complex can be a high-rise, a low-rise or townhouse-style.

It is more difficult and complicated to find the right condominium than it is to find a single-family house. Consider each of the following before committing yourself to a particular condominium complex.

Location Is a Top Priority

Location is always important in choosing real estate, but it is especially important when deciding on a condominium complex. Look for a complex that is:

- Next to or near a park, golf course, lake or open space area

- Adjoining or near a neighborhood of single-family houses

- In an area of other owner-occupied complexes rather than rental complexes

- In an area of compatible architectural styles

- Away from major highways or with a barrier between the complex and the roadway

- Not in a commercial or an industrial area

With the help of your REALTOR®, list all the condominium complexes in your price range and within the area you wish to live. Visit and gather information on the three or four most attractive complexes.

The location of your home within the complex is also important. Decide whether you prefer to be near or away from the recreational facilities. Some people feel a condominium overlooking the pool or tennis courts is in a prime location. Others would rather not be near any recreational facilities. What is your preference? Be aware of the direction your home will face. Do you enjoy the morning sun or the afternoon sun? Will the patio be hot or shaded? Check the views from your windows. Is this the view you want to see every day?

Decide whether being upstairs is an advantage or a disadvantage. In a low-rise complex many people prefer the top floor; it gives a better view and no one lives above you. However, carrying things up stairs can be difficult. If you are a parent, how do you get a child, stroller and groceries up those stairs?

Know What You Are Buying

Tour the entire complex so you know what amenities are included and the condition of the property. Take the time to read and understand the declaration and the bylaws. Also have an attorney well versed in condominium law review them for you. The documents will contain a number of restrictions. Are the restrictions reasonable? Request a title commitment and check to see that there are no exceptions that may adversely affect your interest in the property.

Know What the Maintenance Fee Covers

The monthly maintenance fee may cover a wide range of expenses. However, no two complexes are exactly alike, so don't assume that what you have heard about one complex applies to another. Some of the things your maintenance fee may or may not cover are:

- *Water.* Does the fee pay for all the water used by the entire complex, or just the water used for the common areas—lawns, pool, clubhouse, etc.? Is each owner billed additionally for his or her own water?

- *Sewer service.* This is usually paid for the entire complex. Is it included in your maintenance fee?

- *Electricity and gas or heating oil.* Does the fee pay for all utilities, or is each unit metered separately? Will you have your own utility bill to pay?

- *Garbage or trash removal.* Service is usually paid for the entire complex. If the complex is a high-rise, where is the trash chute? Will you have your own trash cans or will you take your trash to a dumpster? Where is it located? How often is it emptied?

- *Snow removal.* Does "removal" mean to your front door and your private parking place, or just the sidewalks and private roadways within the complex?

- *Lawn care.* What is included? Is there a place you can plant your own rose bush or tomato vine?

- *Day-to-day maintenance and repair.* What is not included that you may have to pay for yourself?

- *Insurance.* What does the master insurance policy for the entire complex cover? Is liability coverage adequate? Usually the master policy does *not* cover personal possessions or personal liability for the individual owners.

- *Taxes.* Your individual property taxes usually are *not* included in the maintenance fee. You will have to pay the taxes yourself. Find out what they are expected to be or have been in the past.

- *Management expenses.* Collecting fees, paying bills and negotiating contracts must be taken care of properly and may be very time-consuming. Is any of this your responsibility? Often a management company is hired for large complexes. Even for smaller complexes it is recommended that competent help be hired rather than expecting some of the homeowners to volunteer their time.

- *Preventative maintenance.* Contracts for maintaining elevators, boilers and air conditioning systems are very important. These should always be included in the budget.

- *Lease payments.* Are the homeowners leasing property or facilities that they do not actually own? What is the length of the lease? Can the lease payments be increased?

- *Reserves.* Some maintenance jobs occur only every few years or at even longer intervals. However, they are costly when needed. Some examples might be painting the exterior of buildings, reroofing the buildings, refurbishing common areas, such as the clubhouse, gym and pool areas, recarpeting halls and stairways and resurfacing the private roadways and parking areas. The monthly budget should include money for reserves. If these big jobs are not budgeted for by the association, special assessments will be needed periodically. Remember, there is no one but the homeowners to pay the bills. How they are paid is up to the association, but you should be aware of what expenses to expect.

You have a right to ask questions about the homeowners' association before you enter into a contract to purchase your home. The budget, the various contracts for services and the insurance policy should be available for you to read.

Of course, you don't want the maintenance fee to be excessive. But you also can't expect to get something for nothing. Be skeptical of very low fees, particularly if the complex is new and fees are being estimated. A very low figure may be used to help sell the units, or the first budget may be very unrealistic because of lack of experience. In the past, high inflation has caused havoc with condominium association budgets. Increased expenses were passed along to the homeowners because there was no one else to pay them.

In most instances, the maintenance fee is a real bargain; the owners do get their money's worth. If the entire complex looks attractive and well cared for, the owners are proud and happy to call it home.

Pay Extra Attention to the Quality of Construction of Condominiums

The quality of any property you are considering should be a major concern, but the quality of construction of a condominium complex is especially important. There are several reasons for this. First, of course, is your health and safety. Also, as a homeowner, you will be responsible for the costs of repairs. Even if there are many homeowners, the cost to each may be substantial. The cost of the hazard insurance carried by the association is based upon the construction quality of the building. Another important consideration has to do with future financing. Lenders can pick and choose those properties on which they wish to make loans. If the condominium complex is anything but a prime property, it may be very difficult, perhaps impossible, for a buyer to get a new institutional loan on your home when it's time for you to sell. This may hurt your attempts to sell your home for the greatest profit.

Because most people do not understand the construction of large buildings, they choose to be unconcerned with quality. Read Chapters 31 and 32 and do a careful inspection of the entire complex before writing an offer on a condominium.

The Financial Health of the Homeowners' Association

Be very concerned about the financial status of the homeowners' association. Each homeowners' association has a budget. The amount of money needed to pay all the expenses for the complex is determined and then each homeowner is assessed a maintenance fee each month so that he or she pays a fair share of all the expenses. But what if a homeowner doesn't pay the maintenance fee or the fee is not paid on time?

Most declarations provide for this possibility; a late fee is charged for late payments and usually a lien can be placed against the owner's property for the delinquent amount. Eventually the delinquent fees and the additional legal costs will be collected when the unit is sold. However, few if any associations have the authority or the resources to foreclose on a property.

But what if the condominium owner stops paying the maintenance fee and the mortgage and the lender holding the first mortgage forecloses? Then all junior liens are rescinded; the homeowners' association is just out of luck and will not get the maintenance fees owed to it. Every owner in the complex loses.

If the mortgages on only one or two units in a large complex are foreclosed, the situation is not serious; the loss is spread out among the many owners. In the past few years, however, foreclosures have wreaked havoc for many complexes.

Often the trouble started when the units were offered for sale; loans with very low payments, because of deep buydowns or negative amortization (loan types that will be explained later), enticed purchasers. Often the developer also paid the closing costs. People with lower paying jobs and very little savings could qualify and buy their own homes. This part of the bargain was appealing.

But soon the homebuyer who lost his job, who was transferred, who needed to move, etc., quickly found out that it was almost impossible to sell; buyers interested in a condominium could do better by purchasing directly from the developer. Renting the unit was also difficult. Because the owners had so little money invested in their homes, many who wanted out simply stopped making payments.

Depending on the lender and state laws, it may take a year or more before a property is through the foreclosure process and resold. During this time, the homeowners' association receives no maintenance fee. Soon the fees for everyone else are raised and expenses are curtailed, less lawn care and fertilizer, less cleaning and upkeep, etc.

As the monthly mortgage payments for the condominium owners increase (the payments for the first year or two were artificially low), the maintenance fees increase and the complex itself begins to look a little shabby. The situation gets worse. More homeowners walk away from their properties.

While a variation of this scenario has happened over and over, there are many, many complexes that have not had serious problems. How do you choose a financially healthy complex?

1. Read all the documents, including the budget, carefully. Learn what happens if a maintenance fee is not paid on time.

2. If you are considering a brand new unit, look at the financing that is offered. Is a down payment of at least 10 percent required? Does the loan have level payments? Is the maintenance fee comparable to similar sold-out complexes?

3. If you are buying a resale unit, ask your REALTOR® for information about the homeowners' association:
   • The number of owners who are current with homeowners fees
   • The number of owners who are 30 days late, 60 days late, 90 days late
   • The number of units in foreclosure
   • If all payments were current, what amount of money would be in reserves? What is the actual reserve balance? How is this money to be used?
   • Is a special assessment anticipated soon? In the next three to five years?

Try to attend a homeowners meeting. How many owners are actively involved and go to the meetings? Are problems discussed and solved in a friendly manner? Do you feel the homeowners' association is well-managed and financially sound? Will you feel comfortable living in the complex?

What Are the Policies Regarding Children and Pets?

Many condominium complexes are designed for families and welcome children. They are excellent places to raise children. Some complexes are for adults only; children are not allowed as permanent residents. Sometimes children are allowed to visit for only limited periods and are not permitted to use the recreational facilities. Be sure you are aware of any such restrictions.

Be aware of the policy regarding pets before you decide on a particular complex. Are all types of animals allowed? Are only cats and small dogs allowed? Are no pets of any kind allowed? Find out what special provisions are made for the animals and whether there are leash laws, etc. If you don't care to own a pet, you may be happier in a complex that does not permit them.

Noise—The Number One Complaint

The most frequent complaint of condominium owners is noise. The living units are close together and often stacked on top of each other. Unless the units are well insulated for sound, you will be able to hear a considerable amount of noise from your neighbors.

Some people find the noise of running water particularly irritating. Will you be bothered if you are awakened in the morning when your upstairs neighbor takes a shower? Outside noises are also bothersome, whether they come from the busy street, a busy parking lot or the pool and play areas. Loud stereos cause real problems when the walls are not well insulated. Try to inspect the condominium units when they are most apt to be noisy so you can judge the noise factor for yourself.

Adequate Parking Is Essential

Many complexes have garages or covered parking for the owners. Others have assigned parking spaces convenient to each home. Extra guest parking spaces should also be available.

If the complex has only unassigned parking, be wary. If there are too few parking spaces for the number of occupants, you may have a real problem. Not only is it inconvenient for you and your guests, but lenders will consider the lack of adequate parking to be a high risk factor when considering future loans on the property.

Rental and Resale Restrictions May Be a Problem

Many condominium complexes have no restrictions whatsoever concerning the renting or selling of units. However, some homeowners' associations have the authority to regulate certain aspects of renting and/or selling units and some declarations have right of first refusal clauses.

The most common regulation has to do with "for rent" and "for sale" signs—the size, where they can be placed, etc. Sometimes no signs are allowed; only small notices can be posted on a bulletin board. Some associations require a copy of the lease agreement when a unit is rented.

A right of first refusal provision gives members of the association the option of purchasing the unit for a certain period of time, at the same price and terms offered the seller by an outside buyer. These provisions are cumbersome and time-consuming. They tend to discourage buyers. A right of first refusal clause also severely limits the financing options for homes in the complex.

Be Aware of the Problems of Condominium Financing

By now you probably realize that a condominium buyer must be much more concerned about the future salability of the home than the buyer of a single-family house. There are homes in many condominium complexes that are virtually unsalable because they do not have good assumable loans and no institutional lender will make a new loan in the complex. Many of these condominiums have great livability but extremely limited financing options.

The reasons for this lack of financing are complicated. However, the basic problem is that it takes more of an effort for lenders to satisfy themselves as to the lack of risk factors of a condominium than a single-family house. The declaration and all other documents must be reviewed by legal counsel; often the lender won't be bothered with this unless several loans can be made in the same complex. Also, lenders want only prime properties. Remember, no lender is ever required to make a loan on a certain property; all lenders can set their own priorities and do what is good business for them.

Many lenders prefer to make loans that may be sold easily at a later date. This means VA and FHA loans and loans that meet the requirements of the Federal National Mortgage Association (Fannie Mae), the Federal Home Loan Mortgage Corporation (Freddie Mac), or one of the private-sector companies that buy mortgage loans in the secondary market. If a condominium complex has VA, FHA and/or Fannie Mae approval (Freddie Mac does not give approval as such, but sets strict guidelines), you can be relatively sure, although not positive, that an institutional lender will make a new loan on the property.

Approval by one or more of these agencies is a real plus for other reasons as well. With this approval, you may be assured that when the complex was approved, the property met all code requirements, there were no major risk factors and all the documents were in order. If the property is well managed and maintained in excellent condition, you should be able to sell your condominium with new financing.

Some complexes could be approved by VA, FHA and/or Fannie Mae if the necessary paperwork were completed. For other complexes, the properties or the condominium documents do not meet the necessary requirements for approval. Be on the safe side when buying your condominium and choose a home in a complex that has VA, FHA or Fannie Mae approval. Even if you can get a "steal" or a "real deal" in a complex without one of these approvals, think twice. Work out a plan to sell your condominium in the future before you buy it now.

Special Advice for Cash Buyers

There are times when buying a condominium with cash can be risky. The sellers of a newly constructed condominium complex and the owners of apartment complexes who are converting to condominiums are very eager to have cash buyers. The sellers often try to close the cash transactions as soon as possible so they can use the money to pay bills and meet other financial obligations.

The danger to the cash buyers is that they may become owners of the only condominiums that are successfully sold and closed, at least for quite a while. If the developer cannot get the necessary approvals or meet the lender requirements for a loan commitment, the other would-be buyers, even though under contract, will not be able to close. Other problems, such as a sharp rise in interest rates, could also prevent other closings.

If you are paying with cash, don't be one of the first buyers to close in a newly constructed complex or a new conversion. Wait until the seller has closed a number of contracts using new financing. The lender will have checked out the risks before those closings. Also, cash buyers should be aware of the type of financing that would be available if they were to need a loan.

7. The Townhouse: Perhaps the Best Choice of All

Another type of home that many homebuyers find appealing is the townhouse. The townhouse combines many of the features offered by a single-family house and a condominium. Many eastern cities had whole streets of townhouses long before the West was won.

A townhouse is different from, and should not be confused with, a townhouse-style condominium. When you buy a townhouse, you buy a part of the actual structure (the walls, the roof, the floor, etc.), not just the air space within the walls, as with a condominium.

Townhouses are similar to single-family detached houses in that each is on its own lot—at least the amount of land directly under the home. For this reason, townhouses are never stacked on top of each other, but each may be attached to the next. Two townhouses can share a wall or each can have its own side wall built right next to the other in what amounts to zero lot line zoning.

In newer developments, townhouses are similar to condominiums in that they are part of a complex. Ownership may include the townhouse structure and the lot, plus an undivided interest in all the common areas, often a clubhouse and other amenities, as well as some land.

Townhouses come in a variety of styles—a one-story ranch, a two-story or three-story home or a split-level home. They may or may not have basements; often garages or carports are attached or nearby. Some builders prefer to call their complexes patio homes or cluster homes because they don't look like traditional townhouses.

Each townhouse complex is unique. The declaration, bylaws and budget are similar to the documents used for condominium complexes, but are written to fit the special requirements of each townhouse complex. After reading the declaration you will be able to determine exactly what you are buying.

Each complex has its own homeowners' association that assesses a monthly maintenance fee. Be sure you understand exactly what the fee covers. The same list given in the condominium chapter (Chapter 6) may be applied to townhouse complexes. Even though you own the outside walls, roof, doors and windows of your home, the association might take care of outside maintenance, painting, lawn care and other services to make sure the complex is kept up to standards.

The one major exception is in the area of insurance. The townhouse structures belong to the individual owners rather than being part of the common elements. Therefore, they *may* or *may not* be covered by the association's master insurance policy. Be sure to check. Remember, a master policy does *not* cover your personal possessions or give you personal liability protection.

The information given in Chapter 6 concerning quality of construction, financial health of the homeowners' association, children, pets, noise, lawns and parking areas and rental and resale rights may be applied to a townhouse complex as well as a condominium complex.

Townhouses generally are easier to finance than condominiums—at least it is much easier to get VA, FHA and Fannie Mae approval for the entire complex. All the general information concerning condominium financing may be applied to townhouse complexes. If the townhouse is not part of a complex, financing is handled much the same as for a single-family detached house.

8. Doubles, Triplexes and Fourplexes: Living Space, Income and Tax Shelter

Many people own their own home and one or more apartments that may be rented. A two-unit, three-unit or four-unit residential property may be your best choice when you are looking for a home to buy. Doubles (or duplexes), triplexes and fourplexes come in all styles and sizes, with or without basements, garages and all the other features offered by a single-family house. Most of these properties were built as multi-family homes. However, many houses have been expanded or remodeled to make an additional living unit.

Before you purchase a multi-unit home, be sure that the property is zoned for multi-family residences. Usually single-family zoning does not allow you to rent out an apartment. Check with the zoning department before you agree to purchase a duplex, triplex or fourplex. Other restrictions similar to those for single-family houses may also apply.

Research what comparable apartments in the neighborhood are renting for and how many units similar to yours are vacant before you make an offer. Try to look at an apartment from a renter's point of view. If your property is clean, attractive, well maintained and priced the same as other apartments of the same size, would a renter choose your unit?

Two-unit, three-unit and four-unit residential properties that are owner-occupied may be financed much the same way as a single-family owner-occupied house. Conventional as well as FHA and VA loans are available from various lenders. The rental income and tax savings are considered when qualifying for a loan.

Rental Income and Tax Savings

One real advantage to purchasing this type of home is that a substantial part of the monthly payment may be offset with the income from the rental unit(s). As the property increases in value with improvements and normal appreciation, the rents may be increased to pay an even larger portion of the payment.

Most homebuyers are not aware of the considerable tax advantages available to the owners of income-producing residential property. Interest and taxes from the portion of the property you occupy are tax deductible and treated the same as for any other owner-occupied home. However, an income and expense statement (Schedule E) is used for the rented portion of the property. Since the bottom line is usually a negative amount, the rental income as well as some ordinary income, is tax-sheltered.

On Schedule E, income includes all the rent collected during the year. The expenses include the interest payments, taxes, insurance, utilities paid by the owner, repair and maintenance expenses and depreciation. The owner cannot claim a deduction for his or her own time and labor for maintaining and managing the property. The owner may claim actual expenses for materials and equipment, advertising and stationery supplies, as well as fees paid for repairs, bookkeeping, tax preparation, etc.

Depreciation is a major item in the list of expenses. This concept recognizes that things—buildings, roofs, heating systems, machinery, automobiles, etc.—wear out and lose value; this is real depreciation. However, this wear does not occur all at once, but over a period of time. The IRS takes this into consideration and allows you to list as an expense a yearly sum for depreciation. Only property used to produce income comes under the IRS rules and regulations for depreciation. Since land does not wear out, it cannot be depreciated. The cost basis of only the income-producing part of the property is used in figuring depreciation.

At this time IRS guidelines allow you to depreciate newly purchased residential rental property over 27.5 years using the straight line method. This means that you may depreciate 3.485 percent of the adjusted cost basis for the rental portion of the property each year for 27.5 years. For instance, if the adjusted cost basis is $70,540, you may include an expense for depreciation of $2,458 on Schedule E.

There are alternative ways to figure depreciation; check with your accountant. Internal Revenue Service Publications 946 and 534 give information on depreciation.

III
MONEY LENDERS AND THEIR LOANS

9. Learn All You Can about Money Lenders

The single most important thing you must understand about money lenders is that money lenders want to make *more money*. Lenders have money and are willing to loan it to you if they can make *more money*. They loan money to make *more money*. In this one respect all money lenders are alike.

In most every other way money lenders are *not* alike. Institutional money lenders are governed by different rules and regulations that require them to conduct business in different ways. Therefore, the loans they offer you often may be very different. Don't ever assume that you will get the same loan from money lender "A" as you may get from money lender "B." Learn all you can about money lenders and their loans. Remember, they lend money to make more money.

Some money lenders that may make home loans are:

- State-chartered savings and loan associations
- Federally-chartered savings and loan associations
- Mutual savings banks
- Mortgage companies
- National commercial banks
- State commercial banks
- State savings banks
- Federal savings banks
- Industrial banks
- Insurance companies
- Credit unions
- Finance companies
- Credit corporations

In the last few years most of the rules and regulations governing financial institutions have changed. Banks may now offer money market funds. Savings and loan associations (S&Ls) may provide checking accounts and make many types of loans. You may need to change your ideas about the different lenders. For instance, S&Ls have long been considered "the place" to go for a home mortgage loan. This is no longer necessarily true. Some S&Ls may be more interested in making short-term, high-interest automobile loans rather than long-term home loans. Their mortgage loans may not even be competitive because they may not particularly want this type of business. However, this is not true of all savings and loan associations. Don't assume that ABC S&L is making the same loans as XYZ S&L.

How Do Lenders Make Their Money?

Lenders make money on home loans in three major ways:

1. Lenders charge a fee to originate loans; that is, to do all the necessary paperwork before the borrower actually gets the money. They may also charge separate fees for such items as pictures, notary services, etc., that must be paid before a borrower gets the money. Some lenders charge fairly reasonable fees. Others charge you for this, that and every other thing. More about this in Chapter 10.

2. Lenders make money by servicing loans. They receive part of each monthly payment (often three-eighths of 1 percent) for crediting the account, sending statements, paying the taxes and insurance premiums, etc. Also, lenders usually have the free use of the money escrowed for taxes and insurance premiums until it's time to pay them. Sometimes you can choose not to have money escrowed for taxes and/or insurance. Ask the lender about this.

3. The most notable way lenders make money is by charging interest. This is called **yield**—the earnings the lender gets for letting you use the money. Up-front discount points increase the yield and provide more money.

Of course, lenders also have many expenses, particularly the cost of the money that is used for loans and the costs of operating a business. A lender's major risk is the possibility that a borrower will not repay a loan.

Since institutional lenders are in business to make a profit, they need to keep costs down, minimize risks and provide the services that will allow them to make a profit. Lenders set their own policies and guidelines (within the rules and regulations that govern their particular institution). Most lenders specialize in certain types of loans and prefer certain types of properties. Of course, all lenders want well-qualified borrowers.

Money Supply and Demand

Each year several million homes are financed along with millions of other purchases. Businesses borrow money for new buildings, equipment and materials. The owners of office buildings, apartment complexes and shopping centers finance their buildings. Millions of dollars worth of cars, furniture, appliances and other consumer goods are purchased on credit. Plus, the government borrows billions of dollars. All of these financed purchases create a demand for money that, along with government policies, determines the interest rate. Because government policies and the supply and demand for money can change, the interest rate moves up or down.

Freddie Mac, Fannie Mae and Ginnie Mae

Freddie Mac, Fannie Mae, and Ginnie Mae are often mentioned in articles in the housing section of the newspaper. These are not real people but the nicknames of large quasi-government corporations—The Federal Home Loan Mortgage Corporation (FHLMC), The Federal National Mortgage Association (FNMA) and The Government National Mortgage Association (GNMA), respectively. These agencies were brought into being to act as middlemen—bringing together lenders and investors—to help assure a constant supply of mortgage money for homebuyers. Many local lenders originate loans that conform to the requirements set forth by Fannie Mae, Ginnie Mae or other agencies that purchase loans. To a large extent these conforming loan requirements determine property qualifications, borrower qualifications and the terms and conditions in the loans available to you.

The Amortized Loan

Most home loans are amortized, which means the loan is scheduled to be fully repaid in a definite period of time with equal monthly payments. Each monthly payment is part interest and part principal, known as a PI payment. The interest part of the payment decreases each month and the principal part of the payment increases as the loan is gradually paid off.

For example, $50,000 borrowed at 9 percent interest will be completely repaid in 30 years by making 360 monthly payments of $402.31. The amount borrowed ($50,000) is called the **principal**. The **rate of interest** is 9 percent. The length of the payback period (thirty years) is called the **term**. The term of the loan can also be expressed in months (360 months). The **monthly PI payment** is the dollar amount needed to amortize the loan.

Types of Loans

Institutional lenders make three major types of loans to finance homes: Federal Housing Administration (FHA) insured loans, Department of Veterans Affairs (formerly Veterans Administration) or VA guaranteed loans and conventional loans. All loans made by institutional lenders and not insured or guaranteed by a government agency are considered conventional loans. Not all lenders make all types of loans.

The Farmers Home Administration (FmHA), a part of the Department of Agriculture, makes direct loans for homes in small towns and rural areas to low and moderate income families. The Federal Land Bank, part of the Farm Credit System, also makes direct loans for homes in rural areas. Money is sometimes available for home loans from a variety of local, state and federal government agencies, usually through special bond programs. Ask your REALTOR® about these lending sources.

Increasingly, many homes are financed with private loans. These loans may be available from the seller of the property, from relatives or friends or from any individuals or groups who wish to invest in mortgage loans.

Finally, a great many homebuyers are able to assume the existing financing on the homes they are purchasing, sometimes with the help of additional financing.

Each of the different financing plans is discussed separately in this section of the book.

The Best Loan for You

Now you understand that money lenders are in business to make more money and you know some of the ways in which they do this. You also know the lender is going to make money from you on the amount you borrow. What do you do?

First of all, learn everything you can about loans and all the various costs involved. The Loan Profile in the next chapter will help you do this. Then match up the best type of loan with your situation and the property you want to buy. It is important to know about loans *before* you decide on your new home. After you have a contract, shop for a loan using what you know about lenders and their loans.

Remember, each loan is made on a unique property and for a certain borrower. It is not always possible to obtain the "perfect" loan, but you should compare loans to get the best financing plan available for your special situation.

10. The Loan Profile: Understand and Compare Financing Plans

Real estate is almost always financed by mortgage loans; that is, the property becomes the security for the loan. One of two documents, the **mortgage** or the **deed of trust** (also called **trust deed**), pledges the property as security for the loan. These documents state all the terms and conditions agreed to by the borrower. Whether a mortgage or a deed of trust is used depends on the laws and requirements of the state in which the property is located. The main difference between a mortgage and a deed of trust has to do with the way a foreclosure is handled if the borrower defaults on the loan.

The terms *first* and *second* are often used in reference to loans. A first is really a first mortgage or a first deed of trust; a second is a second mortgage or a second deed of trust and represents a second loan for which the property is pledged as security. The first or second (or third, fourth, fifth, etc.) indicates the investor's position or claim on the property. If a foreclosure is necessary, the holder of the first mortgage or first deed of trust will have his or her claim to the property completely satisfied before the holder of the second can have his or her claim satisfied, and on down the line. As you can see, a first is a safer investment with less risk for the investor than a second, third or fourth.

The **promissory note** is the companion document to the mortgage or deed of trust. By signing the note, the borrower promises to repay the loan according to the terms outlined.

The term *mortgage* is often used to refer to the loan documents—to either a mortgage or a deed of trust and the promissory note.

The Loan Profile—
Understand All the Features of a Loan

Mortgage loans may vary in many ways. It's important that you, the borrower, are aware of *all* the various terms and conditions of a loan. The following Loan Profile, with its twelve features, is designed to help you understand a mortgage loan. With a complete Loan Profile you can compare the features of various financing plans and determine which loan will give you the greatest value and be the least expensive for your special situation. Each of the twelve features in the Loan Profile is explained here:

1. Down Payment. The borrower is usually required to invest some of his or her own money when buying a home. This is called the **down payment**, the amount determined by the **loan to value ratio**. The contract price of the property or the appraised value (whichever is lower) is used to determine the property value. If the lender will loan you 80 percent of the property value, you will need a 20 percent down payment. If you can obtain a 95 percent loan you need only a 5 percent down payment. A loan with a lower loan to value ratio may have a lower interest rate, but you will need a much larger down payment.

Also, the buyer can usually make a larger down payment than the minimum amount required by the lender.

2. Interest Rate. The interest rate is quoted as a certain percent per year and is paid each month on the remaining principal balance. This rate of interest is called the **contract interest rate**. Differences in the rates of interest are not necessarily the most important consideration when comparing loans.

Interest rates change frequently, often daily. Some lenders will guarantee the interest rate at the time you make application for the loan or, if rates are expected to fall, will guarantee the rate and also agree to charge the lower interest rate as of a specific date. This is by far the best for the borrower. Other lenders will guarantee the interest rate when the loan is approved, and still others will determine the interest rate only at closing. *Beware!!* If the market changes you may not have the opportunity to shop again for a more favorable loan, leaving you in a very vulnerable position.

Some lenders require a nonrefundable commitment fee to hold a certain amount of mortgage money at a specific interest rate for a definite period of time. If you are having a new home built and it will be several months until completion, the commitment fee may be necessary.

3. Interest in Arrears or Interest in Advance. Most loans have payments due the first of each month. If the April 1 payment pays the interest for the month of March, the loan has interest paid in arrears. If the April 1 payment pays the interest for April, the interest is being paid in advance. Interest paid in arrears is an advantage for the borrower. The savings are substantial—almost equal to one month's interest payment.

4. Term of the Loan. The length of time over which the loan is amortized is called the **term** and usually is expressed in years or months, such as 30 years or 360 months. A longer term means smaller monthly payments for the same principal amount and also gives the borrower more flexibility and control. If and when the borrower wishes, additional principal payments can be made to repay the loan sooner (see Chapter 25). The date the loan will be repaid in full is called the **maturity date**.

5. Balloon Payment. Sometimes a clause is written into the loan agreement requiring the remaining principal balance to be paid on or before a certain date, usually several years after the loan is originated but before it is repaid in full. One large final payment of this type is known as a **balloon payment**.

Often lenders choose not to use the word *balloon*. Instead they use the words *call*, *maturity date* and *refinance time* when explaining the financing plan with a balloon payment. Don't be misled!

Avoid a loan with a balloon payment (by whatever name) if possible. If you can't, give yourself plenty of time before the balloon payment is due—five years to eight years is not uncommon. Also, try to include refinancing provisions such as terms, conditions and new loan costs in writing in the loan documents. Plan to refinance or sell the property well before the balloon payment is due.

6. Mortgage Insurance. Ordinarily, institutional lenders cannot have more than an 80 percent risk in a property; they cannot make more than an 80 percent conventional loan. The reason for this is that if a borrower defaults on a loan the lender should be able to sell the property for at least 80 percent of value and recover the money for the investor.

Private mortgage insurance (PMI) makes higher ratio loans of 90 percent and 95 percent available by insuring against the possibility of a default. If you do not have the money for a 20 percent downpayment, you may be able to buy PMI to enable you to qualify for a higher ratio loan. Private mortgage insurance may also be used with a lower ratio loan to offset a high risk property or a high risk borrower.

The cost of PMI can vary. The fee is usually one-half of 1 percent (.5 percent) to 1 percent of the loan amount for the first year's premium paid at closing, plus one-quarter of 1 percent (.25 percent) for each year thereafter. One-twelfth of this amount is added to each month's payment, then escrowed by the lender and used to pay each succeeding year's premium. Sometimes just one fee, perhaps 2 percent of the loan amount, is paid at the time the loan is originated.

Sometimes loans insured with PMI are called "magic loans" because Mortgage Guarantee Insurance Corporation (MGIC) was the first company to offer this insurance.

Because PMI insures just that portion of the loan above 80 percent of value, it is logical to assume that you can stop paying PMI once the loan to value ratio drops below 80 percent. This could happen in only a few years as principal payments, appreciation and/or improvements build equity in your property. Sometimes it is possible to drop PMI. More often the one-quarter of 1 percent PMI just becomes part of the loan and you must go on paying it year after year after year. (The lender is making *more money*.)

Choose a lender that will let you buy PMI with a small up-front fee and monthly payments—and arrange to pay PMI for only as long as necessary. You will have to ask for permission to drop PMI; a lender is not going to send you a notice. An adjusted appraisal may be required at that time to justify that the loan to value ratio is under 80 percent.

7. Up-front Loan Costs. This is the amount of money needed to obtain the loan. These costs can vary greatly from one lender to another and may include the loan origination fee, loan servicing fee, discount points and all the other charges for inspections, appraisal, survey, title work, lender's attorney, pictures, credit checks, recording and filing fees, etc.

Many of these fees are necessary. It is not unusual to pay a 1 percent to 1.5 percent loan origination fee and the actual costs of the credit reports, appraisal, survey, title work, inspections, recording fees and transfer fees. However, some lenders require much more paperwork and/or charge separately for services other lenders provide without additional costs.

Up-front discount points are charged for many loans. One **point** is equal to 1 percent of the principal amount of the loan; one point for a $50,000 loan is $500. These discount points increase the yield of the loan and may be considered prepaid interest. In fact, you can usually buy down the interest rate by paying additional up-front points. Points are paid by the borrower or seller, depending on circumstances, and can vary greatly from lender to lender. Most people are so concerned about interest rates that they don't ask about discount points. This enables some lenders to make *more money* by requiring heavy discount points. If you don't expect to own your home for the term of the loan, you may save money by paying a slightly higher interest rate rather than high up-front costs.

8. Loan Repayment Schedule. The repayment schedule for the ordinary long-term, level-payment, amortized loan is simple. A principal and interest (PI) payment of the same amount is due each month until the loan is repaid.

Many of the new creative financing plans, however, have graduated or adjustable repayment schedules that can be complicated. If the loan has graduated payments and negative amortization, you should know what your payments will be at each adjustment period and how much the principal amount of your loan will increase. If the payments are to be adjusted according to an index, the name of the index, how the adjustments are determined using the index, the maximum amount of the adjustment and the time and way the borrower is to be notified of the adjustments should all be clearly explained to you. In fact, lenders who offer adjustable rate mortgages (ARMs) to borrowers are required by Regulation Z (the truth-in-lending regulation) to provide this information. Also ask for a worst case scenario so you know the maximum amount your payments can be. The repayment schedule should be completely outlined with clear and precise wording in the loan documents.

9. Assumption Clause. Some (but not all) loans may be assumed by a new buyer. However, three things may or may not happen:

1. The interest rate may increase. Your 9 percent interest rate won't be so attractive to a new buyer if it suddenly becomes 11 percent or 12 percent.

2. The new buyer may have to qualify just as though he or she were getting a new loan. Many buyers, for a variety of reasons, need to assume a loan for which they are not required to qualify. Also, the lender may state in the clause that only an owner-occupant may assume your loan, thereby excluding investors.

3. An assumption fee may be charged to the new buyer. Assumption fees may vary greatly but should be reasonable—in the range of $100 to $500, or probably not more than one-half of 1 percent (.5 percent) of the unpaid balance.

Be wary if you are told that a particular financing plan is fully assumable at the lender's option. What the lender means is that the loan is *not* assumable, unless, of course, depending on market conditions at the time of the assumption, it would be in the lender's best interest.

A good assumption clause is an important advantage. It may be the difference between selling or not selling your home in the event of another era of high interest rates like those of 1980–1982.

10. Due on Sale Clause. If the loan document has a due on sale clause, the loan cannot be assumed. When you sell the property the loan balance becomes due and must be repaid. Also, don't try to assume a loan that has a due on sale clause unless you receive a written waiver from the lender. (See Chapter 17.)

11. Prepayment Penalty. This is the "sting" in many loans. *Beware!* Everything is fine until it comes time to sell your home. Then the investor who is holding your loan reminds you that you may be charged three months' or even six months' interest on the unpaid balance when the loan is paid off.

Be wary of a lender who tells you that the prepayment penalty may be waived later. Have the lender put all provisions to waive the penalty in writing. If provisions to waive a prepayment penalty are part of the lender's policy and not in writing, the lender can change the policy. Or your loan may be transferred to another institution with a different policy.

Most new loans do not have prepayment penalties; they can be paid off at any time without penalty. Shop for a loan without a prepayment penalty.

12. Interest Calculations and Late Payment Charges. Most first mortgage loans are amortized loans and have a payment which is due on a specific day of each month, such as February 1, March 1, April 1, etc. An interest payment of one-twelfth of the annual rate is charged each month regardless of the number of days in that month or if the payment is made a few days before or a few days after that due date.

When you accept a loan you are obligated to make the payments as agreed. The lender should have the right to charge you a late penalty to encourage you to make your payments on time and to pay the added expenses if you don't. However, you should have a few days' grace period—often 10 days to 15 days—and the late charge should be reasonable, probably no more than 4 percent to 6 percent of the payment. Be sure you understand when the payment is considered to be late and what the penalty will be.

The interest on many loans, particularly second mortgage loans made by institutional lenders, is calculated on a daily (360 days per year), simple interest basis. The payment is due on a specific day each month. However, the interest is calculated daily and credited on the day it is received, whether it is a few days before or a few days after your payment due date. The remaining amount of your payment (after interest is paid) is subtracted from the principal balance.

When interest is calculated by the daily, simple interest method, there is no late charge as such; you are automatically rewarded or penalized according to when you make your payment. If you fall behind in your payments, the lender can take certain actions as outlined in your loan agreement.

Annual Percentage Rate (APR)

Do not confuse the contract interest rate you are paying for your loan with the annual percentage rate (APR). Lenders are required by Regulation Z in the Truth-in-Lending Act to reveal the APR. It is figured by using the contract interest rate plus certain finance charges paid by both the borrower and the seller, and the time the borrower will have use of the money.

The intent of the federal government in requiring disclosure of the APR was to give borrowers an easy and accurate way to compare the actual costs of several different financing plans. However, like so many other protections arranged for us by the government, the APR does not work very well. It is neither an easy nor accurate way to compare loans when buying your home. Because many owners do not plan to own their homes for the full term of the loan, and there are so many exceptions to the rules and errors in arithmetic, the APR should not be used as a comparison tool.

Instead, use the Loan Profile to compare loans. A complete Loan Profile for each financing plan you are considering will let you know which loan is best for your special situation.

Once you have accepted a certain loan with a certain monthly payment, these payments must be made each and every month until the entire obligation is repaid. It is usually possible to increase the size of your payment or to pay an additional principal amount periodically or whenever you prefer. These additional amounts of money reduce your loan balance and save you interest money over the life of the loan, but they do *not* excuse you from making the next month's PI payment. Additional principal payments shorten the length of the term, but they do not decrease the size of the monthly PI payments. If your mortgage or deed of trust has a prepayment penalty, be careful not to incur a penalty by exceeding the allowed principal prepayment amount.

11. FHA Loans Are for Everyone

The purpose of the Federal Housing Administration (FHA) insured loan programs is to make affordable housing available to all United States residents. If you are of legal age, can meet the FHA credit requirements, and the property you choose meets FHA requirements, you may obtain an FHA loan to buy your own home.

FHA itself does not "make" loans. Instead, it insures loans, originated by different lending institutions, against default. Each borrower is required to pay for the mortgage insurance for his or her loan. FHA sets the maximum loan amount that may be borrowed; maximum loan amounts vary from area to area but are in the range of $100,000 to $115,000 for a single-family house. Higher loans are available for properties with two-family, three-family or four-family units. The features of the various FHA programs are regulated by the Secretary of Housing and Urban Development (HUD).

The most frequently used FHA program and the one most people are familiar with is the **203B Mortgage Loan Program**. The 203B loan has a low down payment, level monthly payments, a 30-year term and may be assumed if the new borrower meets the FHA qualifying requirements. The **203B2 Mortgage Loan Program** is for veterans. This loan is very similar to the 203B except that the down payment may be up to $750 less. All veterans with 180 days active duty service, whether or not they have VA entitlement, may use the 203B2, often called the FHA-Vet loan.

An **FHA Adjustable Rate Mortgage (ARM)** has a lower beginning interest rate that may be increased or decreased a maximum of 1 percent each year and a maximum of 5 percent during the term of the loan. The adjustments are determined by an index using the weekly average of the U.S. Treasury securities. A **margin** (which stays the same for the term of the loan) is added to the index's interest rate to determine the rate of interest the borrower will pay. The initial interest rate, the margin and the discount points are determined by the lender. The lender is required to provide complete information about the loan including a worst-case-scenario payment schedule. Consider an FHA-ARM only if you expect your income to keep pace with possible payment increases.

An **FHA Urban Homesteading Program** is a cooperative effort between HUD and certain local governmental agencies. It is designed to help cities revitalize older declining neighborhoods and reduce the number of vacant properties with defaulted mortgages. The **FHA 203(k) Loan Program** provides 30-year, level-payment loans for the purchase and rehabilitation of properties that do not meet FHA normal property requirements.

Although all lenders do not originate all types of FHA loans, an FHA loan officer should be able to help you obtain information on the various FHA loan programs available in your area.

Buyer Eligibility and Qualifications

Any United States resident of legal age can apply for an FHA loan. All applicants must be given equal consideration without discrimination. There are, of course, certain credit requirements. The borrower or coborrowers must show they are willing and able to repay the loan. All income that can be verified and is likely to continue from the borrower or the coborrowers will be considered. For the loan programs discussed here, the borrower or at least one of the coborrowers must move into the property with the intention of making it his or her principal residence.

If the borrower (or the coborrowers) has a good credit history and he or she (or they) can meet the ordinary 25 percent and 33 percent ratios (as explained in Chapter 20), there should be no problem qualifying for the loan. Actually, FHA credit guidelines, while more complicated, are also more lenient and may work out to be as high as 29 percent and 41 percent. If you have questions regarding your credit worthiness or the largest loan amount you can borrow, talk to an experienced and knowledgeable FHA lender.

Property Requirements

The various FHA loan programs may be used for single-family houses, two-unit, three-unit and four-unit family dwellings and condominiums and townhouses in FHA-approved complexes. If you want an FHA loan for a property being built, FHA requires certain paperwork before and certain inspections during construction. These requirements can be waived if the improvements are built under the Home Owners Warranty Program (HOW) or the Home Buyers Warranty Program. If this requirement is not met or waived, an FHA loan may be possible with a larger down payment. FHA property requirements are quite strict. For example, properties located near industrial or commercial buildings may not be approved for a loan. Also, the properties must be in good repair. FHA does not want the borrower to have additional expenses immediately after buying the home. FHA loans in these programs are not available for "fixer-upper" properties.

An **appraisal** made by an FHA staff appraiser or an FHA-approved fee appraiser is required for all properties. (FHA may accept a VA appraisal.) Sometimes the appraisal will require that certain repairs be made prior to loan approval. These repairs may include such things as painting, repairing tile and countertops, replacing worn carpet, reroofing the home and even replacing an entire heating system. If repairs are required, the property must be reinspected by the appraiser or an approved loan officer before the loan can be made. Even though FHA property requirements are quite strict, FHA or the appraisal in no way guarantees or gives any warranties as to the condition of the property.

FHA Lenders

Many different institutional lenders originate FHA loans. FHA allows certain lenders, called "direct endorsement lenders," to give loan approval if the loan package meets certain requirements. This considerably shortens the time needed for loan processing and approval. Whether or not your loan may be lender-approved, use the most knowledgeable and experienced loan officer available since a well-documented loan package will help you secure loan approval.

Loan Profile for FHA Loan Programs

FHA has many different lending programs, and each one has its own variations. Information in this Loan Profile is only for FHA 203B, 203B2 and ARM mortgage loan programs.

1. *Down payment.* The minimum required down payment for an FHA borrower may be as little as 3 percent, depending on the sale price or appraised value (whichever is less) of the property and the FHA program. The down payment for most FHA borrowers is between 3 percent and 5 percent.

2. *Interest rate.* The maximum interest rate for FHA loans is not set by law. Often the lender, the borrower and the seller negotiate the interest rate and the discount points.

3. *Interest in arrears or interest in advance.* Interest on FHA loans is paid in arrears.

4. *Term of the loan.* The maximum term is 30 years.

5. *Balloon payment.* FHA loans do not have balloon payments.

6. *Mortgage insurance.* All FHA loans are insured against default, and all FHA borrowers are required to pay the mortgage insurance premium (MIP). The "up-front" MIP premium is an amount

equal to 3.8 percent of the loan. This may be paid at closing or it may be added to the loan amount and financed for the term of the loan at the contract interest rate; it is paid each month with the PI payment. In addition, FHA requires an additional .5 percent of the loan amount per year. The length of time it is paid depends on the loan to value ratio and the fiscal year of loan origination. This additional amount is added on to the monthly payment.

Depending on circumstances, a portion of the MIP may be refunded after the loan is repaid. The lender who provides the payoff statement can tell you what information is needed and file HUD form 2344 on your behalf.

7. *Up-front loan costs.* The FHA borrower may pay a 1 percent loan origination fee plus only those closing costs that are allowed by FHA rules. Discount points may be paid by the FHA borrower or the seller. A portion of the closing costs may be financed and paid with the monthly payments.

Ask your loan officer to figure the amount of money you will need for the down payment, closing costs and escrows at the time of closing. Your loan officer can also tell you the total amount you can borrow and the monthly payment.

8. *Loan repayment schedule.* FHA 203B and 203B2 loans have equal PI payments due each month until the entire loan is repaid. The PI payments for the ARM loans may increase or decrease each year to reflect the adjusted interest rate. Some FHA loans may have buydown interest rates for the first year or the first few years, or the payments may be subsidized by the seller. (See buydown mortgages in Chapters 13 and 20.) The repayment schedule for each loan is explained in the mortgage documents.

9. *Assumption clause.* FHA loans originated after December 15, 1989, may be assumed only if the new buyer meets FHA qualifying requirements. The interest rate and other terms and conditions of the loan will remain the same. The assumption fee may be no more than $500.

10. *Due on sale clause.* Many older FHA loans do not have due on sale clauses and may be assumed by any buyer. While the more recently originated FHA loans do not have due on sale clauses, they do require that the new borrower meet FHA qualifying requirements. If the terms and conditions stated in the loan documents are not met, the loan can be called.

11. *Prepayment privilege or penalty.* FHA loans may be rpepaid in full or in part at any time. However, the lender may (and most often will) charge interest to the end of the month.

12. *Late payment penalty.* A late payment penalty (most often 4 percent) can be charged according to the terms written into the mortgage documents.

12. VA Loans:
Good News for Veterans

Department of Veterans Affairs (VA) loans, or GI loans if you prefer, have the best terms and conditions of any loans available today. If you are a veteran, you can probably buy your home with a VA loan, even if it has been many years since you were in the service, even if you have already received a VA loan and even if you are not buying the traditional house.

The Department of Veterans Affairs works for veterans by helping them and their families obtain homes with reasonable financing. VA loans are originated by many lenders and guaranteed against default by the federal government according to each veteran's entitlement (eligibility). This chapter gives guidelines that can be used by most veterans who are buying a home for a principal residence. If you have unusual circumstances or needs, write, call or visit the nearest VA office. You may receive personal help with your problems from a VA representative.

At one time, veterans were told they could obtain only one VA loan in their lifetime. That is no longer true. The rules have been changed and the entitlement has been increased several times to 46,000 as of December 18, 1989. Unless you have purchased a home after that date, you probably have at least partial entitlement still available.

Entitlement Eligibility

Veterans who were discharged under honorable conditions and who have served the required minimum time of continuous active duty are eligible for entitlement. This means you must have served a minimum of 90 days during the periods from September 10, 1940, to July 25, 1947 (World War II), and from June 27, 1950, to January 31, 1955 (Korean Conflict), or a minimum of 181 days during the periods from July 25, 1947, to June 27, 1950, and from January 31, 1955, to September 7, 1980. Beginning September 7, 1980, the minimum time of service was increased to two years. If a veteran is presently in service, the requirement is 181 days of continuous service.

Veterans discharged as a result of a service-related disability are eligible for entitlement. Unmarried widows of veterans who died while in service or as a result of a service-related disability are eligible for entitlement. Spouses of POWs and MIAs also may be eligible. However, service personnel with only Active Duty for Training (ACDUTRA) do not have entitlement.

Veterans may have two entitlements if they served in two or three of the following: World War II and the Korean and Viet Nam wars. If the veteran has used one entitlement to purchase a home, he or she may have full entitlement to purchase another home. Check with your VA office. Furthermore, two veterans can combine their entitlements to purchase a property if both are going to live in the property.

All qualified veterans with or without VA entitlement can choose to use the FHA-Vet program and obtain a regular FHA loan with a lower down payment. (See Chapter 11.)

Reinstatement of Entitlement. If you once owned a home financed with a VA loan, and that loan has been paid in full and you no longer own the home, your entitlement may be reinstated. Even if you don't know for sure, but have reason to believe the loan may have been paid off, contact your VA office and ask a representative to check for you. The VA will need your name, service identification number and the property address of the home that was financed with the VA loan. Also, supply as much of the following additional information as possible:

- VA case number for the loan
- Date or approximate date of purchase
- Date or approximate date you sold the property
- Mortgage holder, address and loan number
- Name of buyer who assumed your VA loan

If a veteran's VA loan is assumed by another veteran with at least as much entitlement as the first veteran, the second veteran can substitute his or her entitlement and the first veteran's benefits will be reinstated. The VA office can provide the necessary forms.

Partial Entitlement. Many veterans who have obtained a VA loan and whose benefits cannot be reinstated may still have a partial entitlement. Entitlement has been increased several times from the original 4,000 on June 22, 1944:

- To 7,500 on March 20, 1950
- To 12,500 on May 5, 1968
- To 17,500 on December 31, 1974
- To 25,000 on October 1, 1978
- To 27,500 on October 1, 1980

- To 36,000 on January 31, 1988
- To 46,000 on December 18, 1989, for loans above $144,000 and to 36,000 for loans of $144,000 and below

(The VA may raise entitlement at any time. When this happens be sure to note the date and amount.)

Once a veteran has obtained a loan, each increase gives the veteran additional entitlement. For instance, a veteran who bought a home in 1969 and used the full entitlement of 12,500 at that time now has a remaining partial entitlement of 23,500 (36,000 − 12,500 = 23,500).

Lender Policies

Lenders can usually make VA loans that are four times the amount of the veteran's entitlement. For veterans with partial entitlement, many lenders calculate the loan amount in a manner that results in a larger loan. If this is important to you, ask your REALTOR®'s help in locating such a lender. A veteran with full entitlement may purchase a home for up to $184,000 with no down payment, provided other credit and property requirements are met.

Buyer Credit Requirements

The veteran must meet the VA credit requirements. The VA uses its own qualifying formula, which is more lenient than the underwriting guidelines used for conventional loans.

The VA is concerned with net effective income—the amount of money remaining after subtracting federal and state income tax, social security or retirement payments, debt service (over six months), insurance premiums, child care expenses and estimated housing expenses. The remaining income should be enough to support the veteran and his family. All income of the veteran and his or her spouse is considered. Some of the things the VA will consider are the family's previous and expected life-style, the increase in shelter expenses, number and age of dependents and local economic conditions. Each loan application is evaluated on an individual basis.

The VA wants to help veterans obtain adequate housing, but must guarantee that the mortgage loan will be repaid. If the veteran can show that he or she needs the housing and will repay the loan, the VA will make a special effort to make the loan.

Veteran-Nonveteran Loans

The veteran buyer may have a coborrower to whom he or she is not married. However, the VA will guarantee only that portion of the property belonging to the veteran. A larger down payment may compensate for that portion of the property not guaranteed by the VA. Your lender can determine the amount of down payment needed.

VA Automatic Loans

Many lenders have been approved by the VA to make automatic loans. These lenders may originate, approve and close VA loans before submitting all the paperwork to the VA. This eliminates much of the red tape and saves a great amount of time. If time is a big factor in obtaining your new home, your REALTOR® can help you locate a lender who can make automatic VA loans.

Loans requiring more complex documentation because of the particular property, the borrower's special situation or some other reason may not be approved automatically. Consider using an automatic lender for these loans. Automatic lenders have more experience in putting together loan packages. This can be a real advantage to you in getting loan approval.

Property Requirements

The types of properties eligible for VA loans are single-family detached houses, condominiums, townhouses and patio homes in VA-approved complexes or areas, and two-unit, three-unit and four-unit family dwellings. Two veterans can combine their entitlements and purchase a larger apartment property if both will make it their principal residence. The VA will make loans on newly constructed homes if certain guidelines are followed during construction. Check with a knowledgeable loan officer before beginning construction.

A Certificate of Reasonable Value (CRV), which is the VA appraisal form, must be completed by a VA-approved appraiser. (VA may accept an FHA appraisal.) The appraisal must show that the property does or does not meet the minimum requirements. It is possible for a VA buyer to purchase a "fixer-upper" home and do the repair and renovation work. Contact a knowledgeable REALTOR® or loan officer for details on how to handle the transaction for a "fixer-upper" property.

The VA loan cannot exceed the CRV. If the CRV is lower than the contract price of the property, a reconsideration can be requested. (See Chapter 42.)

Certificate of Eligibility

The veteran will need his or her Certificate of Eligibility before the VA loan can be approved. If one has not been issued, it can be obtained from the VA office. (Your loan officer can help you obtain it.) The veteran will need form DD214 (separation papers) and a VA form 1880.

VA Loan Profile

All VA loans and their costs to the veterans are alike. However, lenders' policies concerning discount points and down payment requirements for partial entitlement and properties over $110,000 may vary.

1. *Down payment*. The loan amount cannot exceed the CRV and is limited by the VA borrower's entitlement and ability to repay the loan. There is no down payment if the property and veteran meet lender guidelines. The loan to value ratio can be as high as 100 percent.

2. *Interest rate*. The interest rate cannot exceed the maximum permitted by law, but may be lower.

3. *Interest in arrears or interest in advance*. Interest on VA loans is paid in arrears.

4. *Term of the loan*. The maximum term is 30 years.

5. *Balloon payment*. There is no balloon payment in a VA loan.

6. *Mortgage insurance*. VA loans are guaranteed by the federal government, according to the veteran's entitlement, at no cost to the veteran.

7. *Up-front loan costs*. The veteran buyer may pay the 1 percent loan origination fee, the .5 percent to 1.25 percent VA funding fee (depending on the loan to value ratio and not required in certain instances), plus other closing costs allowed by the VA. The veteran may pay for the appraisal (CRV) only if it is ordered in his or her name. Discount points may not be paid by the borrower.

8. *Loan repayment schedule*. For level-payment VA loans, the same PI payment will be due each month until the entire loan is repaid. Sellers can buy down the interest rate for the first year or the first few years of a VA loan. The repayment schedule for buydown loans will reflect the lower interest rate(s). Some VA loans may have principal payments that increase according to the terms of the loan.

9. *Assumption clause*. VA loans originated after March 1, 1988, may be assumed only by a new borrower who follows the VA qualifying procedure and is approved by the VA. The interest rate will not increase. An assumption fee (usually $500) will be charged. If the veteran wishes to retain his or her entitlement, the loan should be assumed by another veteran who can substitute his or her entitlement by following the necessary procedure.

10. *Due on sale clause*. VA loans do have due on sale clauses if they are assumed without VA approval.

11. *Prepayment privilege*. A VA loan can be fully or partially prepaid at any time without penalty.

12. *Late payment penalty*. A late payment penalty (usually 4 percent) can be charged according to the conditions written into the loan documents.

13. Some Conventional Loans Are Very Unconventional

Institutional lenders make many types of conventional loans. The old-fashioned, level-payment, 30-year loan, preferred by most home-buyers, is available from many lenders. Borrowers may choose from a wide variety of conventional loans that have adjustable rates, graduated payments, shorter terms, buydown features, biweekly payments or a combination of these.

Lenders determine the size of the loans they will make. Some lenders will not make loans under $50,000, or they may charge a higher interest rate for these loans. Loans over $202,000 are usually considered jumbo loans. Some conventional lenders specialize in these larger loans and offer special terms to well-qualified buyers. Your REALTOR® can help you find a lender for your special situation.

It is important to remember that lenders may establish their own guidelines and lending policies. They may also change their policies whenever they wish. While lenders design their mortgage plans to fit their particular requirements, the terms and conditions can sometimes be negotiated. Also, different lenders offer different variations of financing plans, such as the adjustable rate mortgage.

Of all the mortgage plans, the level-payment, 30-year assumable loan is still the best option for most homebuyers, provided the interest rate is reasonable. You should consider other options and choose the financing plan that makes the most sense for your situation. Then shop for the lender who offers that particular plan with the best terms and conditions.

Borrower Eligibility and Qualifications

To qualify for a conventional loan the borrower must be a United States resident and of legal age in the state where the property is located. All borrowers and coborrowers must be treated alike and given equal consideration without discrimination.

Lenders may set their own qualifying guidelines. Ratios of 25 percent and 33 percent are often used, although the ratios can be as high as 29 percent and 38 percent. (Ratios are explained in Chapter 20.) Often lenders intend to sell their loans in the secondary mortgage market and the potential buyer (Freddie Mac, Fannie Mae, or a company from the private sector) determines the borrower qualifications. If the lender is originating loans for a specific investor, the guidelines and ratios are determined by that investor. Ordinarily, coborrowers, cosigners and gift letters may be used.

Property Requirements

Single-family houses, condominiums, townhouses and two-unit, three-unit and four-unit family dwellings may be considered for owner-occupied conventional loans. In most instances, the properties must meet all building and zoning requirements as well as minimum property standards.

Lenders may set their own guidelines and determine the types of properties and the individual properties within each group on which they will make loans. For instance, a lender's guidelines may enable a loan to be made on condominiums in one complex but not in another. Also, lenders determine which appraisal reports they will accept. Some use only reports from their own staff appraisers.

High Risk Lenders and Loans

In almost every metropolitan area there are a few lenders who specialize in high risk loans. These lenders make loans on properties that almost no other lender in town would touch. The properties may be considered high risk for any one of a number of reasons: zoning and/or building code violations; very poor location; structural problems; inadequate wiring, plumbing, heating, etc.; lacking or risky services, such as an inadequate or bankrupt water and sewer system; inadequately maintained roads (perhaps not plowed in the winter); ground water problems; or potential flood problems. The list could go on and on.

Of course, these lenders charge a higher interest rate or expensive up-front points (often both) for these high risk loans. These high risk lenders are known to others in the real estate community by reputation and are usually used only in special, rare situations with full disclosure by reputable REALTORS®.

Be aware of high risk lenders. Do not purchase a home that requires a high risk lender. There are sellers who will pay the extra premium, as well as a bonus or an additional fee, to a real estate salesperson so they can dump a bad property on an unsuspecting buyer. Don't be that unsuspecting buyer. It is very important to have competent, professional help to look after your interests.

There are times when special loans may be justified and in fact are necessary. A good example would be an older home that you plan to rehabilitate. Because the property is in bad condition now, it may not qualify for a normal conventional loan. However, when the rehab work is finished, the home will be in top condition and may be refinanced.

Some very reputable lenders have a certain amount of "non-conforming" money available for such situations. Often the lender may agree to replace the loan with a standard conventional loan as soon as the property meets all qualifications. Your REALTOR® will help you find a reliable lender who will make financing available, provided it can be justified by the property and your plans for it.

Give Careful Consideration to Creative Financing Plans

Lenders are in the business of selling financing and, of course, are always looking for new products to sell. Many different financing plans, some with several variations, are available. Because these financing plans are not the normal, level-payment, long-term, amortized loans, you must understand all the unusual provisions, terms and conditions. Some of these mortgage plans have provisions that benefit borrowers. Remember, though, lenders want to make *more money* and some provisions are definitely in the lender's best interest.

Some of the loans described here may not be available in all states or may be known by different names in your area. Amortization tables cannot be used for many of these plans.

The Qualifier Loan. This conventional loan is designed to help single people and families obtain a slightly higher-priced home than one for which they might otherwise qualify. The loans have terms of 30 years; however, for the first five years of the loan, the monthly payment covers only the interest. Beginning with the sixth year, the monthly payment increases and begins to pay both principal and interest. The entire principal amount is amortized over the remaining 25 years. For example, with an $80,000 loan at 9 percent interest for 30 years, payments 1 through 60 (interest only) are $600.00; payments 61 through 360 (principal and interest on a 25-year schedule) are $671.36.

With this financing plan, the payments for the first five years will be less and the borrower will be able to qualify for a higher-priced property. When the borrower accepts the loan, he or she should know exactly when and how much the payment will increase. The only disadvantage to this loan is that there will be no equity built up from principal payments for the first five years.

The Pledged Savings Account Financing Plans. Pledged savings accounts are used in two different financing plans. One variation uses a portion of the borrower's down payment in order to allow smaller monthly payments for the first few years of the loan. A large part of the down payment is placed in a pledged savings account, where it will earn interest and is used as additional security to help the buyer qualify for the loan. This money is gradually withdrawn to supplement the monthly principal and interest (PI) payments made by the borrower. When the entire savings account is depleted, the PI payment is increased and the borrower pays the full principal and interest amount each month.

Another mortgage program, available in some areas, requires a sum of money—perhaps 5 percent to 10 percent of the price of the property—to be placed in a pledged savings account as additional security for the loan. The lender may then make the loan, sometimes with a loan to value ratio as high as 100 percent, without requiring mortgage insurance. The money placed in the savings account may belong to the buyer, the seller or a third party, such as a relative of the buyer. The money must stay in the savings account (the owner may receive the earned interest) until a certain amount of the principal balance of the loan is repaid.

The Graduated Payment Mortgage with Negative Amortization. Conventional loans with graduated payment schedules and negative amortization were very popular in the 1980s, when interest rates were very high. They allowed many homebuyers to qualify for loans with very low monthly payments the first few years. During this time the loan balance was increasing to make up for the low payments. Unfortunately, as home values leveled off and began to fall, many owners realized they owed more for their homes than they were worth. Since the properties could not be sold for the amount of the loans, many owners let their properties go into foreclosure.

Few if any lenders are making new loans with negative amortization. In any case, don't accept this type of financing.

The Adjustable or Variable Rate Mortgage. There is an almost unlimited variety of adjustable rate mortgages. Even though it may take considerable time to shop the many lenders, the right adjustable rate mortgage also may be very good for you, the homebuyer, depending on your special situation.

One very important consideration is the length of time you plan to own your home. If you expect to sell your home within five to ten years, by all means consider an adjustable rate mortgage. Only by comparing the various plans and working out the payments will you know which plan will save you money.

Begin by shopping for a level-payment, conventional loan with the lowest interest rate available. Remember up-front discount points affect the interest rate. When you write down the lender's name and the interest rate, be sure to note the discount points. Then shop for an adjustable rate mortgage using the same principal amount and the same up-front discount points as the level payment loan. Look for an adjustable rate mortgage that:

- has a low first year interest rate;

- is adjusted 1 percent or no more than 2 percent each adjustment period;

- will be adjusted only every three years, two years or one year (the longer adjustment period may be an advantage); and

- has a lifetime cap of 5 percent or 6 percent. This means that the interest rate can never be more than 5 percent or 6 percent higher than the beginning interest rate.

Other things to consider: The lender usually chooses the index on which the adjustments are based. Ask for the name of the index and the present index interest rate when you shop for the loan.

Ask about the margin, the amount that is added to the index interest rate at each adjustment. The margin, usually from 1 percent to 3 percent, stays the same for the life of the loan.

Remember that the interest rate can be adjusted down as well as up. Also, it might not be changed the entire 1 percent or 2 percent at each adjustment period.

Some adjustable rate mortgages have convertible clauses, meaning the loan may be converted to a level-payment loan at certain times.

Since adjustable rate mortgages differ in so many ways, working out a worst case scenario will help you compare financing plans and choose the one that is best for you. Table 13.1 compares a 30-year, level-payment, conventional loan with an adjustable rate mortgage. (These are loans available in 1992.)

This example shows that in the worst possible situation, with the adjustable rate mortgage raised to the maximum amount each adjustment period, these two loans will cost the same at about seven and a half years. If you keep your home less than seven years, you will save money with the adjustable rate mortgage. If you plan to keep your home longer, you need to decide which financing plan you will be most comfortable with.

Another consideration: Since the adjustments and cap are based on the beginning interest rate, it may pay to buy down the first year interest rate with points. If in this example we had opted to pay one point of $800 (1 percent of the $80,000) to reduce the interest rate by .5 percent, we would have saved even more. In the first seven years the monthly payments for the adjustable rate mortgage, starting at 5 percent, would have been about $2,335 less, a savings of about $1,535. Also, the highest interest rate the loan could have would be 11 percent.

The payments on the level-payment loan with an interest rate of 8.25 percent would be about $2,380 less for the first seven years, a savings of about $1,580. If you have additional money available at the time of

Table 13.1

Price of home: $100,000. LTV: 80 percent. Down payment: $20,000. Loan amount: $80,000. Term: 30 years. Up-front costs: 0 points, 1 percent loan origination fee, normal closing costs.

Level-payment loan: 8.75 percent interest. Monthly PI payments of $629.36.

End of Year	Interest Rate	Monthly PI Payment		Months	Payments for Year	Total Payments
1	8.75%	$629	×	12	$7,552	$7,552
2	8.75	629	×	24	7,552	15,105
3	8.75	629	×	36	7,552	22,624
4	8.75	629	×	48	7,552	30,192
5	8.75	629	×	60	7,552	37,740
6	8.75	629	×	72	7,552	45,288
7	8.75	629	×	84	7,552	52,836
8	8.75	629	×	96	7,552	60,384

Adjustable rate mortgage: First year interest rate of 5.5 percent, adjusted every year with a maximum adjustment of 1 percent and a cap of 6 percent.

End of Year	Interest Rate	Monthly PI Payment		Months	Payments for Year	Total Payments
1	5.50%	$454	×	12	$5,448	$5,448
2	6.50	506	×	12	6,072	11,520
3	7.50	559	×	12	6,708	18,228
4	8.50	615	×	12	7,380	25,608
5	9.50	673	×	12	8,076	33,684
6	10.50	732	×	12	8,784	42,468
7	11.50	792	×	12	9,504	51,972
8	11.50	792	×	12	9,504	61,476

closing, and you plan to own your home for several years, figure out how much you will save by buying down the interest rate.

Shared Appreciation Mortgage Plans. Shared appreciation mortgage plans seem to have real benefits for both the occupant-owner and the investor-owner, but present a lot of unanswered questions.

Many shared appreciation plans have been devised. In some cases, the investor-owner puts up some or all of the initial investment money and/or pays part of the monthly payments. The occupant-owner is expected to pay his or her share of the monthly payments and maintain the property in top condition. Both the investor-owner and the occupant-owner receive certain tax advantages from the arrangement.

Shared appreciation mortgage plans can be win/win situations. The occupant-owner is able to buy a home at a lower cost; the investor-owner receives tax benefits and expects a good return on the investment in the future.

However, the big problem is uncertainty: What if housing prices level off and there is very little or no appreciation? If interest rates drop, can the occupant-owner refinance? How will the appreciation (or lack of it) be handled then? How will home improvements, added and paid for by the occupant-owner, be handled when the time comes to divide up the appreciation? What if the occupant-owner is transferred and must sell sooner than stipulated in the agreement? How would an assumption be handled? What happens if one of the parties wants out or wants to buy out the other? Will the occupant-owner be required to sell or refinance the home at a certain time? Are all other situations covered?

If you choose a shared appreciation mortgage plan, be sure you understand all the provisions, restrictions, terms and conditions. Probably the two most important questions you must ask yourself are: Is this a win/win situation with advantages for each party? Are the documents written clearly and precisely so they will be interpreted the same way by both parties?

Shared appreciation plans can work well in many family situations. For instance, parents who wish to help their children buy homes can use the shared appreciation concept to everyone's advantage. The young adult/homebuyer/borrower will live in the property and fulfill the owner-occupant requirement. The parents become the investors and can receive excellent tax benefits.

FHA loans, as well as conventional loan plans, can work well in these situations. Each transaction must be structured to fit the special situation. Obtain competent professional help when drawing up the necessary documents.

Buydown Mortgages. Many home sellers, particularly builders selling new homes, advertise buydown mortgage plans. A loan with lower interest rates for the first few years is offered. The 3-2-1 buydown is the most common, but there are also 2-1 buydowns, 2-1-1 buydowns and many others.

In a 3-2-1 buydown, the interest rate is 3 percent less the first year, 2 percent less the second year and 1 percent less the third year. For an example, let's consider a $90,000 loan at 9 percent interest amortized over thirty years. The monthly PI payment is $724.16. However, with a 3-2-1 buydown, the first year's interest rate is 6 percent and the monthly PI payment is $539.60. For the second year, the interest rate will be 7 percent and the PI payment will be $598.77. In the third year, the interest rate will be 8 percent with a monthly PI payment of $690.08. For the remaining twenty-seven years the interest rate will be 9 percent with monthly PI payments of $724.16. The borrower will save more than $4,100 during the first three years.

Besides offering actual dollar savings, buydown mortgages allow more buyers to qualify for the properties being offered for sale. Most lenders use only the first year's monthly payment when qualifying the borrower.

Buydown mortgages are a good marketing tool for the seller and also offer many benefits for the buyer. However, not all mortgages with buydowns are level-payment, long-term loans described in the above example. Be sure you do a complete Loan Profile so you understand all the advantages and disadvantages of the buydown mortgage being offered.

Balloon Mortgage or Call Mortgage or Early Maturity Mortgage. Any financing plan requiring a balloon payment—one final large payment that will repay the entire loan before the loan is completely amortized— can be called a balloon mortgage, a call mortgage or an early maturity mortgage. Often, the borrower must refinance or sell the property before the balloon payment is due. If the borrower cannot come up with the necessary money or sell the property, the lender may foreclose on the property.

Often lenders choose not to use the word "balloon." Instead the words "call," "maturity date" and "refinance time" are used when the balloon financing plan is explained. Don't be misled!

The Two-Step Option Mortgage. A new loan that many lenders are offering is the two-step option. This is a 30-year mortgage with a new twist. The borrower agrees to take a little lower interest rate for the first five or seven years and then accept an adjusted interest rate for the remaining 25 or 23 years. The only adjustment comes at the end of the five or seven years, whichever plan the borrower chooses. Then the interest rate will be .5 percent higher than the Fannie Mae Index for Reset Options. There will be no additional costs to the borrower at that time.

This mortgage plan definitely has more advantages for the lender. With interest rates lower than they have been in years, the lender is asking the borrower to take a big risk and agree to accept whatever the interest rate may be in five or seven years. The interest rate could jump to 12 percent, 14 percent or higher; there is no cap, no built-in protection for the borrower.

At this time, the two-step option interest rates with no points range from 7.5 percent to 8.5 percent—only .5 percent lower than a level-payment, 30-year conventional. The index is at 8.43 percent—within the range and close to market interest rates. A much better option if you plan to sell your home in five to ten years may be an adjustable rate mortgage with a low first year interest rate, a maximum adjustment of 1 percent or 2 percent and a lifetime cap of 5 percent or 6 percent. If you plan to own your home for 15 to 30 years, consider a level-payment, conventional loan. Before accepting a two-step option mortgage, look at all alternatives.

The Fifteen-Year Mortgage and the Biweekly Mortgage. Some lenders advertise the 15-year mortgage and the biweekly mortgage as better mortgage plans that will save money for borrowers. These mortgages may be level-payment loans or a wide variety of adjustable rate loans; the one thing they have in common is a shorter term. Borowers definitely save money over the life of the loan because the loan is repaid sooner.

The 15-year mortgage is amortized over 15 years rather than the more common 30 years. The 15-year term requires a larger payment each month until the loan is repaid. For instance, the monthly PI payment for a $100,000 loan at 9 percent for 30 years is $804.62, as compared with $1,014.27 for 15 years. The $210 a month difference pays the loan off in one-half the time. The savings is substantial:

> 360 PI payments of $804.62 equals $289,663
> 180 PI payments of $1,014.27 equals $182,567
> The overall savings equals $107,095

The biweekly mortgage requires a PI payment every two weeks of approximately one-half of the normal 30-year monthly payment. However, the borrower makes 26 biweekly payments a year instead of 12 monthly payments; this is the equivilent of an extra payment each year. Usually the lender requires that the biweekly payments be transferred automatically from the borrower's bank account to the lender.

Shorter-term loans are an advantage for the lender, and the borrower should not be expected to pay anything extra for the shorter term. In fact, borrowers should receive a lower interest rate, lower points or both for accepting a shorter-term loan. Also, borrowers can usually arrange to have the monthly mortgage payments transferred automatically from their bank account to the lender at no charge.

The 30-year term loan is a better choice for most borrowers because they will have lower monthly payments and more flexibility. If they wish to repay the loan sooner, they can include an additional amount of money each month that will reduce the loan principal. (See Chapter 25.)

Many Lenders Make Second Mortgages

Many lenders who originate first conventional loans also make seconds. Other institutional lenders specialize in second mortgage loans. Lenders usually charge a higher interest rate (1 percent to 3 percent above conventional rates) for a shorter term (seldom longer than 15 to 20 years) for these loans. Up-front costs may amount to several points. Remember, lenders like to make *more money*.

Lenders may set the property and borrower requirements and the terms and conditions of the loans. Usually the combined first and second mortgages may be no greater than 80 percent of the appraised value of the property. Seconds are not necessarily level-payment loans; often they have adjustable interest rates. *Beware!* The monthly PI payments for seconds may be very high for the amount of money borrowed. Try to obtain your second from the seller or a private investor; you may be able to negotiate a longer term and a more reasonable interest rate.

Shop carefully for a second and use the Loan Profile. Be sure you know what the combined monthly payment for your first and second mortgages will be. Most foreclosures on homes are due to expensive seconds that the borrowers cannot afford.

Loan Profile for Conventional Loans

A complete Loan Profile will give the borrower the terms, conditions and costs of the financing plan he or she is considering. Use Chapter 10 (Loan Profile) along with the information given here to evaluate each mortgage plan.

1. *Down payment.* Most conventional financing plans require a 20 percent or 25 percent down payment. Higher ratio loans of 90 percent that are insured with private mortgage insurance or with the additional security of a pledged savings account are available from some lenders. You can make a larger down payment if you wish.

2. *Interest rate.* The interest rate is set by the individual lender. The quality of the property, the financial strength of the borrower, the amount of the down payment, market conditions and the particular financing plan are all determining factors.

3. *Interest in arrears or interest in advance.* Interest can be charged in arrears or in advance on conventional loans, depending on lender policy. Interest in arrears is an advantage for the borrower.

4. *Term of the loan.* The term can vary with each lender; 30 years and 15 years are most common.

5. *Balloon payment.* Conventional loans may include a balloon payment. Check with the lender for the details of each financing plan. The mortgage or deed of trust may or may not spell out the conditions, including costs, under which the original lender will refinance the loan at the time the balloon payment is due.

6. *Mortgage insurance.* Private mortgage insurance is usually required for 90 percent and 95 percent loans. Sometimes it is used with a lower ratio loan to offset a high risk property or a high risk borrower.

7. *Up-front loan costs.* Up-front costs can vary greatly depending on the lender, the particular loan program and the interest rate. Either the borrower or the seller can pay the discount points and other costs for a conventional loan.

8. *Loan repayment schedule.* For level-payment loans, the same PI payment will be due each month until the entire loan is repaid. For many mortgages the payments will *not* remain the same. The repayment schedule should be clearly explained by the lender and written into the mortgage documents. Regulation Z, the truth-in-lending regulation, requires the lender to provide complete information on ARMs at the time of loan application.

9. *Assumption clause.* These clauses can vary from one loan program to another. Many, but not all, conventional loans may be assumed by a new buyer. Often the buyer will be required to qualify. The interest rate may or may not be raised. The assumption fee can range from zero to 1 percent or more of the loan balance. When a loan is assumed, the new borrower usually assumes the same terms, conditions, adjustments, payment schedule, etc., of the original loan.

10. *Due on sale clause.* Due on sale clauses are becoming more common in conventional loans. If the mortgage documents contain a due on sale clause, it means the loan must be paid off when the property is sold.

11. *Prepayment privilege or penalty.* Conventional loans have a variety of prepayment privileges and penalties. Ask the loan officer to explain each financing plan. All provisions and requirements should be stated clearly in the loan documents.

12. *Late payment penalty.* The late payment penalty written into conventional loans may vary as to when the payment is late and what late payment fee may be charged.

14. FmHA Loans:
Help for Small Town and
Rural Buyers

The Farmers Home Administration (FmHA), a part of the United States Department of Agriculture, provides many different lending services for rural areas throughout the United States, Puerto Rico and the U.S. Virgin Islands. The FmHA home loan program helps low-income and moderate-income families in rural areas obtain adequate housing. The loans, secured by first mortgages on the properties and insured by the United States government, are sold to investors. This money is then used to replenish the revolving loan fund.

FmHA personnel originate, close and service loans in more than one thousand county offices. Applications for loans should be made to the FmHA office that services the county in which the property is located. All applicants are given equal consideration, without discrimination.

Buyer Eligibility and Qualifications

The FmHA borrower must be in the low-income or moderate-income range, as determined by FmHA, and may not presently own a home. Also, the buyer must be unable to obtain a loan from an institutional lender with terms and conditions he or she can reasonably be expected to repay.

The buyer must have sufficient income, however, to make the loan payments and pay other necessary living expenses. He or she must also possess the character, ability and experience to meet loan obligations. Cosigners may be used. There are many judgmental factors that determine the eligibility of the applicant. The final decision is usually made by the FmHA county supervisor.

FmHA uses a two-part buyer qualifying system. First, the applicant's adjusted gross income is determined to see if he or she can qualify to meet FmHA program guidelines. Then the applicant's total income is used to determine the monthly payments he or she can reasonably be expected to pay.

Total income is determined by combining the income received by all adult household members who will live in the property. Most sources of income must be included. Check with the FmHA office for complete information.

Property Qualifications

At the present time, FmHA loans are available only for single-family houses. The property must be located in an open rural area or in a rural town with a population of 10,000 or less and may not be associated with a large metropolitan area. Some rural towns with populations up to 20,000 are included in this program because there are no other mortgage lenders.

An FmHA loan may be used to purchase an existing house on a lot or to purchase a lot and have a house built by an approved contractor. The lot may be in an open tract or it may be in a subdivision. With FmHA approval, a fixer-upper house may be purchased and the repairs completed with FmHA loan money.

Property standards are set by the Farmers Home Administration. The home should be modest in size and cost, but should be adequate to meet the needs of the family.

FmHA Loan Profile

1. *Down payment.* There is no down payment for FmHA loans. The loan to value ratio is 100 percent.

2. *Interest rate.* The interest rate is set by law and is usually lower than the conventional rate.

3. *Interest in arrears or interest in advance.* Interest on FmHA loans is always paid in arrears.

4. *Term of the loan.* The term is 33 years.

5. *Balloon payment.* FmHA loans do not have balloons.

6. *Mortgage insurance.* FmHA loans are insured by the government at no cost to the borrower.

7. *Up-front loan costs.* The up-front costs for an FmHA loan are minimal. The borrower pays for title services, legal fees, the credit report, survey, inspection reports, recording fees, etc. There is no loan origination fee.

8. *Loan repayment schedule.* FmHA loans are level-payment, long-term loans. The same principal and interest payment must be made each month until the entire loan is repaid.

9. *Assumption clause.* An FmHA loan may be assumed only by a buyer who meets the qualifications of the FmHA program. There is no assumption fee, but the interest rate may be adjusted to the FmHA interest rate at the time of the assumption.

10. *Due on sale clause.* FmHA loans do not have due on sale clauses. However, if the loan is assumed by a borrower who does not meet FmHA requirements, the loan may be called.

11. *Prepayment privilege or penalty.* The loan may be prepaid in full or in part at any time without penalty.

12. *Late payment penalty.* A late payment penalty may be charged if the monthly payment is not made as agreed.

15. The Federal Land Bank: Loans for Rural Borrowers

Since making its first loan in 1917, the Federal Land Bank has been providing credit to farmers and ranchers for a variety of needs related to agriculture. As part of the nationwide Farm Credit System, the Federal Land Bank system is organized into 12 districts. Each district has a large number of local Federal Land Bank Associations. The local associations are owned and operated by the people who use the services.

The Federal Land Bank is not a government organization and government money is not used in its operation. Each district is operated more or less independently. Funds for loans are obtained through the sale of bonds on the open market. The entire organization is financially self-sustaining.

Each district, with the approval of the Farm Credit Administration, can offer programs which meet the needs of its particular area. Many of the local Land Bank Associations provide financing to rural borrowers in two areas:

1. Loans for single-family houses in small communities or in unincorporated areas not in the path of development.

2. Loans for properties that produce or have the potential to produce agricultural income. However, the Federal Land Bank is not interested in financing agricultural assets that are being held primarily for speculative appreciation. The determination is made by Land Bank personnel.

Borrower Qualifications

There are no absolute rules and regulations governing borrower qualifications. Of course, borrowers must demonstrate that they are willing and able to repay the loan. Borrowers are expected to have outside income in addition to agricultural income.

Each borrower is required to become a member of the local Federal Land Bank Association, and often is required to buy shares of stock or participation certificates in the association. A stockholder-member has a voice in the affairs of the Federal Land Bank Association and is eligible to vote for its directors.

Property Requirements

The local Land Bank Association determines which properties it will finance. Appraisals are made by Land Bank personnel.

Loan Profile for Federal Land Bank Loans

Each Federal Land Bank district sets its own lending guidelines and policies. For more detailed information call the local association. It will be listed in the white pages as Farm Credit Service or Federal Land Bank Association.

1. *Down payment.* Most Land Bank loans have down payments of at least 15 percent to 20 percent, sometimes higher. The loan to value ratio is determined by the Federal Land Bank district.

2. *Interest rate.* The interest rate is set by each Federal Land Bank district and may be a point or two below the conventional rate. The interest rate may be adjusted up or down during the life of the loan.

3. *Interest in arrears or interest in advance.* Interest on Land Bank loans is paid in arrears.

4. *Term of the loan.* The maximum term is 40 years but most Land Bank loans have shorter terms of 15, 20 or 30 years.

5. *Balloon payment.* Land Bank loans do not have balloon payments.

6. *Mortgage insurance.* Mortgage insurance is not necessary.

7. *Up-front loan costs.* All Federal Land Bank loans are first mortgage loans originated and serviced by the local association. The Land Bank districts set their own policies and make an effort to keep loan costs to a minimum.

    Many Land Bank associations require the borrower to buy shares of stock or participation certificates in the association. Often the cost of the shares or certificates, as well as the loan origination fee and other loan costs, may be added to the loan and the entire amount may be amortized.

8. *Loan repayment schedule.* The repayment schedule is usually for monthly payments but may be arranged to fit the borrower's needs with payments due annually, semiannually or quarterly. A special feature of many Land Bank loans allows the borrower to deposit money in a special account to be used for future installment payments in case of adverse economic conditions. This money earns interest at the same rate as that of the loan.

9. *Assumption clause.* Loans usually may be assumed with the approval of the local Land Bank association.

10. *Due on sale clause.* Usually there is no due on sale clause in a Land Bank loan; however, the loan may be called if the new borrower does not meet qualifying requirements.

11. *Prepayment privilege.* Borrowers are encouraged to make additional principal payments. There are no penalties.

12. *Late payment penalty.* A penalty can be charged if the payment is not made as agreed.

16. Tax-Exempt Bond Programs: A Great Idea

Traditionally, tax-exempt bonds have been used to finance water and sewer projects, new streets, schools, hospitals and other community needs. These bonds are usually repaid with tax money collected from the community.

Tax-exempt bonds are also used to generate mortgage money for homebuyers at a lower interest rate. However, the housing bond programs work a little differently and *no tax money* is needed to repay the bonds. In simplified terms, the program works like this: First, the bonds are sold to investors; then the money received from the sale of the bonds is used to make home mortgage loans. These mortgages become the security for the bonds. Both the interest on the bonds and the principal amount of the bonds are repaid by the homeowners as they make monthly principal and interest (PI) payments.

Each government entity is able to design the bond program to meet the needs of the community while complying with all applicable laws and regulations. Borrower qualifications and property requirements vary from program to program. One or more local lenders usually originate and service the loans—conventional, VA and/or FHA loans have all been used. As with other tax-exempt bond programs, the investors who buy the bonds do not have to pay federal (and often state) income tax on the interest income. This tax-exempt feature usually attracts investors, even though the interest rate may be lower than for other investments.

Many bond programs are designed to help lower-income and moderate-income persons purchase homes. Some are designed for specific groups, such as people with commuity service jobs (teachers, medical personnel, police officers, firefighters, etc.). Other programs help only first-time homebuyers. Some communities issue the bonds for the primary purpose of increasing employment in the construction industry, thereby helping all segments of the local economy. In these instances, the mortgage money may be available to many different types of borrowers.

There has been some opposition to these programs on the grounds that the federal government is losing tax money because the investors who buy the bonds do not pay federal income tax on the interest income. Many people, however, see these bond programs as an excellent way to provide housing money for owner-occupied home loans, and feel they should be allowed to continue. Any "lost" tax revenue is usually offset by increased income taxes from workers employed as a consequence of the bond program and the decrease in required unemployment and welfare expenses.

Your REALTOR® should be able to tell you whether bond program money is available or will become available in your area, and he or she can help you obtain all the necessary information.

17. Be Wary of Pitfalls When You Assume a Loan

Many times the purchaser may take over, or assume, the existing loan on the property he or she buys. The difference between the sale price and the loan amount may be paid to the seller in cash or in some other way.

Before agreeing to take over a loan, however, there are many things the buyer needs to know. First, there are two ways to take over existing financing: (1) The buyer can "assume and agree to pay" the loan. The new purchaser accepts the responsibility for paying the balance of the loan and becomes legally liable for the loan. (2) The purchaser can buy the property "subject to" the existing financing. In "subject to" situations, the new buyer accepts the responsibility for paying the balance of the loan, but the original borrower remains legally liable for the loan. If the new borrower should default, the lender can go back to the original borrower for the payments. In either case, the new purchaser accepts responsibility for making the loan payments.

Whether the buyer assumes the existing loan or purchases the property subject to the existing loan usually depends on the type of loan and the terms and conditions written into the original mortgage or deed of trust. In either case, *assume* is the word used to mean that the new buyer takes over the financing already on the property.

Many loans may be assumed quite easily with no changes in the terms. The interest rate and all conditions of the loan remain the same. Most VA loans originated before March 1988 and many FHA loans originated before December 1989 may be assumed in this manner with an assumption fee. VA loans originated after March 1, 1988, may be assumed only by a VA-approved borrower. FHA loans originated after December 15, 1989, may be assumed only if the new borrower qualifies under FHA requirements.

Many conventional loans also may be assumed without a change in the interest rate or other loan conditions. The assumption fee may vary but should not be excessive. Lenders are not supposed to make *more money* on assumption fees. The new buyer may or may not be required to qualify in order to assume the loan. This act of qualifying is more a formality than a restrictive requirement if the loan to value ratio is less than about 75 percent. The lender usually may not turn down the borrower if the lender's risk in the property is less than this amount.

Many loans may not be assumed without a change in the conditions of the loan. Usually the interest rate may be increased.

The mortgage or deed of trust will state the exact terms and conditions of the loan. Unless these are illegal (discriminatory or contrary to law) or the lender agrees to waive them, the new buyer must comply with all terms and conditions. The seller will probably have a copy of the original mortgage or deed of trust. Since these documents are recorded, a copy is available from the county in which the property is located. Your REALTOR® or attorney can help you obtain a copy.

Read the entire document carefully or ask your REALTOR® or attorney to read it and explain it to you. Be sure to consider all the loan conditions *before* you write the offer on the property. Pay particular attention to the interest rate (and whether it may be increased), the prepayment penalties and assumption requirements. Ask if the private mortgage insurance (PMI) payments may be dropped when the loan is assumed if the loan to value ratio is below 80 percent. Be sure there is not a clause that calls for a balloon payment.

Many of the creative financing plans with interest rates and/or payments that can be adjusted are not good loans to assume. Read the mortgage or deed of trust carefully. If the wording is unclear, or may be interpreted in several ways, avoid it. Be sure you know how often and to what extent the interest rate may be raised. Also be sure you understand which index is used for the adjustments. It's always a good idea to have your attorney read the loan document and write out for you in plain language what you are agreeing to *before* you sign a contract. Don't be so anxious to buy a home that you assume a loan that is not in your best interest.

If there is a due on sale clause, it means the loan cannot be assumed; however, you may ask the lender to waive the due on sale clause. Even if the lender will give you a written statement waiving the due on sale clause, be sure to consider the other pros and cons of assuming the loan.

All the creative, foolproof ways of getting around the due on sale clause are extremely risky for you, the buyer. Most were designed to help a seller get rid of a property. You may not even have a clear title recorded in your name. You don't need the worry and the risk. Either get a new first mortgage loan for that property or find another home. If your REALTOR® insists that an installment land contract (by whatever name) or a vivos trust or some other arrangement is OK for you, get another REALTOR®.

18. Consider a Private Lender

Private lenders are a very important source of mortgage money; a great many homes are financed entirely or in part by private loans. Any individual or group of individuals (rather than an institutional lender) who will make a direct loan to a homebuyer is considered a private lender.

The single largest group of private lenders are home sellers. It's good business for a seller to finance, or help finance, his or her own property. The property may sell faster and the owner financing may enhance both the desirability and value of the property. Also, the seller may make more money because the rate of return on the mortgage may be greater than that of other long-term investments, such as certificates of deposit or bonds. Certain tax advantages are also available to sellers who meet IRS guidelines. A loan made directly by the seller of a property to the purchaser is often called a **purchase money mortgage**, and may be a first, second, third, etc.

Relatives and friends of the homebuyer who provide a loan become private lenders. Many individuals or groups of individuals invest in first and second mortgages on high-quality properties with well-qualified borrowers. Your REALTOR® may be able to locate a private investor.

The privately financed loan may be a first or second mortgage (or a third, fourth or fifth, etc.). When the seller owns the property free and clear, or can pay off all liens, the new loan is a first mortgage or first deed of trust. The majority of private loans are seconds. By obtaining a new first conventional loan or assuming the already existing first loan on the property, then obtaining a second from a private lender, the buyer is able to purchase the property with a smaller amount of cash.

A private loan may be tailor-made to fit each situation. The interest rate, term, and other terms and conditions may be negotiated between the private lender and borrower. The up-front costs are usually very reasonable, as many of the fees charged by institutional lenders may be eliminated. Private loans may and should be win/win situations, with advantages for both the purchaser-borrower and the investor-lender.

All necessary documents should be drawn up by the real estate brokers and/or attorneys. Special care should be taken to protect the interests of both parties. Use the Loan Profile in Chapter 10 and the information on the various documents in Part VI when writing the agreement. Also, consider the special concerns listed at the end of this chapter.

Wrap-Around Mortgages: Proceed with Caution

Wrap-around mortgages have been used by sellers to sell their homes to new buyers. Wrap-arounds have proven very beneficial for sellers; in many situations they also may be advantageous for buyers.

A wrap-around mortgage should be a second mortgage that secures the amount of the first loan plus an additional amount. This mortgage usually has an interest rate greater than that of the first. An example will help you understand what a wrap-around mortgage is and how it works.

Mr. Seller is selling his property for $75,000. The property presently has a VA loan with a balance of $22,600 at 7 percent interest with a remaining term of about 10 years. The monthly principal and interest (PI) payment is $179. Ms. Buyer would like to own Mr. Seller's home and has $5,000 that she can use for the initial investment.

Mr. Seller will accept a down payment of $4,500 and a $70,500 wrap-around mortgage at 9 percent interest amortized over 30 years with monthly PI payments of $575. Ms. Buyer will use the additional $500 for a homeowner's insurance policy and the closing costs. Mr. Seller will continue to make the $179 payment from the $575 he receives each month from Ms. Buyer. In reality, Mr. Seller is loaning Ms. Buyer $47,900 ($70,500 $22,600) and receiving $396 ($575 − $179) each month, and making about 9.25 percent interest. If Ms. Buyer continues to own the property and makes the $575 monthly payments, Mr. Seller will be able to keep the entire $575 monthly PI payment when the first mortgage is paid off in approximately 10 years.

Is this wrap-around mortgage in the buyer's best interest? That depends on a variety of circumstances. Another option Ms. Buyer should consider is new financing—a new FHA loan. If the property appraises for the $75,000, Ms. Buyer can apply for the largest loan available. Her $5,000 will be used for the down payment, some closing costs, a one-year hazard or homeowner's insurance policy and the tax and insurance escrows.

FHA will let Ms. Buyer include the 3.8 percent mortgage insurance premium and some of the closing costs in the loan she will receive. The monthly payment also will include the additional .5 percent mortgage insurance premium that FHA requires. At this time the FHA interest rate with no points is 9 percent; the monthly payment for this loan is about $637, excluding taxes and insurance. This FHA loan will cost about $62 more each month than the wrap-around mortgage used in this example.

A third option for Ms. Buyer to consider is to assume Mr. Seller's VA loan and then obtain a second mortgage with favorable terms and conditions. A major benefit would be that the first would be paid off in ten years and Ms. Buyer's monthly payments would decrease by $179.

However, institutional lenders ordinarily will not make a second mortgage on a property, even with private mortgage insurance, if the loan to value ratio of the first and second combined is more than 90 percent. Ms. Buyer would need a down payment of $7,500 for this option to work.

In this particular example, it appears that Ms. Buyer should accept the wrap-around mortgage from Mr. Seller. However, there is a built-in risk in this wrap-around mortgage that Ms. Buyer should be aware of. If Mr. Seller does not make the $179 payment on the first mortgage, the first mortgage holder may foreclose on the property without Ms. Buyer being aware of it. (Ms. Buyer's loan is a second.) Ms. Buyer can protect herself by requiring that an escrow company or institutional lender service the loan and credit her with the correct principal and interest amounts each month, pay the $179 to the first mortgage holder for Mr. Seller and give Mr. Seller the balance. Ms. Buyer should ask her attorney to put this in her wrap-around contract.

Not all wrap-around mortgages, however, are good or even safe situations for the buyer. Sometimes the wrap-around mortgage instrument is not a second, but a third, fourth, fifth, etc. (Consider only a *second*. Stay away from thirds, fourths, etc.)

If the first underlying mortgage that is to be wrapped contains assumption restrictions, a due on sale clause or any other restrictive condition, the wrap-around could be extremely risky for the borrower.

Get a copy of the first mortgage or deed of trust from the seller or from the county recorder's office (your REALTOR® or attorney can get a copy for you) and read it carefully. Be sure to have *your* attorney check not only the first mortgage, but also the wording of the wrap-around document. It will contain all the terms and conditions to which you are agreeing. Watch out for balloons! Use a wrap-around mortgage only if it is the best available financing and is safe for you, the buyer. Insist that the seller have an escrow company or institutional lender accept and credit the payments and do the bookkeeping for the loan. *Write this into the contract; don't accept a verbal agreement.* Again, consider all conditions described at the end of this chapter.

Conditional Sales Contracts Are Too Risky

Some homeowners offer to sell their property "on contract." In reality, this is a **conditional sales contract**, also known as an **installment land contract**, a **real estate contract** or a **contract for deed**. In a sale of this type, the seller retains title to the property until the full purchase price or an agreed upon amount of the principal balance and interest has been paid and the buyer has complied with the other terms of the contract.

Usually, a very small down payment and no credit check are the only advantages to the purchaser with a conditional sales contract. The risks for the purchaser, on the other hand, are many. If the purchaser defaults on the contract or breaches any of the provisions, the seller may keep all payments and the purchaser may lose the right to obtain the deed. If the purchaser wants to sell the property before the contract is fully complied with, the purchaser may have problems because he or she does not have title to the property. If the seller dies before the purchaser receives title, he or she may have to go to court to retain the property. These are just a few examples of the many, many possible risks.

It is strongly recommended that purchasers *do not* buy homes with conditional sales contracts. This is another instance of a situation that is good for the seller but not in the best interest of the buyer. Rather than buying a home in this way, find another REALTOR® who will help you find another home.

If you must use a conditional sales contract, have *your own attorney* oversee the transaction. You must obtain a title commitment to be sure the seller owns the property and see what encumbrances are on the property. Also, you must get a copy of the mortgage or deed of trust and be sure there is no due on sale clause or any assumption restrictions. All the terms and conditions should be spelled out clearly in the contract. An institutional lender should be named to do all the bookkeeping for the loan account. (Read the rest of this chapter carefully.)

Be sure the seller signs the deed properly and has it notarized at the time the contract is signed. The deed should be delivered to you, the purchaser, by the seller (a technical point, but extremely important), and then placed in escrow until you have complied with all the terms and conditions of the contract. The contract *must be recorded immediately* to give notice that there is such a conditional sales contract. If these precautions are not taken, the seller could further encumber the property or sell it again to another party. Be careful and protect yourself. Better yet, don't get involved in a conditional sales contract.

Lease with Option Is Great for the Seller

Sometimes it's suggested that people without a large down payment should find a home they can lease now with an option to buy in a year or two. Usually the plan works something like this: The would-be purchaser agrees to lease the property for an above-the-market monthly rent amount and also gives the seller one to several thousand dollars for the option. In return, the seller agrees to sell the property to the would-be purchaser at a set date and for a set price. The seller also agrees to credit the would-be purchaser with the option money and a certain amount of each month's rent payment when the sale takes place.

The lease with option to buy is another situation that has many more benefits for the seller than the buyer. The seller has someone living in the property who may take good care of it, has the use of the option money and is receiving a high rental income. Also, the seller receives all the tax benefits of owning income property. At the same time the would-be purchaser is paying dearly for the privilege of buying the seller's property. He or she has given up the option money, is paying too much rent and is not entitled to the many benefits of owning a home. The advantage is not having to move when the sale is completed. If for any reason the would-be purchaser is not able to complete the sale, all the money would be lost and he or she would probably have to move.

A much better alternative for the purchaser would be to actually buy a home using some of the suggestions in Chapter 21. Otherwise, he or she should rent a home for a reasonable amount of money while building up a savings account with regular deposits. Always keep control of your own money!

If you do rent with an option to buy, the option agreement should clearly state all the terms and conditions of the sale, much the same as a purchase contract. See Chapter 36. Use your own attorney and record the agreement for your protection.

Special Concerns When Considering Any Type of Private Financing

Sometimes sellers provide financing on properties that otherwise would be unsalable or could be financed only with a high-risk premium. Try to evaluate the property the way an institutional lender would. Also, take extra care to be sure the entire transaction is handled properly and is in *your* best interest.

Quality of the Property. Concern yourself particularly with the quality of the property when considering any type of private financing. Is the seller trying to cover up a problem or potential problem? Is the property in a flood-prone area? Is the well and/or septic system adequate and in good condition? Does the property meet all zoning and building code requirements? Would the property pass an appraisal inspection by an institutional lender?

Be particularly skeptical of condominium complexes, including condominium conversions. Some do not meet minimum building code or lender requirements. The condominium documents might not comply with state or federal laws. The declaration, bylaws or budget may or may not contain certain provisions that make the property too risky for an institutional lender. Only if a condominium or townhouse complex meets FHA, VA or Fannie Mae requirements can you be relatively sure (although not positive) that new institutional financing will be available in the future when you want to sell your home.

Value. Ask yourself if you are getting good value for your private financing. Are you paying too much for the property just to get the private loan? If you were forced to sell your new home in six months or a year, would you have to take a loss? Some sellers offer private financing so they can sell their properties at much higher prices than they could expect to get otherwise.

Documents. Consult *your* attorney in preparing all documents for the real estate transaction involving private financing. Remember, just because it is legal doesn't mean it is in your best interest!

Servicing the Private Loan. There is one important additional consideration to keep in mind when using private financing: The loan should be serviced in a businesslike manner for the entire term. Each payment is part interest and part principal. Exact records must be kept of each payment showing how much of the payment is interest and how much is credited to principal. You, the borrower, have a right to expect accurate periodic statements from the lender. If a misunderstanding or dispute should arise, anything from mild unpleasantness to a full-blown court battle could result.

It is in the best interest of both the homebuyer-borrower and the investor-lender to have a neutral third party, preferably an institutional lender, accept and credit the payments and do the bookkeeping for the loan. This type of an account is easy and inexpensive to set up with a bank or savings and loan institution that is already servicing mortgage loans. Add a clause to the contract requiring that an institutional lender or escrow company (name it in the contract) will service your loan at the lender's expense.

IV
HOME-BUYING STRATEGIES

19. Four Important Questions That Need Answers

You began your search for a home the right way by determining the life-style you want. Only you should decide the way you want to live and how you want to spend your time and money. Also, you have considered the types of homes and the types of financing that might be right for you. Now it's time to plan your home-buying strategy.

Your home-buying plans must fit your special circumstances. Disregard all the old guidelines and rules of thumb. Your situation, your wants and needs and your future goals must be considered when you determine the best option for you. The four questions below and your answers to them will help you begin to formulate your home-buying strategy. The next seven chapters give additional information and many suggestions for solving specific problems.

**How much money—*cash*—do you have available
for the initial investment in your home? How much
money will you have each month for housing expenses?**

Determine the total amount of cash you can have available, if you so choose, when it is time to buy your home. There are many expenses connected with buying and moving that must be paid. Unless you calculate the total dollar amount you could spend, you cannot decide on the best way to buy a home.

Cash assets may include anything that can be turned into cash when needed—certificates of deposit, stocks and bonds, equity in your present home, savings account, money market funds, cash value of a whole life insurance policy (replace it with a lower cost renewable term policy), things of value that you are willing to sell, such as a car, boat and furniture, and even miscellaneous items to be sold in a garage sale. If you expect to receive a gift of money to help you buy your home, include it, too.

Not all your money should be invested in your home. Some of it should be set aside for a rainy day, some should be available to pay all the expenses associated with moving and perhaps some to pay off bills. The following suggestions may help you use your cash assets wisely.

1. Set aside some cash as an emergency fund that will not be used when you buy your home. The equivalent of two to three months' income is the minimum figure to keep as savings. If you are a first-time homebuyer, this may be impossible; you might need almost all your assets to buy a home. Try to use some of the ideas for buying a home with a small initial investment in Chapter 21. Without a sizable savings account, it is extremely important that you follow a strict savings plan once you move into your new home.

2. You need to determine and plan for moving expenses. Include incidental expenses like telephone charges, utility deposits, costs to hook up appliances, cleaning services, etc.

3. Consider paying off bills that have high interest rate charges. You may want to pay off all bills and loans so you can qualify for the largest mortgage loan. Discuss this with your loan officer.

4. If you plan major purchases in the first year or so after buying your home—appliances, furniture, a new car, etc.—consider setting the money aside now. You may want or need to spend a large amount of money on improvements—a fence, sprinkler system, landscaping, carpet, new decorating, energy-saving items—for the home you choose. Try to avoid high financing charges for these purchases.

5. The remaining cash assets may be used as the initial investment in your home. Or, better still, part of the remaining cash assets may become the initial investment in your new home and another part may be used to purchase an income real estate property that will give you additional tax benefits and help increase your net worth.

The monthly housing expense figure should come from your budget. Remember, your housing expenses will include the monthly payment for principal, interest, taxes and insurance (or maintenance fee if you are buying a condominium) as well as utilities and upkeep costs.

What is your tax situation?

Now, before you purchase your home, is the ideal time to take a long hard look at your tax situation. If Uncle Sam has been taking a hefty share of your income, you may be able to cut your tax obligations substantially. What you don't pay in taxes can be spent in better ways. Chapters 24 and 46 give specific information on the tax benefits of owning your home.

A call to your local IRS office will get you the 1040 forms that you may use to estimate your taxes after purchasing your new home. The time spent working through these forms, using approximate numbers for interest and tax deductions, will be well spent.

What changes do you see in your personal and family situation in the next five years? Over the next 15 years? What changes do you see in your financial situation in the next five years? Over the next 15 years?

You know there will be changes in your life, even if there isn't a crystal ball to predict the future. It is important to consider how any anticipated changes might affect your life-style. Give some serious thought now, before you buy your new home, to your current situation and whatever changes you foresee. Plan for these changes, but don't live in the future. The home you buy should let you live the life-style you want today and for the next few years. While it is good to anticipate change and plan for it, don't let future considerations dominate your plans. For example, don't stretch your budget and give up things you'd like to do now in order to pay for a three-bedroom or four-bedroom house if you won't need the space for five or six years. Instead, buy a home that fits your needs and life-style now and still leaves money for other things. Do try to buy a home that will be easy to sell when the time comes, or perhaps buy a home that can become a rental in a few years. Your home-buying strategy should give you the most options and the most benefits.

How long do you plan to own your home?

This is a major consideration. If you plan to stay put and live in your home for 20 to 30 years or longer, and would feel most comfortable owning it free and clear, put a reasonable amount of your assets into your home. You may wish to double up on principal payments so you can pay off the loan as soon as possible (see Chapter 25).

Most people, however, own their home for only a few years. If you think you will sell your home in a relatively short period of time, consider these points:

- Plan for only the foreseeable future. Purchase the size home you need now and will need for the next few years. You can always buy a larger home when you need the space. In the meantime, you will have lower housing expenses.

- Buy a home that will be easy to resell. A smaller down payment and financing that can be readily assumed by a new owner may be an advantage. Avoid prepayment penalties if at all possible.

- Try to avoid expensive up-front points when purchasing a home for short-term ownership. It is usually less expensive in the long run to pay a little extra each month (a higher interest rate) than to pay large up-front costs.

- Consider buying a home now that can become a rental property. Buy with a small initial investment and save as much cash as possible to use for your next home purchase, so this home won't have to be sold in order for you to be able to afford another.

20. Qualifying Guidelines and More Useful Information

If you are a typical homebuyer, you will finance your purchase with a new first mortgage loan. Many first-time buyers think this means getting all dressed up in your best suit, arriving at the lender's opulent palace well before the appointed time (heaven forbid you would be a moment late) and beseeching the revered banker for just enough money to buy your home.

Nonsense! Lenders no longer belong on an ivory pedestal, if they ever did. Don't be intimidated! Lenders are business people and should be respected, the same as you and your colleagues, for conducting business in a competent, honest, courteous, businesslike manner. Lenders want to make loans, but must be concerned that the money will be repaid as agreed. Borrowers who can show they are good credit risks—both willing and able to repay the loan—should have no trouble obtaining a loan.

To guard against taking undue risks, lenders are required to follow strict guidelines when determining the maximum amount of money any borrower may receive. You, as the borrower, should look upon the lender's guidelines as a technical requirement that you must meet before you can get a loan. Only you know how much you can comfortably afford for your monthly housing expenses because you have spent considerable time and effort working out your personal budget.

The amount of money you feel you can spend each month may be more or less than what the lender thinks you should spend. The lender's figure will include principal, interest, taxes and insurance payments (PITI). Your housing expenses must also include utilities, maintenance and upkeep.

If the amount you want to borrow falls within the lender's guidelines, you should have no problem getting a loan. If you honestly feel you can handle larger monthly payments, there are several other ways of satisfying qualification requirements. These are outlined below.

General Requirements for Loan Qualifications

In general, loan qualifying requirements are quite simple: the borrower must be a resident of the United States, must be of legal age in the state in which the property is located (from 18 to 21 years, depending on state law) and must demonstrate creditworthiness. An institutional lender may not discriminate against a potential borrower because of race, color, religion, national origin, sex, marital status or age. To do so is a violation of the Equal Credit Opportunity Act. Also, the lender must give full consideration to coborrowers, whether or not they are married.

Of course, each lender can decide which loans or type of loans he or she wants to make and may set underwriting guidelines, but all borrowers must be treated alike.

When determining your creditworthiness, lenders are concerned with your attitude toward meeting your financial obligations and your ability to make monthly payments. The lender will always obtain a credit report that shows your debts and record of payments. Close attention will be given to any negative items, such as late payments, bankruptcy or foreclosure. You will be given the opportunity to explain the circumstances and outcome of each negative item. It is always best to clear up all financial problems before applying for a loan.

Lenders also take into consideration how much credit you use even if all payments are made on time. If you always have a rather large balance on several or many credit card accounts, and never seem to be able to get them paid off, the lender will take a dimmer view of your creditworthiness. You may be sending the message that you have a hard time controlling your spending and living within your means. You must use credit wisely. An ounce of prevention will do wonders when you are planning to buy a home.

Many first-time homebuyers do not have a history of credit use. This is OK. Don't be misled into thinking you must go out and charge something just so you have experience paying off a loan. If you do not have a credit history, the lender will probably ask you to write a letter of limited credit. This is just a short note stating you prefer to make purchases with cash rather than on credit.

Estimating Maximum Loan Amount

Different lenders use different formulas to determine your ability to make monthly payments, but most formulas use total monthly income and total monthly debt.

Total Income. Yearly total income is the total income from all sources *before* taxes, FICA or any other deductions. All income received by the borrower or coborrowers that can be verified and is likely to continue may be used to qualify for a loan. If the money is received weekly, multiply by 52; if it is received monthly, multiply by 12.

Total income includes:

- salaries, wages, commissions and bonuses for both full-time and part-time work;

- overtime income if your employer will state that it is likely to continue;

- tips and self-employment income to the extent it is reported on federal income tax returns;

- interest and dividend income;

- net rental income;

- alimony, separate maintenance payments and child support payments. (If you do not choose to use this income as a basis for repayment of the loan, this income does not have to be revealed.);

- disability and retirement payments, annuities, pensions, social security payments and other such income;

- veterans' educational benefits. If you are attending classes and receiving VA educational benefits, you can usually add this to your total income because it is assumed your income will increase once your schooling is finished; and

- usually, income from government-sponsored work/study programs.

Add together the annual income from all these sources to obtain total annual income. Divide this figure by 12 for total monthly income.

Determining qualifying income for borrowers who are self-employed and/or obtain income from commissions or the operation of a business is more difficult. Lenders usually ask to see the last two to four years' income tax returns and current profit and loss statements. Self-employed borrowers ordinarily must qualify on the basis of income, not just on the strength of substantial assets.

Total Monthly Debt. Your total monthly debt is the amount of money needed each month to meet your credit obligations. To determine your total monthly debt, list each one of your debts showing: who you owe money to; the total now owed; the payment amount due each month; and the number of months until the debt is paid in full.

Every debt and everyone you owe money to should be listed. This includes car loans, furniture and appliance loans, vacation loans, credit union loans, education loans, revolving charge card and credit card loans, and mortgage loans. Also include dentist, doctor and hospital bills, and all other payments for which you are responsible, such as alimony, separate maintenance and child support payments. (If you are selling a home and the loan on it will be repaid before you buy another home, the loan on your present home will be excluded when figuring total monthly debt.)

Add up the amount of money due each month to these creditors. This is your total monthly debt. Many lenders, while they need to be informed of *all* your debts, will disregard the debts that will be paid off in six months or less if the amount is not excessive.

Lender Ratios. Traditionally, lenders making conventional loans have used 25 percent and 33 percent ratios to qualify borrowers. This means that the PITI or PITM may be the lesser of:

25 percent ratio—Your monthly payment, PITI (principal, interest, taxes and insurance) or PITM (principal, interest, taxes and maintenance fee if your home is a condominium), can be 25 percent of your total monthly income.

Total monthly income × .25 = PITI or PITM

33 percent ratio—Your monthly PITI or PITM *plus* your total monthly debt service can be 33 percent of your total monthly income.

Total monthly income × .33 − total monthly debt = PITI or PITM

You may carry a PITI or PITM based on the lower figure of these two ratios.

Often higher ratios are used. Fannie Mae/Freddie Mac *conforming loans* are originated by many lenders throughout the country. These loans conform to strict uniform standards for documentation, loan limits and qualifying and may be sold into Fannie Mae/Freddie Mac loan pools. Fannie Mae/Freddie Mac conforming loan ratios are 28 percent for housing expenses (PITI or PITM) and 36 percent for total monthly debt.

The ratios for FHA loans are approximately 29 percent for housing expenses and 41 percent for total fixed payments (the FHA wording for total monthly debt). The VA's method of qualifying applies only a 41 percent ratio limit to all fixed payments. The ratios for many *affordable housing programs* are 33 percent for housing expenses and 38 percent for total fixed payments.

Sometimes exceptions are made. If you are single with no dependents, or a married couple and each is contributing substantially to the joint income, and if you have good credit and minimal debt, some lenders will qualify you at the higher ratio. It's interesting to note that the FHA may allow a 2 percent increase in the qualifying limits if the applicant does not own a car.

Translating the monthly PITI or PITM into the total amount that may be borrowed is more difficult. Property taxes and insurance premiums vary, as does the maintenance fee for a condominium complex. Your REALTOR® can give you the actual figure to use for a particular property or a ballpark figure if you are estimating.

By far the largest percentage of each payment is for interest. The available interest rate at the time you are looking for a home will have a big effect on the amount of money you may borrow. The loan amount (principal) may be determined from the amortization factors (given near the back of this book) if you first subtract an amount for taxes and insurance or a maintenance fee from the PITI or PITM. Divide the remaining amount (the PI payment) by the interest rate/term factor for the available loan.

Other Qualifying Options

Some borrowers cannot meet lenders' requirements for obtaining a loan as large as they need, but honestly feel they will have no trouble making the payments. Several other qualifying options are available.

Coborrower. Consider finding a coborrower to buy the property with you, thereby helping you qualify for the loan. With a coborrower, you enter into a partnership arrangement with benefits for both parties. The coborrower may contribute money for the initial investment and/or monthly payments or just contribute creditworthiness.

A coborrower is an owner of the property and signs both the mortgage or deed of trust and the promissory note. The coborrower's name is on the deed, and when the property is sold, he or she (or they) must deed out of the property. Some situations in which a coborrower may be beneficial:

- Two or more individuals buy a home that they will share.
- A student buys a house or condominium in the college town with his or her parents as coborrowers. The student and roommates can make the monthly payments and the parents can derive excellent tax benefits. For instance, if the student and his or her parents buy the property as equal coborrowers, the parents may depreciate two-thirds of the property, as well as take part of the interest and tax deductions. (See Chapter 8 for general rules on investment real estate.)
- A senior citizen buys a home with an adult child as the coborrower, with benefits for both.
- Rather than accept a cash gift, a young couple can have the parents be coborrowers so the parents can have the tax benefits of owning part of the property. Several years later the parents can "gift" their portion of the property to the children.

Cosigner. The borrower or borrowers may obtain a cosigner for their loan. A cosigner can be any individual(s) or a corporation whose financial qualifications are satisfactory to the lender. The lender may require the cosigner to supply the same information necessary for a loan application. Sometimes only a financial statement is required.

The cosigner is not an owner of the property. His or her name does not appear on the deed. The cosigner signs the promissory note and is obligated only if the borrower defaults on the loan.

Pledged Savings Account. A pledged savings account can be used as additional security for a loan. For instance, Uncle Andy's Certificates of Deposit (CDs) may be held by the bank that is making his niece a mortgage loan. The interest on the CDs will be paid to Uncle Andy as usual. The lender may take money from the savings account only if his niece defaults.

Lenders using Federal National Mortgage Association (Fannie Mae) funds to make mortgage loans may accept a pledged savings account equal to 36 monthly payments to qualify the borrower.

Income Exchange Account. Qualifying for a new loan is often difficult for retired persons because they cannot meet the income ratios. Some lenders may set up income exchange accounts and use the income received to make the monthly mortgage payments. The income accounts most often will be mortgages taken back by the retired persons when they sold their homes. However, other income-producing securites can be used, such as bonds, mutual funds, annuities, CDs, etc.

Private Mortgage Insurance (PMI). PMI is most often used to insure the investor's risk in 90 percent loans. It may also be used to insure against a qualifying problem, allowing the borrower to obtain a larger loan.

Buydown Mortgages. Many builders or developers offer new home-buyers buydown loans as a way of marketing their properties. A typical 3-2-1 buydown means that the interest rate for the first year is 3 percentage points less than the actual rate; the second year 2 percentage points less; and the third year, 1 percentage point less. For the remaining 27 years, the interest rate will be the actual rate. (See Chapter 13.)

Any home seller who is willing to pay the extra costs may pay for points that will lower the interest rate for the borrower or may provide the purchaser with a buydown loan. This may be negotiated into the contract. Buydown loans may be VA, FHA or conventional loans.

FHA and VA Loans. Both the Federal Housing Administration and the Department of Veterans Affairs use qualifying formulas that are more complicated but also more lenient than those used by lenders for conventional loans. You may not have a problem when applying for an FHA or VA loan for the amount you need since each loan application is approved on an individual basis.

21. You Can Still Buy a Home on a Shoestring (Well, Almost)

Some people still believe they need a 20 percent down payment or at least $10,000 to $15,000 to buy a home. However, many homes have been purchased with initial investments in the $500 to $3,000 range. If you have some savings, a steady income and good credit, you should be able to buy a home. One or a combination of the ideas given here is sure to work for you.

You may think you do not have enough income to pay for all the costs of owning and maintaining a home, or you may prefer to spend less of your income for monthly housing expenses. If you want to own a home but find yourself in this situation, consider the many helpful suggestions in the second part of this chapter.

Remember, whatever your special situation, the first step in finding the right home is finding a good REALTOR® who is willing to help you.

Buying a Home with a Small Initial Investment

If you can make only a small initial investment, choose a smaller, less expensive home. Even though you think a particular home may be perfect for you, the fastest way to get it might be to buy a less expensive "starter" home now, let it appreciate while you live there and improve it and then use your increased equity to buy your dream home.

If you're a veteran, consider a VA (no down payment) loan with minimal closing costs (see Chapter 12). Veterans may also use the FHA-Vet program with a lower down payment than a regular FHA loan (see Chapter 11).

If you are not a veteran, consider buying a home with a new FHA loan. The minimum down payment is less than 5 percent and a portion of the closing costs may be included in the loan amount (see Chapter 11). Perhaps a special mortgage bond program is or will be available in your area with special benefits for low-income and moderate-income homebuyers (see Chapter 16). If you live in a small town or rural area, you may qualify for a Farmers Home Administration (FmHA) loan with a minimal initial investment and lower monthly payments (see Chapter 14).

A wide variety of conventional loans requiring only a 10 percent, and sometimes only a 5 percent, down payment are available from institutional lenders (see Chapter 13). The added cost of private mortgage insurance (PMI) is a reasonable trade-off when you need a loan with a small down payment. Affordable housing programs are available in many areas as well as many special financing programs that help first-time homebuyers (this often includes people who have not owned a home for three years) purchase homes. Your REALTOR® can tell you if there are such programs in your area.

Another way to buy a home with a small initial investment is to find a seller who will carry the financing on your new home. Negotiate a small down payment in the contract. If there is a low interest first mortgage that you may assume, the seller may carry back a second. If the property is free and clear, the seller may give you a first. Also, the cost of obtaining a loan from a private investor is often much less than the cost of a new loan from an institutional lender (see Chapter 18). A wrap-around mortgage with a small down payment may be another alternative. However, be very careful here. Not all wrap-arounds are in the buyer's best interest. Read *all* of Chapter 18.

If a relative or friend will loan you second mortgage money at a reasonable rate, you could use the money to assume a first mortgage loan. Another possibility is to assume a low-interest first mortgage, obtain a second from an institutional lender (this money is then given to the seller) and have the seller carry back a third. This is often called a 1-2-3 financing plan.

If you are able to do home repairs, find a seller with a home that needs repairs you can do. Ask the seller to carry the financing at a reasonable interest rate with no down payment. In return, promise to invest your money and time to repair and upgrade the home. This will build equity for you and decrease the risk for the seller carrying the financing. If necessary, you can promise to refinance the home when the repairs are completed and the value of the property has increased considerably. (Be sure to give yourself enough time and flexibility before refinancing is necessary.) If you prefer a new home, another possibility is "sweat equity." Sometimes builders will let the buyer complete certain jobs in exchange for a portion of the down payment.

If you want to buy a fixer-upper home with a new loan and do the repair work yourself, but you won't have enough money after closing for the materials, ask for a repair allowance. Increase the contract price to reflect the value of the property after the repairs are completed and ask the seller to pay you the difference in cash at the time of closing. The allowance must be stipulated in the contract and the appraisal and be approved by the lender. (The lender may want to escrow the money and give it to you as the repairs are completed.)

Energy-saving improvements may be handled in the same way. If the home needs storm windows, a glass fireplace screen, more insulation, etc., and you will not have enough money for these improvements after you move in, they may be included in the purchase offer. Ask the seller to credit you with a certain amount of money, based on firm cost estimates, at closing. These improvements should be reflected in the appraisal and approved by the lender. (Again, the lender may want this money held in an escrow account until the improvements are completed.)

If the home you want to buy needs decorating, ask the seller for a decorating allowance in the contract rather than negotiating a lower price. Take the new loan at the higher asking price, then have the seller pay you a cash decorating allowance at closing. The amount may vary from several hundred dollars to several thousand dollars.

To save on closing costs, you might choose a home in a new development where the seller is paying part or all of the closing costs. In fact, you can ask the seller of any home you are buying to help you out by paying the closing costs. This may be part of contract negotiations.

Some people buy a home with a friend and pool resources. Many new condominiums and townhouses with two master bedroom suites are designed for this arrangement. If you choose to do this, work out your arrangements with the help of an attorney to protect each individual's interest.

It is also possible to form a partnership with an investor in order to buy a home. The investor often provides the initial investment while you live in the home, take care of it and make the monthly payments. The investor will be able to depreciate his or her interest in the property (see Chapter 8), and you may split the other benefits as previously arranged.

Remember to shop carefully for a lender (see Chapter 40) since loan costs may vary. Some lenders in some cities may pay the loan origination fee and other loan costs to attract business. Ask your REALTOR® if a lender in your area offers these incentives.

Finally, you may be given the opportunity to buy a home with a very small down payment using a conditional sales contract, also called a contract for deed, an installment land contract or "on contract." Don't do it! Few conditional sales contracts are in the buyer's best interest. Read *all* of Chapter 18.

Buying a Home with Low Monthly Housing Expenses

Many people can manage only a small amount of money each month for housing expenses. If there is money for the initial investment, they may still find a home that fits their situation. Here are some suggestions.

First, consider a smaller home. Not only will it cost you less initially, but other housing expenses—taxes, insurance, utilities, etc.—will be less. Buy a home that is in good condition and will not be expensive to maintain. Give special attention to energy-saving features in any home you buy. Utilities constitute a major portion of monthly housing expenses.

Also, look for a property with a low-interest, assumable loan. Some older VA, FHA and conventional loans may be assumed without qualifying and without an increase in the interest rate. (See Chapter 17.) There are still some loans with interest rates in the range of 6 percent to 8 percent that may be assumed. If you find a low-interest, assumable loan on a home that has more room than you need, you may also be able to find one or two other people who will move in and share your expenses.

If you have a sizable amount of money for a down payment, but not enough for the entire difference between the loan on the property and the asking price, ask the seller to carry back a second mortgage for you. Or perhaps a relative or friend might loan you the second money at a favorable interest rate.

Another choice is to buy a small income property and live in one of the units. Find a situation where you do not have to qualify for a loan, if possible. You will be able to manage it efficiently because you are living on the property. You may even be able to live rent free.

Another alternative is to form a partnership with an investor and buy a duplex, triplex or fourplex. You will be able to get favorable owner-occupied financing because you will live in the property. The investor can qualify for the loan and depreciate his or her part of the property (see Chapter 8). Split the other responsibilities and benefits as you choose. Ask your attorney to draw up the agreement to protect each partner's interest.

Some additional suggestions include taking advantage of a mortgage bond program loan for lower-income homebuyers (see Chapter 16) or buying a home in a small town or rural area with a low interest FmHA loan (see Chapter 14).

Even though you have little money to buy a home or for monthly housing expenses, *never* try to save money by acting as your own REALTOR® or attorney. Real estate fees are paid by the seller so you can get help from a good REALTOR® at no cost to you (see Chapter 27). When you are buying a home on a shoestring, you are in a vulnerable position and need all the help you can get. Your REALTOR® will understand and perhaps offer more suggestions so you can own a home as soon as possible.

22. The "Buy Now, Refinance Later" Strategy

Some builders, REALTORS® and lenders are touting a new strategy: "Buy now! You can always refinance later." Homebuyers are being urged to accept financing plans that offer very low payments for the first few years and then many pitfalls. Buydowns often make graduated payment loans, adjustable rate mortgages (ARMs) and loans with balloon payments look very attractive at first glance.

Be wary when an enthusiastic sales agent tells you, "This is just the home for you now and with these low payments you can't pass it up. In a few years you'll be making more money, the home will be worth a lot more, and you won't have a problem at all. Besides, you can always refinance." Before you grab any loan you can qualify for now, and decide to worry about any problems when the time comes, learn about refinancing.

One of the advantages of owning your home is being able to mortgage it. You have the right to place a loan(s) on your property and to refinance the loan(s) when you want. If you refinance with a first mortgage or first deed of trust, all previous liens must be paid off. If you refinance with a second, only the original first remains on the property. The refinanced loan may be larger or smaller than the total of the liens being paid off.

Refinancing is similar in many ways to getting a loan to purchase a home. You shop for a loan and set an appointment for the loan application. You must qualify for the loan and the property must be appraised to determine its value. Probably the biggest difference between getting a loan to purchase a home and a refinanced loan is the total cost to you. You must pay *all* the expenses for a refinanced loan: loan origination fee, credit report charges, title insurance fees, points, appraisal fee, recording and filing fees, etc. There is no seller to pay for points, title work, releases, etc. The borrower is required to pay all points for an FHA or a VA refinanced loan. Sometimes, however, the borrower is able to refinance a loan large enough to cover all the loan costs.

The Best Time to Refinance

Of course, the best time to refinance a loan is when interest rates are low and points are reasonable. Sometimes you may work with a loan officer and time the closing of the refinanced loan to obtain the best interest rate and points. However, you may not have this option if a balloon payment is due. Also, refinancing is not always possible; you must still qualify for the new loan at the available interest rate. In the past, during periods of very high interest rates, many people were unable to refinance balloon mortgages. Because the real estate market was slow, they were not able to sell their homes, either, to pay the balloon. Many of these people lost their homes through foreclosure.

Be Realistic and Wary

Before accepting a loan that features very low payments, take a good look. The seller is using the financing plan to sell you a home. Nobody gets something for nothing. You may be paying a high price for the home and the loan. Ask yourself these questions: Is the property overpriced to compensate for the financing? Will you be able to make the payments as they increase each year? Are you accepting a risky loan just because it looks attractive at first glance? Will you be forced to refinance or sell your home in a few years? Will you be able to refinance the loan or sell your home?

Don't accept the "buy now, refinance later" strategy unless you have a plan for making it work for you. Find a home you can afford and shop carefully for a lender. Use the Loan Profile so you understand all the terms and conditions of the loan you accept. When it's necessary to refinance, shop carefully for a lender and use the Loan Profile.

23. Do You Buy First or Sell First?

Many homeowners must sell their present home in order to buy another. Coordinating the selling and buying often presents many problems. Which comes first, the buying or the selling? The answer depends on your circumstances.

Begin by taking a realistic look at the salability of your property and the real estate market. Is the property you have to sell clean, uncluttered, attractive and well maintained? Is it in a desirable location? Is the existing financing assumable and desirable compared to available new loans? Are you willing and able to carry back a second mortgage? Or are you willing to sell the property with a new VA or FHA loan and pay some points?

What is the status of the real estate market? Is it a buyer's market with a surplus of homes for sale? Are homes selling in a reasonable period of time? How realistic are you about your asking price? How motivated are you, as the seller?

As a seller, there are several attitudes you may take:

- You know what your home is worth and you're going to hold out for every last penny. (By all means, sell your home first. Don't bother to read the rest of this chapter.)

- You are very realistic about your property and the real estate market. You will be cooperative and reasonable in negotiating the sale price.

- You want to move and are willing to do all that's possible to get your property sold. If you lose a thousand or two by not taking more time, so what? It's only money and you can make it up some other way.

Before you decide whether to buy first or sell first, get a realistic idea of how long it may take to sell your property. Discuss your answers to the above questions with a competent REALTOR® or REALTORS® in your area. The salability of your property, the market conditions and your personal motivation must all be considered.

Selling First

Sell first if finding a new home will not be too difficult, if you are moving to a new city and must pay all or most of your own expenses or if you are in a slow real estate market.

By selling first, you reduce the pressure on you to sell your home. You may bargain for a higher price. Furthermore, you will know exactly how much money you will have for a new home. Finally, you will be able to write a firm contract and be in a good bargaining position when buying.

The disadvantages of selling first include less control over the moving date and pressure to quickly buy a home that might not be the best for you. Also, you may need to move twice—first into a rental in order to give up possession of your sold home and then again into your new home.

Buying First

If you have special requirements that may make it difficult to find just the right home, you should find your new home before committing yourself to sell your present home. Also, if your new home must be built, start on it first. Construction can often take from six to nine months or longer, so you should have time to sell. If you are being transferred to a new city, you may need to buy without waiting for your present home to sell, as you will want to move your family and get settled as soon as possible. Many companies pay moving expenses.

If you buy first, you will know all about your new home—what and where it is, when it will be available and how much it will cost. You will be able to move when it is convenient for you. If you are in a rising real estate market, you may be able to buy at a lower price and sell your present home later at a higher price. This works best if there is a long period between contract time and closing.

On the other hand, if you buy first, you do not know when your present home will sell or for exactly how much. If the purchase of your new home is contingent on selling your present home, you will not be in the best bargaining position. You may be put under pressure to sell your home at a lower price than you could otherwise receive.

However, you may be able to use a guaranteed buyout plan or obtain bridge financing. Either one of these programs will allow you to write a firm offer on the home you wish to purchase. Any additional costs you might have may be well worth it if you can buy the home you want.

The Guaranteed Buyout Plan

Some builders and real estate companies may offer to buy your home so you may purchase another. Usually, the real estate company will list your home for a certain period of time and try to sell it for the normal commission. If the property isn't sold by a specified date, the real estate company may buy your home for an agreed upon amount of money and take over all responsibility for the property. You may then use the money to purchase the new home. Some companies can arrange buyout plans even if the home you are purchasing is not in the same city as the home you are selling. If you are moving to a new city, ask about this type of buyout plan before you choose the real estate company.

Buyout plans vary from one company to another, but there is always one important thing to keep in mind: real estate companies are not in business to lose money. The amount of money you receive from a guaranteed buyout plan will probably be less than if the property were sold during the original listing period. Before you agree to the buyout, know what expenses you may have to pay and the exact amount of money you will net from the sale. If this amount seems reasonable considering your own situation, ask for a written agreement outlining all the terms and conditions of the buyout sale. When both you and the broker for the real estate company sign this agreement, you have a firm, binding contract.

The Bridge Loan

Many homebuyers need equity from their present home to purchase a new home. A bridge or equity loan may help solve this problem. The purchaser may arrange to borrow an amount of money that is less than the net proceeds he or she expects to receive from the sale of his or her present home. This money is then used for the down payment and closing costs for the new home. When the present home is sold later, the loan plus the loan costs are repaid. However, if the present home should sell and close before the scheduled closing of the new home, usually the purchaser is not obligated to the lender. These loans are called bridge or equity loans because they bridge the time between buying one home and selling another. They are secured by the equity in the property.

Your REALTOR® can help you locate lenders who specialize in this type of financing. Some real estate companies offer bridge financing as a way to get new business while providing a service to their clients.

Sometimes the owner of the home you want to buy will provide bridge financing. If an existing first mortgage is to be assumed, the sellers may be able to carry back a second for a short time, until your property is sold. The seller's second is secured by liens on both properties that will be paid off when your first home is sold.

Bridge loans differ from most mortgage loans in that they are not amortized loans and there are no monthly payments. Ordinarily, the money is not handed directly to the borrower but is provided to the escrow company, title company or real estate broker at the time the transaction on the new property is closed. At the same time, a lien is recorded against the purchaser's unsold home. The total amount of the loan and loan expenses is repaid in a lump sum when that home is sold and closed. The lien is removed from the property when a release is executed and recorded.

The cost of bridge loans varies depending on who the lender is. Interest usually is figured on a daily basis and the borrower pays interest only for the number of days from one closing to the next. Some institutional lenders and real estate companies charge one or more points to make the loan. Lenders who do not charge up-front points usually charge a higher rate of interest. Shop around and select the lender who will make the loan you need at the most reasonable cost.

When considering whether to buy first or sell first, plan for the worst and work for the best. Get a good REALTOR®. REALTORS® have experience handling these situations. Usually everything works out fine if everyone stays in a cooperative frame of mind and you are realistic about what your present home is worth and the time it may take to sell it.

24. Tax Strategy: Know the Rules

Owning your own home is a good tax strategy. The interest portion of your monthly payment and the real estate taxes are deductible on your federal income tax return and probably on your state income tax return. Some closing costs are deductible—your accountant will be able to tell from your settlement statement which items are deductions. The improvements you make to your home will lessen your tax bills later on (see Chapter 46). Then, when you sell your home, you can postpone and possibly avoid entirely the tax on the profit you receive by following certain IRS guidelines.

Rules for Postponing Capital Gains

Many people must sell their present home when they purchase a new home. Many properties have appreciated since they were purchased; many homes sold today show a profit that sometimes amounts to thousands of dollars. Fortunately, for home sellers who are going to buy another home, the entire tax on the profit from the sold home may be postponed if:

- the seller completes the purchase of another principal residence within 24 months, either before or after the sale of the previous principal residence; *and*

- the cost of the new principal residence is equal to or greater than the adjusted sale price of the previous principal residence.

The cost of the new home includes the contract price and certain expenses associated with the purchase of the property. The cost of capital improvements made within the 24-month time period may also be added to the cost of the new residence. The adjusted sale price of the previous residence is the contract price minus certain selling expenses.

Ordinarily, the IRS allows you to postpone the tax on the profit from the sale of your residence only once every 24 months. However, if the sale of your home is for employment reasons and you can meet certain IRS guidelines, this ruling may be waived.

113

If you are selling a home and buying another that is less expensive, you may still defer part of the tax on the profit. Only that portion of the profit not offset by the cost of the new home will be taxed.

Note: Nowhere does it state that you must take the money from one home and reinvest it in another in order to take advantage of the deferred profit tax benefit. You may purchase your new home with as large or as small a down payment as you wish. You may even use a 100 percent VA loan with no down payment. This is perfectly permissible. The tax on the profit may still be deferred.

The Once-in-a-Lifetime $125,000 Capital Gains Exclusion

The $125,000 once-in-a-lifetime capital gains exclusion is another tax benefit for homeowners. Up to $125,000 of the profit realized when the home is sold may never be taxed if certain IRS guidelines are met:

- You are at least 55 years old on the date of the sale.

- Neither you nor your spouse has already elected this exclusion after July 26, 1978.

- You have owned the home for at least three years immediately preceding the date of sale.

- The home has been your principal residence for at least three of the five years immediately preceding the date of sale.

If you and your spouse own the property jointly and file a joint tax return, only one of you must meet the age, ownership and use tests for electing the exclusion. If you do not own the property jointly, only the owner must meet these tests.

Most people assume this tax exclusion is to be used only when the last home they plan to own is sold. However, some accountants are suggesting that eligible clients use their $125,000 exclusion now when selling their home, whether or not they plan to buy another.

The reason for this recommendation is that deferred capital gains (up to $125,000) of all the homes they have owned can be wiped out with this exclusion. When they buy another home the basis will be the same as the cost of the home. Of course, if this next home increases in value, there might be some capital gains taxes due when it is eventually sold. However, these taxes may be relatively small since the basis will be the same as the original cost of this property plus capital improvements. If the $125,000 exclusion is not used now and the homeowners are not able to meet all the requirements later with the new property, they may lose the $125,000 exclusion entirely. Ask your accountant about all tax matters.

IRS Requirements

A special tax form, Form 2119—Sale or Exchange of Personal Residence—is to be used when filing your federal income tax returns after you have sold your home. IRS publications that provide additional information and may be useful are 523—Tax Information on Selling Your Home—and 530—Tax Information for Homeowners.

25. Every Borrower Can Save Thousands in Interest Payments

Home mortgage loans are amortized; each payment is part interest and part principal. Each month, the interest due on the loan is subtracted from the payment amount. The balance of the payment is then applied to the principal and the loan is reduced by this amount. In this manner, the entire loan is gradually repaid.

Example A in Table 25.1 shows the first 12 months of payments for a $50,000 loan. The interest rate is 11.5 percent and the loan has a term of 30 years. A total of 360 monthly principal and interest (PI) payments of $495.15 will repay the loan in full.

If you increase the principal payment, the loan will be paid off sooner. For instance, in Example B, $25 was added to each PI payment for the 12 monthly payments shown. If the additional $25 a month is continued, the loan will be paid off in 267 months (22 years and 3 months) rather than 360 months (30 years).

The savings in Example B are quite substantial. You will have spent an additional $6,675, figuring $25 a month until the loan is repaid (267 months). However, the 93 payments (7 years and 9 months) of $495.15 that will *not* have to be made will save you $46,049.

Virtually every company servicing amortized loans uses a computer that automatically figures the interest due and credits the balance of the PI payment to principal. Every borrower may pay an additional amount to reduce the principal balance whenever he or she desires. (If your loan has a prepayment penalty, determine how much principal may be repaid each year without penalty.) You may use your amortization schedule and make the next month's principal payment. However, this is not necessary. The additional payment does not have to be a set amount, nor does it have to be made on a regular basis. For instance, you may wish to use the overtime pay you occasionally earn or an annual bonus to make additional principal payments that will reduce your loan balance.

Even if you have had your loan for a number of years and have never paid anything extra, you may start now. The one thing you must understand is that even though you make additional principal payments, you are never excused from making the next month's PI payment. The

Table 25.1

Example A: **$50,000 loan, 11.5% interest, 360 payments of $495.15**

	Payment Amount	Interest Due	Principal Payment	Loan Balance
1	$495.15	$479.15	$16.00	$49,984.00
2	495.15	478.99	16.16	49,967.84
3	495.15	478.84	16.31	49,951.53
4	495.15	478.69	16.46	49,935.07
5	495.15	478.53	16.62	49,918.45
6	495.15	478.37	16.78	49,901.67
7	495.15	478.21	16.94	49,884.73
8	495.15	478.05	17.10	49,867.63
9	495.15	477.88	17.27	49,850.36
10	495.15	477.72	17.43	49,832.93
11	495.15	477.55	17.60	49,815.33
12	495.15	477.38	17.77	49,797.56

Example B: **The same loan as in Example A above, but with an additional $25 principal payment each month.**

	Payment Amount	Interest Due	Principal Payment	Loan Balance
1	$520.15	$479.15	$41.00	$49,959.00
2	520.15	478.76	41.39	49,917.61
3	520.15	478.36	41.79	49,875.82
4	520.15	477.96	42.19	49,833.63
5	520.15	477.56	42.59	49,791.04
6	520.15	477.15	43.00	49,748.04
7	520.15	476.74	43.41	49,704.63
8	520.15	476.32	43.83	49,660.80
9	520.15	475.90	44.25	49,616.55
10	520.15	475.48	44.67	49,571.88
11	520.15	475.05	45.10	49,526.78
12	520.15	474.62	45.53	49,481.25

additional payment will shorten the term of your loan, but will not reduce the required monthly PI payment. Also, to avoid any confusion, be sure to let the lender know you are making an additional principal payment; clearly mark the amount so it will be credited properly.

If you are getting a new loan, take the longest term available, unless you can receive some extra benefits by accepting a loan with a shorter term—perhaps a reduced interest rate or lower up-front costs. The longer term loan will give you a lower monthly PI payment and more flexibility. You may always shorten the term yourself by making the extra principal payments.

If you would like to pay off your loan within a certain number of years by increasing your monthly payment by a set amount each month, you may estimate that amount by using the amortization factors near the back of this book. Locate the interest rate of your loan and pick the term nearest the time you would like to have your loan repaid. Multiply the present balance of your loan by the rate/term factor. Increase your monthly PI payment to this amount. If your monthly payment includes an escrow for taxes and insurance or taxes and maintenance fee, be sure to add the escrow to the new PI amount. Tell your lender the additional amount is to be credited toward the principal balance.

There are some instances when you probably should *not* make additional principal payments. If you don't have a substantial savings account or a rainy-day kitty, any extra money should be used to build up a readily available fund that may be used in an emergency. Also, if you plan to sell your home in a few years it may be better to invest your money in another way. Finally, if the interest rate on your loan is lower than the interest you can earn by investing your money in some other way, you should probably not pay down your loan.

However, if you have a healthy rainy-day kitty, plan to live in your home for a long time and would like to own it free and clear, now is the time to take action. Make an additional principal payment every month or whenever you are able. You'll save yourself thousands of dollars in interest charges and own your home free and clear much, much sooner.

26. Cash Buyers Must Be Wary

There are times when buying a home with cash may be risky. Although it may be easier to pay for your home, own it free and clear and avoid the hassle of getting a loan, cash buyers must be aware of certain problems.

Buying a newly constructed home is a prime example. Before anything is offered for sale, the developer-builder often arranges financing for the potential buyers of the new houses, townhouses or condominiums. However, the builder must meet certain requirements before the lender will actually make a loan and the first sales can be closed.

It is not unusual for the builder to court cash buyers, make extra concessions to them and finish up their units first. Of course, the cash buyers are led to believe the builder respects their financial status and is just giving them due attention. Too often, what the builder respects is their cash. Cash sales may be closed without the lender's approval of the property, and the builder might need the money to meet payroll or other expenses.

Most of the time there are no major problems with cash home sales. Before long the builder meets the lender's requirements and the financed sales begin to close. However, there have been plenty of instances where the builder was unable to get final lender approval and the only sales that were closed, at least for a long time, were those for cash buyers. So if you are a cash buyer, be wary! Don't be one of the first to close and move into a new development. Even if it is a great inconvenience to wait, don't close your cash sale until several of the financed sales have closed.

Cash Buyers, Especially, Need Competent Professional Help

In one respect, a cash buyer goes it alone when buying real estate; he or she doesn't have the added protection of a lender's interest in the purchase. Even though cash buyers need not be concerned about getting a loan, they must not overlook many of the documents routinely required by a lender: title commitment and title insurance policy, survey, tax certificate, inspection reports, etc. Cash buyers, especially, need competent professional help to make sure their entire transaction is handled properly.

Some Buyers Should Not Purchase
Their Homes with All Cash

Unless you have a substantial savings account with money that is more readily available, or other assets that can be converted to cash when needed, you should not tie up all your money in your home. It is quite difficult to get access to the equity in your home. If there is any chance you will need the equity in your home, and you may not be able to qualify for a loan later on (for instance, if you will be retired), invest only part of your money in your home and get a loan now. Put the remaining money in an income-producing investment and use the yield to make the payments on your home loan.

Finally, if you are in a high tax bracket, consider putting a mortgage loan on your home and using your extra cash to buy income-producing real estate. The income will make your home loan payments and you will receive considerable tax savings.

V
THE SUCCESSFUL HOME HUNT

27. Choose Your Own REALTOR® and Attorney—and Go for the Best

There is no question about it—buying a home is a big undertaking. Not only is your home going to determine your life-style to a great extent, your home is going to be expensive and the real estate transaction will be complex. This is no time for a do-it-yourself project. You need help. You need your own REALTOR® and your own attorney.

It is important that you learn to recognize knowledgeable, competent, honest and helpful professionals, know how they work, how they are paid and how they can help you. It is important that *you* choose your own REALTOR® and attorney; don't just accidently become their client. You need your own REALTOR® who will help you find the right home, not just a real estate salesperson or REALTOR® who is selling you his or her listing. Sometimes it seems more convenient and less expensive to just let the seller's attorney handle all the paperwork. Remember, even though it's legal, it may not be in your best interest. It is always better if the buyer and seller are *not* represented by the same professionals.

Who should your REALTOR® be? It is almost impossible for one person to be knowledgeable and proficient in all areas of real estate. Since you are buying a home, you need a salesperson who specializes in residential properties and enjoys working with homebuyers. You also need a salesperson who has an honest concern for your situation and is truly interested in helping you find the right home.

In addition, your REALTOR® should be something of a community expert in the area where you want to live. He or she should know current home values, have a basic, working knowledge of the types of construction used in the area, be able to spot problems or potential problems and be willing to point them out to you.

A competent REALTOR® is knowledgeable on all current, available financing. She or he understands the different types of financing plans, the many rules and regulations and how they apply to your special situation. Also, she or he understands all the paperwork involved in the real estate transaction, is technically competent and is the type of person who follows through and makes the extra effort to get things done.

Your REALTOR® should be a full-time salesperson, committed to the real estate industry and willing to spend the time for educational courses and meetings necessary to keep current with the market. He or she should also be affiliated with a real estate company that is committed to doing the best job possible for its clients. Big or small, the size of the company does not matter; however, the professionalism of the company matters a great deal. Avoid real estate companies that have part-time salespeople. With so much to learn and keep up with, a person unwilling to make a full-time commitment cannot do the best job. A company more interested in making money from part-time employees than in giving its clients the very best services is not a professional organization.

The National Association of REALTORS®

About 720,000 REALTORS® belong to the National Association of Realtors, an organization dedicated to upgrading the professional standards of the real estate industry by making available a wide range of educational courses and other services. The state and local chapters provide many special services to their members (REALTORS®). The most well-known service is the multiple listing service, which gives all REALTORS® updated information on each of the properties listed for sale by other members. Through your own REALTOR®, you may inspect and compare the properties that fit your unique requirements, regardless of which company has the property listed for sale.

REALTORS® also have access to updated financial information and are kept informed, through their organization, of court proceedings, tax rulings, new or modified rules and regulations, etc., that could have an effect on your real estate transaction. In addition, all REALTORS® are expected to honor a strict code of ethics. Because of their professionalism and access to information, REALTORS® often make the best sales people.

Find Your Own REALTOR®

Probably the best way to find a REALTOR® is through a relative or friend who has recently purchased a home and was pleased with the way the entire transaction was handled. Ask for the name and company of the REALTOR®, then call and arrange to meet him or her.

Another way to find a REALTOR® is to drive around an area where you would like to live and look for "open house" signs. Stop and inspect the property and meet the salesperson. Engage the salesperson in conversation so you can judge how helpful he or she might be.

Or, use the real estate ads in the newspaper. Find a property that might fit your needs and then call the agent or office listed in that ad. Plan on spending a few minutes talking to the salesperson to find out if that person is interested in helping you. Did the sales agent ask about your situation and what you are looking for in a home? If the person is not interested in helping you, try another.

When you find a REALTOR® who seems competent and helpful, arrange a face-to-face meeting to discuss your special needs. Ask the REALTOR® questions. Does he or she seem experienced and knowledgeable? Will you be comfortable working with her or him?

There are a few things to avoid when looking for a REALTOR®. If you broadcast to everyone that you are going to buy a home, you will probably be beseiged by real estate people, and these people may not be the best for you. You may be put in the awkward position of working with an associate at work who is a part-time agent, or a friend's mother or brother who has just decided to make extra money by showing houses on weekends. Remember, you want the most competent and professional REALTOR® available. And you want only *one* REALTOR®. If you think you can have every salesperson working for you, you are wrong. The competent, experienced REALTORS® can easily spot the buyers who want every REALTOR® to cart them around town and show them houses. Good REALTORS® cannot afford to waste their time and talent if you are not going to be honest and open with them. Perhaps this point would be clearer if you knew how a REALTOR® works and is paid.

The great majority of REALTORS® work only on a commission basis. They are paid only when the real estate transaction closes. Traditionally, the seller pays the entire sales fee or commission out of the money he or she receives when the home is sold and the buyer does not pay the REALTOR® anything.

Ideally, there are two REALTORS® involved in every transaction, one who represents the seller and has the property listed, and another who represents the buyer, but who is also a subagent for the seller. It doesn't really matter if these two REALTORS® are with the same or different companies. The sales fee is divided between the two REALTORS® and their companies in some previously agreed upon manner. It actually costs you, the buyer, nothing to have the services of a REALTOR®. This is the way the industry operates. When you buy a home, you will invest your money, agree to make payments worth thousands of dollars and accept the responsibility for a property that will have a great effect on your life-style. You need a REALTOR®'s experience and expertise to help you find the right home and follow through with the entire transaction until the last closing document is signed. Don't you want the services of one of the very best REALTORS®?

Subagent for the Seller

Your REALTOR® will be a subagent for the seller. How will this affect you, the buyer? The REALTOR®-buyer relationship is informal and nonbinding. The buyer has no monetary obligation to work with a certain

REALTOR® and the REALTOR® offers his or her time, experience and expertise in expectation of obtaining a fee when the sale is closed. Since this fee will be paid by the seller, your REALTOR® has certain obligations to the owner of the property you are shown: (1) Your REALTOR® must represent the property at the listed price and terms. However, if the seller has said to bring an offer, your REALTOR® may repeat the seller's request for an offer. (2) Your REALTOR® must not use privileged information concerning the seller's situation to the detriment of the seller. (3) Your REALTOR® should know that you are financially capable of buying the property. It would be unfair to the seller to take the property off the market for an unqualified buyer.

Being the subagent for a seller does not give a REALTOR® the right to misrepresent the property or withhold information concerning defects or problems with the property. Your REALTOR® may point out attractive features and potential problems, help you compare different properties, suggest the best financing plans and answer honestly all the questions you ask.

When you decide to make an offer on a property, remember that your REALTOR® is working for the seller and should encourage you to make the highest possible offer. The best way to handle this is for you to decide what you will offer. Give the price and all other terms to your REALTOR® and/or attorney so they can be included in your offer. Be firm and expect the seller to accept your offer. At this time, don't tell your REALTOR® what you will do if the seller doesn't accept all the terms of your offer; you will be able to make a counteroffer later if necessary. (See Chapters 35 and 36.) After the contract is finalized, your REALTOR® will help you each step of the way to a successful closing.

Consider a Buyer's Agent

In many parts of the country it is possible for homebuyers to use the services of REALTORS® who are not subagents for the seller. A REALTOR® who is working exclusively for the buyer is called a buyer's agent or a buyer's broker. Buyer's agents are in a position to make suggestions and negotiate the very best deal for you, the buyer. However, you may be required to compensate the buyer's agent for the lower contract price.

Although the buyer's agent movement is strong and growing, there are no set rules throughout the country for buyer's agents. Local customs and state real estate laws vary greatly. Some REALTORS® act as both subagents and buyer's agents at different times, depending on the circumstances. If working with a buyer's agent appeals to you, ask your REALTOR® more about it. Be sure you understand all the advantages and disadvantages for you, the buyer.

Buyer's agents may be compensated in several different ways: by the buyer, by the seller or a combination of both. Also, the buyer's agents' compensation may be based on the value of the property, the amount of time required or some other factor. Be sure you understand your obligation to a buyer's agent before you look at properties with him or her.

Buyer's agents are now used quite extensively in commercial and investment real estate transactions and are becoming more common in residential transactions. It would be in your best interest to employ your own agent when looking for a home with special or unique features or in a high price range, where it is more difficult to determine value. It is unethical and usually illegal for a REALTOR® to accept compensation from the buyer if there is not full disclosure to all parties concerned.

A Word about Compensation

Whether your REALTOR® is a subagent for the seller or a buyer's agent working exclusively for the buyer, I strongly believe that the home-buyer should know what the REALTOR® will be paid for the transaction. I have no problem with REALTORS® making a great deal of money; they should be paid well for their expertise and time. It is not unusual for REALTORS® to make in excess of $100,000 a year. Of course, they must pay many expenses from their earnings.

Buyers should know, however, that REALTORS® may be paid varying amounts of money, depending on the property the buyer selects. For instance, your REALTOR®'s total compensation may or may not be more if you choose a property listed by your REALTOR®'s company. Some properties listed in the multiple listing service carry a bonus to encourage REALTORS® to show and sell the properties. In my area, HUD has often paid the buyer's REALTOR® 6 percent of the sale price—much more than the REALTOR® would probably make on a property listed by a real estate company. Sometimes REALTORS® are paid more when they sell a brand new home in a new area. Builders need to sell their homes, so their marketing plans may include a very healthy commission for the REALTOR® who brings a qualified buyer to purchase a home.

The real estate market is free and open; there is nothing wrong with sellers paying REALTORS® different amounts of money. In fact, to do otherwise would be illegal. The problem is when a REALTOR® pushes or encourages a buyer toward a certain property, not because it is the best property for the buyer, but because the REALTOR® will make more money.

If REALTOR® and buyer talk openly about this issue, the buyer can take a more objective look at each property. The buyer can decide which property is really best for him or her, regardless of how the REALTOR® is paid. Good REALTORS® are more interested in helping their buyers and building a good reputation. They know they will be well compensated in the long run.

Help Your REALTOR® Help You

When you find a REALTOR®, be open and honest and help him or her get to know you: your likes and dislikes, the things you enjoy doing and those things you really don't want to do, the special interests and needs of your family and your complete financial situation. All of this information is necessary for your REALTOR® to know so he or she may help you find the right home. Share your lists from Chapters 2 and 3.

If your credit history is less than sterling, discuss it. There is usually a way to straighten out problems. The more time your REALTOR® has to help you the better. You will probably save a substantial amount of money if you let your REALTOR® help you in the financing department. Also, he or she may offer sound advice for your long-term financial planning.

Take your REALTOR®'s advice and suggestions. For instance, when looking at homes, don't engage the seller in conversation. Let your REALTOR® get the answers to questions for you. Don't visit the property without your REALTOR®. Even if you are buying newly constructed property, check with your REALTOR® before going to the site.

Sometimes things don't go as well as they should. If you run into a bad situation or an unusual circumstance, call your REALTOR® and discuss it. Clear up misunderstandings as soon as possible. If you feel your REALTOR® is not giving you the help you need, or is using selling techniques more to his or her advantage than to yours, by all means take the time to find another REALTOR® and begin your home search again.

Select Your Attorney with Care

In many states you are required to have an attorney handle a real estate transaction. The attorney must either write the contract completely or approve the paperwork drawn up by the REALTOR®. In other states the real estate broker or a licensed sales agent may write and negotiate the contract if state-approved forms are used and only changes within certain guidelines are made. Whatever the requirements, it is to your advantage to have your *own* attorney. Don't ever try to save money or time by using the seller's attorney.

The attorney you choose should practice real estate law. Your attorney should also have time for you when you need it. If he or she is not available to write the contract, answer questions, or do other necessary work, you may not be able to buy the property you want. Ask the attorney you are considering using if she or he will be available when needed. Your attorney's responsibilities are to make sure the documents are properly prepared and executed, that title is transferred correctly and that you are protected from other legal problems.

Most attorneys never see the property and do not know market values. You must tell your attorney what is included in the sale price, what inspections you want and what type of financing is available. Your REALTOR® will help you list the things that should be included in the contract.

You always have the right to ask about fees before you select an attorney. By calling several law firms that specialize in real estate law, you may find there is a wide range of fees. Shop around, but do not sacrifice competence in order to get the lowest fee. Sometimes, too, it is possible to pay the attorney over a period of time.

Select your REALTOR® and attorney carefully. Be open and honest with them. They will help you find that just right home and have a successful real estate transaction.

28. Home-Hunting Tips

Picking the right REALTOR® is the most important part of your home-hunting experience. Whether his or her style is formal ("We'll sit down in my office and discuss a few things") or more informal ("Let's begin by driving through some neighborhoods and just talk"), your REALTOR® needs to get to know you and your family, your values, the life-style you want, your financial situation, the work you do, your hobbies, your special interests, your likes and dislikes—almost everything about you. The lists you made in Chapters 2 and 3 will be a great help. With all this information, your REALTOR® will be able to show you the homes that fit your special requirements.

Here are some more tips that will make your home hunting easier:

Don't Limit Your Options

Take a good look at a variety of housing choices. Discuss your needs and preferences with your REALTOR® as you consider the different types of homes. Before long, you'll be able to identify the right home for you. By giving yourself the freedom to choose, you will be more confident and happier with your final decision.

Work with a Map

A large map of the community in which you will be living is a necessity, particularly if you are not familiar with the area. If your REALTOR® does not have a map for you, check with the chamber of commerce or a bookstore. Some bus route maps are also good.

Mark your place of employment, various recreational facilities, shopping centers, schools and all other places of special interest. Your REALTOR® will be able to point out neighborhoods you may be interested in and/or condominium complexes that have the amenities you desire.

Also, use the map to mark the areas you want to avoid because of poor or inadequate water and/or sewer facilities, excessively high taxes, the possibility of flooding or any other problems your REALTOR® thinks you should know about. When you find homes that spark your interest, mark them on the map.

Don't Force the "Reluctant Looker"

If you are married, it's usually better if both you and your spouse go with the REALTOR® to inspect properties. You will both profit from the experience by getting a clear idea of what is available, a feel for value and a chance to discuss what each likes and dislikes about each property.

Sometimes, however, one party is a "reluctant looker." Whoever it is, the reluctant looker really dislikes going in and out of houses, has complete confidence in his or her mate's ability to pick a home and can see no need to house hunt. Instead, the reluctant looker is willing to look at the final choice or choices and give the new home a stamp of approval.

If you are home hunting with a reluctant looker, consider the trust a compliment and do the major part of the home hunting yourself. Some REALTORS® insist that both husband and wife be present for the home inspection tour because it usually works to the salesperson's advantage. A reluctant looker is more willing to buy a house, any house, just to end the whole affair. (The third house will probably be just fine, no matter what it is.) A great many "good" REALTORS® sell houses in this manner rather than helping a family find the right one.

Look Only at Homes That Meet Your Requirements

You have given a lot of thought to the life-style you want and to your financial situation. There will always be larger and more costly homes that are fun to see but don't fit your special situation. Don't insist on seeing these homes.

Also, if you are inspecting a property and it is not right for you, leave the property as soon as possible and forget about it. Concentrate only on those homes that you might buy.

Avoid the Seller

When inspecting a home, look pleasant and smile a lot, but *don't* talk to the seller. Don't let yourself be drawn into a conversation with the seller. Also, don't let the sellers hear you make any negative comments about the property. The reason for this is that you want the seller to have a favorable impression of you, but you don't want the seller to know how much you want or need the property.

You may have questions about a home that need to be answered. Ask your REALTOR® the questions and let her or him get the answers for you, but not while you are on the property if the seller might hear you. You'll have time to discuss the property after you get back in the car, and you can always see the property again. This is a very important point and will work in your favor when it is time to negotiate the contract.

Don't Be Overly Influenced by Decorating

When looking at homes, try to look past the lovely furniture and beautiful decorations or the messy housekeeping and unattractive furnishings. Look past the carpeting, also. More people decide to buy or not buy a home because of the color and condition of the carpet than for any other reason—a mistake! If the home is right for you in other ways, you may be able to buy it and have new carpeting installed. Remember, when you move into a home, it will be empty. Even some walls in very attractive homes will require repainting or repapering, so plan to do some decorating of your own in any home you buy.

Be Aware of Energy Costs

Monthly housing expenses include the cost of heat and air conditioning, electricity and water. Ask to see all utility bills for the past year to get an accurate estimate of these expenses. The energy efficiency of each property will be different, depending on the quality of construction, the type of heating/air conditioning system, the amount of insulation and the addition of such things as glass fireplace screens, water heater covers, storm windows, etc. If additional insulation and energy-saving items are needed, the cost of these items may be taken into consideration when the price is negotiated. After the improvements are made you should have lower utility bills. You may want to find a home situated in a way that will allow for the addition of solar features.

You Can't Mix and Match!

It might work when choosing a wardrobe, but it sure doesn't when choosing a home. You can't have the fantastic kitchen from house A, lovely patio and yard from house B, huge game room and magnificent fireplace from house C and the spectacular view from the house high on the hill all in one home. Don't waste your time and energy on wishful thinking. Realize that no home is going to be perfect in every respect. Look at each home you inspect realistically for its good and not-so-good features.

Play the First Choice, Second Choice, Third Choice Game

As you inspect each home place it in your order of preference—either first, second or third. Any home that would not be one of your first three choices should be forgotten about completely. As soon as you know you are not interested in a particular property, leave and forget about it. If you drive up in front of a home and realize you definitely will not buy it, don't even go in. Ask your REALTOR® to make your apologies to the owner.

Inspecting many different homes can be confusing. Try to concentrate on and remember only those homes you are truly interested in buying. Leave time at the end of your home inspection tour to return to the homes that are on the top of your list. This will help you forget the others and create a clearer picture of the homes that are right for you.

View Model Homes with a Discerning Eye

The professionally decorated show models are so appealing that many buyers forget to actually look at the property. For example, one baby's room was absolutely precious, with an expensive crib and dresser, matching hand-embroidered curtains, baby quilt and pillows and attractive wall decorations. Some potential buyers were not aware, however, of the room's small size. Will a youth bed fit in the room when the baby outgrows the crib?

In a model townhouse, the country kitchen seemed to have everything: antique furniture, wine glasses, recipe books, a hand-decorated tea kettle, lovely plants, a color TV, even a home computer. It wasn't until the buyers moved in that they noticed what was missing: a light over the sink and conveniently placed electrical outlets.

Realize that the decorating in show homes is a sales tool. You must look beyond all the fancy fixings and envision the property as your home. Be aware of the size of the rooms, window placement or lack of windows, amount of counter and cupboard space, etc.

Before you make a final decision to buy in a new development, ask your REALTOR® to make arrangements for you to see your plan in an undecorated state. This will give you a better idea of the builder's workmanship and the home's features.

Remember You Are Buying Your HOME!

With so many things to be concerned about, it is easy to lose sight of what is most important—you are buying a home for you (and your family, if you have one). You want a home that you really like, that you are comfortable with—a home that makes you feel special, that makes you proud to be the owner.

Keep your concerns about construction imperfections, component parts, warranties, energy costs, special features, the right price and financing terms in perspective. These are real and legitimate concerns, but they are only subheadings under the main topic—Finding the Home You Really Like. If you genuinely like the home, the location is right, the quality is good and it is within your financial capabilities, you have found your home!

29. What about Buying a "For Sale by Owner"?

A For Sale by Owner (FSBO—pronounced "fizbo") is a home offered for sale by an owner without the assistance of a real estate agent. Should you, the homebuyer, consider buying a FSBO? The answer is yes, if the FSBO seems to meet your requirements. You should give it the same careful attention you are giving all the other properties that seem to meet your requirements.

However, just because a home is offered for sale by the owner without professional help does not mean you, the homebuyer, do not need professional help. You still must inspect the property, compare homes to obtain the best value, write the offer, negotiate the contract, arrange financing and do all the other necessary things before you actually take title to your new home. You need your REALTOR®'s help.

Resale Homes

If you know of a FSBO you would like to see (or if you've already seen the property), tell your REALTOR® about it and ask him or her to get all the information about the property. Since the owner wants to sell, he or she will probably work with your REALTOR®. When your REALTOR® has obtained and verified all the information concerning title, financing, etc., proceed as you would with any other property. If this is the home for you, have your REALTOR® present your offer, negotiate the contract, etc.

What if the owner does not want to work with your REALTOR®? An owner who won't work with you through your REALTOR® is taking a very unrealistic approach. Probably the objection is to paying a fee or commission. Actually, the fees for marketing real estate are very reasonable; marketing expenses for most other products you buy are much greater.

If you want to buy the FSBO property and the owner won't pay your REALTOR®, work out an agreement and pay your REALTOR® yourself. Your REALTOR® is then a buyer's agent, working directly for you. He or she can negotiate the best contract possible and probably save you more money than the buyer's agent fee. And you will have your REALTOR® to make sure the entire transaction is handled correctly.

New Home Developments

Buying a home in a new development from an on-site sales agent is a special "for sale by owner" situation. The sales agent is hired by the builder to sell only that property. The agent is not interested in finding the best property or the best financing for you; he or she must make the property for sale sound as attractive as possible so you will buy it.

When model homes are available the attitude often is, "What you see is what you get"—but without all the fancy wallpaper, mirrors, built-in bookcases, upgraded carpet, beautiful furniture and very attractive accessories. You are expected to have enough imagination to picture the plain vanilla, generic condition in which you will receive your home, unless, of course, you want to pay for all the extras.

Homebuyers definitely benefit from having their own REALTOR® when buying from a developer. While builders often offer special financing and good value, there are many problem areas. The on-site sales agent, hired for his or her selling abilities and persuasiveness, is not in a position to point out negative features. (If you ask a question, you should get an honest answer.) The seller's attorney often writes the contract form in favor of the seller. After you finalize the contract, many things must be taken care of before closing. You do need your own REALTOR® and attorney to look out for your interests before you agree to buy and during the time until closing.

Many builders pay co-op REALTOR® fees; they realize that buyers need their own REALTORS®. Also, the builders need the help of real estate agents to sell their homes. If you have questions about this, discuss it with your REALTOR®. If the seller won't pay your REALTOR®, arrange to pay her or him as a buyer's agent. It will be well worth the money.

30. Buying a HUD or VA Repossession or an REO

Government agencies have homes in all parts of the country to sell. Properties that once had FHA insured loans or VA guaranteed loans and were foreclosed by the lenders now are owned by HUD or VA. Homes financed with conventional loans that were foreclosed by the banks or savings and loan associations are often called REOs (real estate owned) and must be resold. When the banks and savings and loans become insolvent, their properties are taken over by the Resolution Trust Corporation (RTC) and the Federal Deposit Insurance Corporation (FDIC). These agencies then have the responsibility of selling the properties.

The Farmers Home Administration is another agency that forecloses on properties when the payments are not made as agreed. Their inventory properties are sold to new FmHA borrowers. Other agencies, such as the U.S. Customs Department and state and local law enforcement groups, acquire properties in various ways, often in drug raids or in connection with other criminal activity. Eventually all of these properties will be sold.

All types of properties are available—single-family houses, duplexes, triplexes, fourplexes (and larger multiunit buildings), condominiums and townhouses—and they range in price from very inexpensive to very expensive. They are located in rural areas, small towns, resorts, cities and large metropolitan areas.

How Do You Find These Homes?

Many HUD, VA and REO properties are listed with real estate brokers and are in the multiple listing service. Your REALTOR® can set appointments and show you the homes that fit your needs. In some areas HUD and VA properties are advertised in newspapers. You can drive by and look; often, real estate agents hold open houses on weekends. Look at the property again with your REALTOR® or let your REALTOR® show it to you the first time. Offers must be submitted on VA or HUD contract forms. Your REALTOR® knows the procedure.

Many properties are sold at auctions which are advertised in newspapers. Usually there is an inspection period for several days before the auction is held. You can pick up the guidelines which tell when the property must be paid for, etc.

Should You Buy One of These Homes?

It is possible that one of these homes is the right home for you. But it is right for you only if it is located in a neighborhood you want to live in and if the home has the space and features you want.

Often people assume that if they buy a VA or HUD repo or an REO they will automatically get a fantastic deal. Usually this just isn't so. Don't get caught up in the hype and forget you are buying your home.

Most of these properties have sat vacant for months, usually through one winter, often two. Many other homes that people are living in and maintaining are for sale. Take the time to see other well-cared-for homes before you make a hasty decision.

Consider Each of These *Dos* and *Don'ts*

- *Do* work with your own REALTOR® because he or she works in and knows the area where you want to live, really cares about helping you find the right home and meets all the other criteria in Chapter 27.

- *Don't* work with a REALTOR® who specializes in HUD and VA properties, and *don't* work with a REALTOR® who holds open houses at VA or HUD properties. While these REALTORS® may know about submitting HUD and VA offers, etc., they usually don't know what else is available in the marketplace.

- *Do* realize that if there are quite a few VA, HUD and REOs available, it is probably a buyer's market and there are plenty of other good buys.

- *Do* look at other resale homes so you have something to compare the repos with.

- *Do* try to determine if the property, in the location and condition it is in, is actually priced lower than comparable properties, taking into consideration necessary repair costs. A few are; many are not.

- *Don't* assume that because homes are offered for sale by HUD or VA that the properties are in any way guaranteed or warranted by HUD or VA. They are not.

- *Do* realize that most foreclosed properties have been vacant for many months; most have sat vacant through at least one winter.

- *Do* have the property thoroughly inspected by a competent home inspector. Once you purchase the property, all the problems, whether you knew about them or not, are yours.

- *Don't* buy a property that needs repairs unless: (1) you can make the necessary repairs yourself and are willing to spend the money, time and energy; or (2) you have a realistic estimate of what the repairs will cost and you are willing and able to pay someone else to make them.

- *Don't* get in a bidding war over a VA or HUD property. What may be a good buy at $56,000 could be a very poor buy at $60,000. You probably can find a better buy at $60,000.

- *Don't* buy a home just because you think it is "such a deal." Use your information from Chapters 2 and 3, and buy only the home that fits your special situation.

- *Don't* make an offer on a foreclosed property unless it is a home you would be willing to pay the market price for.

31. Value Is in the Eye of the Beholder

All homebuyers share the same concerns: "Is the property really worth the price?" "What am I really getting and how much is it really worth to me?" These concerns involve both price and value. Let's take a look at each.

Price is the amount of money, the dollar figure, being asked for the property by the seller. Sellers may put any price on their property. Asking price is determined usually by the seller's personal motivation for selling and the dollar amount the seller wants to get; often it's a little higher than this to leave some room for negotiation.

As the potential buyer, you do not know why the seller wants to sell or how he or she arrived at the asking price. If you have made a good choice in selecting your REALTOR® you probably won't be looking at "overpriced" homes; your REALTOR® probably will not put them on the list of homes to show you.

The benefits you will receive from a certain property give it **value**. Like beauty, value is in the eye of the beholder. The degree of importance you want to put on the various factors determines the overall value of the home you select. A certain home may have greater value for you than for another buyer. Some value factors are:

Location

Location gives a property intrinsic value and is an important consideration when selecting a home. It is easier to find a good location if you go about it in an orderly way. First of all, decide on the general location—the areas of town or sections of a large city where you would like to live. Factors that may help you determine location are your place of work, the schools you prefer, recreational facilities, or subjective reactions—you just like certain areas and feel comfortable there.

Within these larger areas, select the neighborhoods that have homes with the style, size and price range that fit your needs. Next, eliminate neighborhoods with problems (perhaps a creek that overflows regularly) or that do not meet your other requirements—good schools, nearby shopping areas, public transportation, etc. Drive through the remaining neighborhoods on your list. Which ones appeal to you and which ones don't? Pare down your list to two, three or possibly four neighborhoods where you would like to live.

Now start looking for your home. Keep in mind that it is not wise to buy the most expensive home in any neighborhood. If you can afford the most expensive, move up to a higher priced neighborhood. The one exception to this might be if you have a big family and you need lots of space, maybe a large two-story house. Even then, try to find a neighborhood where at least one-fourth to one-third of the homes are of a similar size and price.

The location within the neighborhood is as important as the neighborhood itself. Try to avoid the perimeter areas defining the neighborhood unless the boundary is a park, lake, golf course or a more expensive neighborhood. Also, watch out for the more heavily traveled streets that cut through a neighborhood. Buying next to a school can be a plus or a minus for you. It's a great place to play after school and on weekends, but it can be noisy at recess time. If you are in doubt about the location of a particular home, visit it early in the morning or late in the afternoon during rush hour traffic. It will be worth the extra effort.

Livability

Livability is as important as location when choosing a home. In fact, location is a big part of livability. To determine livability, judge the home on how it will meet the needs of your family. How do you feel about the home and how does the home make you feel? Perhaps you will need to refer back to Chapter 2. What are your needs and priorities, your likes and dislikes?

There are other things, too, such as how you feel about the use of space. Do you like well-defined rooms or large open areas? What about natural light and brightness? Which rooms will get the morning sun; which will get no direct sunlight at all? There is also the practical side to livability. Will the furniture fit? What things can be stored in which closets? Is there enough room in the kitchen for all the cooks to cook at once? Is the home going to be easy to take care of and keep clean?

Decorating

When looking at homes try *not* to be overly influenced by the decorating. Be careful that you are not attracted to a home just because of its charming appearance. When the present owners move out with all their possessions, will the home still be appealing?

When you go into a home that feels drab and gloomy, take a minute and ask yourself if it's the decorating or if the home is drab because of room arrangement, lack of window space, etc. If there are constructional flaws, dismiss the property or get a realistic estimate on what it will take to correct the problems. If it is a case of poor decorating, and you like the house, imagine what you could do to make it attractive.

Many homes, very suitable in other ways, are passed over by buyers because they are not attractively decorated. REALTORS® even try to get the sellers of these unappealing homes to offer decorating allowances as a helpful marketing tool. It stands to reason that if a decorating allowance is offered for unattractive homes, buyers should not be expected to pay anything extra for attractive, well-decorated homes.

Don't dismiss a home because the carpeting is unattractive. If the carpeting is worn or is a color that does not appeal to you, you might ask for a carpet allowance when making your offer. You may be able to buy the home and have new carpeting of your choice.

If you are buying new construction or a condominium conversion where decorated display homes are available, be aware that developers often have very large budgets for decorating the model homes. Mirrors, lighting, wall decorations and small-scale furniture are all used to give the illusion of greater space.

Doing your own redecorating may be easy and inexpensive when compared to the overall cost of a home. For a start, you might want to spend an hour or two at the library looking at home decorating magazines. Use your imagination and adapt these ideas to your own situation. You'll have a home that's fresh and attractive and reflects your personality. And you'll add great livability to your home.

Physical Condition

The physical condition of a home must be considered. Not every property will have solid brass doorknobs, ceramic tile in the kitchen and bathrooms or even all-copper plumbing. However, the materials that are used should meet minimum standards. Also, each system—water, electrical, heating-air conditioning, waste disposal—must be adequate for the job it is intended to do.

The general condition of the property (how well it's been taken care of), the choice of materials, as well as the quality of materials and workmanship, all help determine value. When it comes to condition, value may be more easily translated into price. You must decide how important condition and quality are to you. Is it "top of the line" all the way with the best money can buy, or will a well-built home without solid oak doors and woodwork fit your needs?

The very least you must do is thoroughly inspect the property so you know what you are buying. Chapter 32 will give you some help. If you still have questions or reservations, get professional advice.

Warranty Programs

Many builders across the country are complying with the high standards of either the Home Owners Warranty Program (HOW) or the

Home Buyers Warranty Program when constructing their homes. The purchasers of these homes receive an insurance-backed warranty protecting them against major structural defects, as well as defects in the plumbing, electrical and heating/cooling systems. The warranty may also cover appliances, fixtures and equipment, as well as materials and workmanship. Parts of this warranty remain in effect for up to ten years, even if the home is sold. Read the warranty carefully.

Many other warranty programs are available to the buyers of previously occupied homes. Some of these are really insurance plans; if the furnace goes out within a certain length of time it will be fixed for a small charge or at no cost. Often, the seller or the listing real estate company will provide this insurance as a helpful marketing tool. These warranties are an added benefit to the buyer and give some protection against a major expense during the first months or year of ownership. The insurance may also be bought by the purchaser. You must weigh the benefits you would receive against the cost.

The purchaser also has the right to expect an implied warranty; that is, that the components of a home will be in working condition when title is taken. The dishwasher will work, the furnace will work when you turn it on in the fall, the plumbing is in satisfactory condition without leaks, etc. However, do not rely on this implied warranty. *Carefully check the property yourself.* It is true that if you take the previous owners to court (this is about your only remedy) the decision should be in your favor. But even if you win in court, you lose in terms of time, inconvenience, legal expenses and frustration. Again, inspect the property carefully.

Available Financing

Financing ranks right up there with location, livability and condition as an important consideration when selecting a home. If the financing available for a particular home fits your needs and circumstances, then it certainly adds to the value of that property.

You must determine the benefits and value a certain home has for you. Don't settle for less than a good location, and be sure the home ranks high on livability. Buy a home you really like!

32. Take Off Your Rose-Colored Glasses and Really See What You Are Buying

Before you make an offer to purchase a home, perform a careful, complete inspection of the property. The purpose of the inspection is to let you know what you are buying—all the good points as well as the bad. You may decide you want a more thorough professional inspection of all or some parts of the property. You will be investing your money and time to take care of the property. You need to know what you are getting.

Ask your REALTOR® to set an appointment when he or she can help you with the inspection, and request that the property owners not be home at the time. You will need a pad of paper, pencil, tape measure, and a good flashlight for your inspection. Binoculars will be helpful when you inspect the roof.

Outside the Home

Walk around the property in bright daylight and inspect the entire home and lot. Take notes on all problems and write down any questions you have.

Foundation, Concrete Areas and Brickwork. Any foundation crack larger than hairline could be a problem if not fixed properly. Vertical cracks can also signal structural problems. Brickwork should be symmetrical with no loose or missing brick or mortar. The chimney should not tilt. Concrete driveways, walks and patios should be level and free of large cracks and signs of flaking. Porches, patios and walks next to the foundation should fit tightly, with the cracks sealed, to prevent water from seeping down next to the foundation.

House Siding and Trim. Look for signs of split and rotted wood. Popped nail heads may indicate settling. The siding and trim should be in good condition with no peeling, chipping or blistering paint. The overall paint job should look fresh, clean and neat.

Gutters and Downspouts. Look for missing or improperly attached gutters and downspouts. It is important for water to drain away properly to protect the roof and foundation.

Roof. Check the condition of the roof. With binoculars you can take a good look. There should be no missing, loose or curling shingles. New asphalt shingles are coated with small rock granules that will wear off over time. If a large percentage of rock granules have worn off and/or you can see blisters or small holes in the shingles, you will need a new roof soon. The roof line should be level and straight. A sagging, uneven or tilting roof line can indicate serious structural or settling problems.

Yard, Landscaping and Fences. It is important that water not be allowed to collect near the foundation. The yard should slope so the water drains away from the house. Trees, shrubs and other plants should look healthy; the lawn should be free of weeds and in good condition. If the property has a septic system, locate and examine the area. More healthy looking grass in this area may signal a problem. The fences should be sturdy and in good repair. If there is a sprinkler system, ask to have it turned on at the end of your inspection so you can be sure it is working properly.

Windows and Doors. Windows and doors should be checked from both the outside and the inside. Basement window areas below ground level should have loose gravel or rock to help water drain properly. All windows and doors should fit tightly with adequate caulking and/or weather stripping. Note whether screens and storm windows and doors are available and inspect their condition. Of course, there should be no broken glass.

Garage. Check the garage in the same manner as the house. Open and close the garage door to see if it works properly.

Crawl Space. If the property has a crawl space you should go down into it. Check for moisture, the condition of the foundation and the floor supports above. Look for signs of warping, rot and termite damage. Dank and musty odors may indicate the presence of mildew and mold. Check the furnace, water heater, etc., which might be located in the crawl space. In cold climates, the floor of the house, water heater and pipes should be insulated. This area should not be a home for bugs and small animals.

Inside the Home

Open the draperies, turn on lights and use a strong flashlight. Don't be afraid to move things if necessary to do a complete inspection. Be aware of unpleasant odors as you inspect the home. Pet odors in carpeting are difficult to eliminate; often, carpet and padding must be replaced.

Basement. A damp or wet basement is a serious problem. Check carefully for any signs of moisture or previous flooding. Nails may be rusty or water marks may show on concrete walls and floors. Be skeptical of recently painted walls and floors.

A sump pump could be a precaution or could indicate a major problem. If a sump pump must run almost continuously during wet weather, it can be both expensive and a noisy nuisance. If in doubt about a possibly wet basement, don't buy. At least wait until after a heavy rain to do a more thorough inspection.

The basement floor should be smooth and level with no cracks larger than hairline. An uneven floor may indicate heaving or settling—either one could be a serious problem. Any crack in the walls larger than hairline could be a problem. If vertical cracks get larger as they go up, there may be structural problems. While in the basement, check the floor joists above. Their size and placement can give a good indication of the home's construction. Look for popped nails, warping, rot and termite damage.

Floors, Ceiling and Walls. Walk heavily across floors and jump to see if they feel level and solid. Floor squeaks are often difficult to eliminate. Examine the walls and ceilings carefully for cracks, loose plaster and any stains that indicate leaks.

Attic. Go up into the attic and use a flashlight to check the condition of the rafters. Stains can indicate leaks in the roof. Note the type and amount of insulation so you can determine later whether it is adequate. There should be vents in the attic and they should be covered with screen. Look for signs of small animals, birds or insects.

Windows and Doors. Look at the windows and doors from the inside of the home. Open and close the windows to see that they work well. Binding may indicate settling. Also check the plaster or drywall around the windows for problems caused by moisture. Check doors to see if weather stripping is necessary. Doors between rooms and closet doors should open and close easily.

Kitchen. Inspect the kitchen carefully. Check all around the sink and dishwasher area for signs of water leaks and damage. Inspect the appliances and turn them on, if possible, to see that they work properly. Also note the amount of cupboard and counter space. Countertops should be in good condition without unattractive burns, cuts, chips and stains. Cupboard doors should hang properly and close tightly.

Bathrooms. Bathrooms are generally problem areas. Look for signs of water damage. Closely examine the tile, especially in the tub and shower area, for cracks and leaks. Press the tile walls to see if there is any give. Check for unevenness (warping) in the floor, especially around the toilet and tub or shower. Look around and under the sink for water stains and rotting wood.

Floors, Floor Coverings, Carpet. Wooden floors should be smooth and well cared for. A complete sanding and refinishing job can be expensive in terms of time, energy and money. Check smooth floor covering (linoleum, tile, etc.) for signs of cracks, peeling and stains.

Is the carpet of good quality, and does the type and color appeal to you? Are there stains and/or worn, discolored areas? The carpet was probably cleaned recently so additional cleaning may not improve its appearance.

Floor Plan. Take another look at the floor plan, room sizes and storage areas to see how they fit the needs of your family. You may want to do some measuring if you have large pieces of furniture.

Plumbing. Locate the areas where water lines enter the property and waste materials leave. Tree roots often cause problems with sewer lines. Ask your REALTOR® to ask the owners if they have ever had such problems and how long ago. Trace the pipes through the house and look for signs of deterioration and leaks. Determine what the pipes are made of. Copper is preferred. Many homes built before the 1940s have galvanized steel pipes. Because of their advanced age, you can expect to have problems with them. Plastic piping has been used in recent years in some areas, and if properly installed and maintained, it has proven satisfactory.

To test for adequate water pressure turn on several faucets at the same time. Also check each toilet by flushing it. Check the floor drain in the basement after the faucets have run five minutes or so; there should be no backup.

The life expectancy of a hot water heater is about ten years, but extra heavy use can result in a shorter life. Try to determine the age of the heater by looking for an installation tag. Also look for signs of rust or corrosion deposits that will signal advancing age. Note whether the heater is gas or electric and its capacity; you will need to determine if it will be adequate for your needs.

Heating System. Heating systems vary greatly, depending on climate conditions, types of available fuel, age of the property, etc. Because of high energy costs, it is important to choose a home with an efficient and well-maintained heating system. Determine the type that is best for your area. If you do not feel competent to judge the system yourself, get help from a utility company representative, a heating dealer or an inspection service. Heat should be distributed evenly to all areas of the home. Ask if there are any rooms or areas that do not receive adequate heat in cold weather.

Electrical System. The electrical system must be safe and adequate to meet your needs. Newer homes constructed by reputable builders usually present no problems. However, if major electrical appliances (air conditioning, electric range, electric dryer, etc.) are to be added, 220 wiring may need to be installed. Copper wiring is preferred. If aluminum wiring is used, all component parts must be compatible to be safe. Aluminum wiring is no longer allowed in home construction. Older homes may need a more thorough electrical inspection.

Cooling-Air Conditioning System. The most practical type of air conditioning is cool breezes coming through open windows. When cool breezes are not available an air conditioning system is necessary. Climate conditions and energy costs determine the best type of system for your area. The system should be in good repair and adequate for the size of the home.

Termites, Radon, Asbestos, Lead Paint, etc. Some problems are difficult to detect. Depending on the area of the country, the age of the property, climate conditions, previous maintenance, etc., you may be concerned about other possible problem areas.

This inspection checklist does not cover every possible problem. It is intended to encourage you to take a better, more thorough look at the property you are considering. You may obtain additional information and help from professional home inspection services, home inspection books, public utility representatives, businessmen in the building trades and community services, such as building inspectors and the fire department.

The American Society of Home Inspectors (ASHI) is a national organization that requires experience, training and adherence to a rigid code of ethics of its member home inspectors. Look under building inspection service in the yellow pages for ASHI members or call 1-800-743-2744 to locate an ASHI home inspector in your area or to get general information about what you can expect in an ASHI home inspection report.

33. More Considerations If You Are Buying in a Large Complex

If you are buying a home in a large complex, you still must make a careful, complete inspection of the property. Use as many of the suggestions in Chapter 32 as can be applied to your situation.

It is more difficult to determine the quality of large buildings, but it is no less important. Is the building structurally sound and are the materials and workmanship of good quality? Are the plumbing, heating, cooling, electrical and mechanical systems in good repair and adequate for the building? Are there safety features to protect you in case of fire?

Unfortunately, there is no easy, inexpensive way to determine these things. It would take a qualified engineering firm several days to do a thorough inspection of a large building—a costly proposition. However, there are some things you can and should do to get a good idea of the quality of the building, how well it is maintained and whether there are adequate safety features:

- Walk around and check as much of the outside of the building as possible. Cracks, uneven walls, loose bricks, missing mortar and/or popped nails may be indications of settling and structural problems.

- Note the physical condition of the parking areas and the lawns. Look for any possible drainage problems. After it rains, does the water drain away or does it collect in some areas? Standing water may cause concrete and especially blacktop to deteriorate. Is the sod in good condition? Are the trees and shrubs healthy looking? It is expensive to relandscape lawns and repave parking lots.

- The reception area and the clubhouse facilities should be appealing, well-decorated and well-maintained. Are the carpeting, walls and ceilings clean, free of stains and in good condition? Is the furniture attractive?

- Does the entire building look well cared for? Are the lawn and parking areas neat and free of debris? Are the inside hallways clean and attractive? If the building is not well-maintained now, things probably won't improve in the future.

- Talk to people living in the building. Try to learn whether they are satisfied with the building and the management. Are there ever problems with the heating, air conditioning or plumbing? Are the problems taken care of promptly? Has there been talk of major problems or renovation projects? Has there been talk of an assessment to pay for problems or improvements?

- Look for safety features. Safety rules and no smoking signs should be posted. Smoking should not be allowed in hallways and elevators. All exits should have lighted *exit* signs. Stairwells should be enclosed and should be lighted at all times. (Incidentally, if you live in a high-rise, occasionally use the stairs when you are leaving the building to familiarize yourself with them in case they are needed in an emergency.)

  Sprinkler systems should be in all hallways, and fire extinguishers should be mounted in hallways. There should be fire walls between floors and between each living unit.

  Solid doors should be used at the entrances to all living units. Living units should have security locks that are *not* dead bolt locks requiring a key for unlocking from the inside. (In case of a fire, broken water pipe or some other emergency, management personnel should be able to enter the unit.)

  All living units should have battery-operated smoke detectors, and they should be checked every few months to make sure they work properly. If each unit does not have a smoke detector, request the homeowners' association to require that they be installed. Smoke detectors should be in the furnace room, storage areas, the laundry rooms, the clubhouse area, etc.

  Good maintenance practices prevent fires and other accidents. For example, the laundry room should be kept clean and neat. Trash chutes should be clean with tight-fitting doors. Trash should be collected in an outside area and removed frequently, and the area should be kept tidy.

  Check the storage room. Paint, varnish and other combustibles should not be stored in the building. The storage areas should not be stacked with junk. Finally, motorcycles should never be allowed inside the building.

34. Homework for Homebuyers

As an added precaution, do a double-check of the services available to the property you are considering. Ask specific questions of the proper authorities and accept only specific answers.

Day-Care, Preschool

Where are nearby day-care and preschool facilities? What types of programs do they offer? Will there be a place for your child? Which days and what times are available? What are the costs?

Schools

Which grade school, junior high school and high school will your children attend? If they must ride a school bus, where will they be picked up? Because of overcrowding, boundary changes, busing for integration or other reasons, the children moving into a home may not be able to attend the closest schools or even the same schools as the children moving out. Call the school district to get accurate answers.

Public Transportation

Is a bus or some other public transportation available? Where are bus stops located? How frequent is the service? Obtain a transportation map so you can determine the routes you may be using.

Recreational Facilities

Will you be allowed to use recreational facilities in the area? Is your new home in a public or private recreation district? Are special memberships required?

Where are parks located and what facilities do they have? Are the parks used by recreational organizations on specific days? Who takes care of park maintenance and security?

Hospital and Medical Services

Where is the nearest hospital? Are emergency medical facilities closer?

Police and Fire Protection

How available are police, fire and emergency services? Is the protection adequate? Will your home be protected by a neighborhood watch program? Does the area have access to a 911 or other emergency telephone number?

Television Reception

Is TV reception adequate? Is cable TV available for those who want it? Are there restrictions on antennae? Can you have your own TV dish?

Telephone Service

Will telephone service be available as soon as you move in? Will a private line be available? What other telephone services are available?

Postal Service

Will mail be delivered to the front porch, to the front curb or to community mailboxes at the end of the road? Will mail be delivered daily? Where is the nearest facility to mail packages, buy stamps, etc.?

Trash Collection

Is a commercial garbage collection service available, or will you have to haul and dispose of your own trash? If dumpsters are provided, where are they located?

Street Maintenance and Parking

Are the roads properly maintained? Will community or county crews plow the roads and keep them open in the winter? Will it be your responsibility to maintain any part of the roads?

Is it a law that sidewalks be shoveled? What are the parking restrictions weekdays, weekends and in emergencies? Can you park directly in front of your home?

Water and Sewer

Are water and sewer facilities adequate? Are there water restrictions?

Property Taxes

What are the property taxes now and what are they expected to be? Is a general tax increase expected?

Special Assessments

Are special assessments anticipated? These could be made for any number of reasons—paving projects, water and/or sewer improvements, drainage improvements, schools, parks, sidewalks. Are you expected to pay for special assessments approved or anticipated?

Zoning Changes and New Construction

Have there been any recent zoning changes? Are zoning changes anticipated? Is new construction planned that will change the appearance of or the traffic flow through the neighborhood?

35. Negotiating Tips That Will Save You Money

Negotiating the contract begins with your first look at the property—or rather, it begins with the seller's and the neighbors' first look at you. Keep these tips in mind. They've proven to be real money savers.

Have the Seller Like You

How you first appear to the seller will have an effect on the final contract negotiations. Assume all sellers are nice people, they like their homes and they want only nice people to live in their homes. As you approach each property, smile, look pleasant and interested. Carry a notepad and pencil as you inspect the home carefully. Write down all questions and comments you have, but *do not* make any negative remarks that the seller might hear. In fact, it's better if you don't make any comments at all that the seller might hear. Above all, don't be drawn into a conversation with the seller.

Later, when you are back in the car, discuss the property with your REALTOR® and get answers to your questions. You'll have another chance to see the property.

Be Interested in the Property—
Not in the Life-Style and Personal Problems of the Seller

Remember, you are buying only the seller's property, not the seller's whole way of life. Concentrate on learning as much about the property as you can.

It isn't necessary to ask the seller why he or she is selling. In fact, don't ask the seller anything! There are good reasons for this. First of all, the seller isn't likely to tell you the main reason. Instead, you will probably hear how much the seller loves the home and what a great place it is and why she or he needs every penny of the listed price. And all the while, the seller is studying you, figuring out just how far he or she can go in demanding full price. So, if you avoid the seller, he or she won't know how much you like and need the home. The seller doesn't have to know anything about you except that you are a nice person. The seller doesn't even need to know if you are from out of state or just a mile away. Above all, don't let the seller know you are going to write an offer. That way, when you do make an offer on the property, the seller will be more objective during negotiations.

Ask your REALTOR® to find out from the listing REALTOR® the real reason the home is for sale.

Know the Market

Home prices are determined by supply and demand. When there are more buyers than there are homes for sale, prices go up. If fewer people have the means to buy a home, and many homes are being offered for sale, the seller becomes more motivated to negotiate and may take a lower price. However, even in a buyer's market, a home in excellent condition and well-located within a desirable neighborhood may sell quickly at close to the asking price. The same may be true of almost any home that is reasonably priced and has excellent financing terms. When you inspect several homes in the same price range, you can develop your own feel for value and the marketplace.

Ask to See Multiple Listing Sold Books

Determine the sale price of recently sold homes that are similar to the home you want to buy. Most multiple listing services publish a list of sold properties each month. Also, your REALTOR® may know of other similar properties that have sold more recently and are not yet in the sold book; she or he can usually get information on these properties. However, this information, as well as that found in the sold books, does not tell the whole story. (For example, a price might reflect a large carpet allowance.) Use this information only as a guide.

Don't Be Intimidated by an Appraisal Obtained by the Seller

An appraisal by an outside expert, no matter how qualified and experienced, does not determine market value! The sale price of the property you buy should be determined only through negotiations between you and the seller. (See Chapter 42.)

Get a Feel for How Negotiations Are Handled

Discuss the negotiating procedure with your REALTOR® long before it's time to make an offer. Briefly, this is the scenario in many areas:

1. The property is presented to you at the listed price and terms.

2. You are free to make any offer you wish. Since your REALTOR® is a subagent for the seller, he or she must encourage you to offer the listed price. However, you have the right to make any offer you wish. Once you initiate the bargaining, your REALTOR® will follow through. Request that your offer be presented to the

seller as soon as possible in a face-to-face meeting rather than over the phone.

3. Your REALTOR® will either give the offer to the listing broker to present or will present it directly to the seller, depending on the custom in the area.

4. The seller now has three choices. He or she can accept your offer as written and sign it, in which case your offer becomes a legally binding contract. Or the seller can reject your offer completely. The third choice is more reasonable: the seller can make one or more changes in your offer, sign it and send it back to you as a counteroffer.

5. You now have the same three choices the seller had: accept and sign the counteroffer and it becomes a contract; reject it totally; or make one or more changes, sign it and offer it to the seller again.

6. Negotiations can go on indefinitely until a binding contract is agreed upon, the buyer decides to call it quits or the property is sold to someone else. (A buyer *cannot* tie up a property with a slow negotiating game.)

Negotiate on All Points

More than just price can be negotiated in a contract. The type and terms of the financing you prefer, what is included or not included in the offering price, the dates of closing and possession, and the contingencies may be negotiated. (See Chapter 36.)

Decide what you really want. A low price? A VA or an FHA loan? (This may cost the seller loan points.) A home you can buy and move into quickly? Then ask yourself what might be most important to the seller. You can probably tell from the way the property is listed.

If you can't meet the asking price, try to give the seller other things. Offer to close when it's convenient for him or her, and don't ask for the refrigerator the seller wants to keep. On the other hand, if you need to move into a home very soon, offer the seller's price; he or she will probably move right away even if it's very inconvenient.

Don't Make an Unreasonable First Offer

You know the asking price and terms. Make your first offer as reasonable as you can. If the seller doesn't accept it, but counters, you can make a second offer close to the first. A completely unreasonable first offer may insult the seller, who may decide not to let you buy the home. Even if negotiations continue, they may become a tug-of-war between personalities instead of reasonable negotiations for the property.

Make Your First Offer Easy to Accept

Give the seller at least some of the things requested, and a relatively short period of time to act on your offer—probably a day or two. Giving more time only allows the seller to stew about it, or try to get slower-moving, interested buyers to make an offer. If you are asking for seller financing or will be applying to a lender for a new loan, give the seller a financial information sheet on you along with the offer.

Make your earnest money deposit larger than is customary. Your check won't be cashed until the contract is finalized. If it is a short time until closing, the small amount of interest you lose will be recovered if you can negotiate a good price and other terms. If it will be two months or more until closing, ask that your earnest money be held in an interest-bearing trust account and that the interest be credited to you at closing.

The Best Negotiating Tip of All:
When You Find the Home You Like and Want, Buy It!

A slightly higher price or the inconvenience of not getting your preferred move-in date is a small price to pay for the satisfaction, pleasure and happiness you will get from living in a home you really like. Anything extra you may pay will more than be made up for in the enjoyment the right home will give you.

36. Write the Contract Right and Avoid Problems

You have looked at several properties. Finally you have settled on just one: the home you want for your own. You will enjoy living in the home and you can manage it financially. You have inspected the property carefully. Although you may still have questions (you can get an inspection report), you are ready to buy. You want to make an offer on the home and find out if the seller will accept your offer.

The Offer That Becomes the Contract

Making an offer is serious business. If the seller accepts your offer as written, you have a legally binding contract, and what is or is not in the contract may have a major effect on the transaction. Therefore, the offer must be precisely and clearly written with all the terms and conditions you want in the contract. The contract, the written agreement between the buyer and the seller, should include everything pertinent to your real estate transaction. The contract can and should be used to protect your interests and avoid potential problems.

The first step in writing the offer is gathering and verifying all the needed information. This is a normal part of your REALTOR®'s job and he or she should be a big help. The information you will need when it is actually time to write the offer includes:

- property address;
- property legal description;
- the seller's asking price, terms and other conditions;
- the exclusions named by the seller in the listing contract;
- the items you would like included in the contract price;
- complete information on the new loan you want or on the existing financing you want to assume;
- inspections you want on the property;
- the dates you wish to close and take possession;
- the amount of earnest money you will provide; and
- anything else you or your REALTOR® thinks is necessary.

The second step is deciding what you will offer for the property: the price, down payment, financing terms, what is to be included or not included in the offering price, the dates you will want to close the transaction and take possession, the contingencies you feel are necessary and the earnest money that will accompany the offer. If your REALTOR® is the subagent for the seller, he or she must represent the seller fairly and not give you privileged information. However, you have every right to make any offer you want. If your REALTOR® is the subagent for the seller, don't tell your REALTOR® how much higher you are willing to go if your first offer is not accepted. Be firm with your offer and expect the seller to accept it. You can make a higher counteroffer later, if necessary. (See chapters 27 and 35.)

Step three is very important: call your attorney. Either your REALTOR® and you will write the offer, in which case you must set an appointment with your attorney to review it, or your attorney will write the offer, and you will need an appointment to give the attorney all the necessary information. Remember, your attorney has not seen the property, doesn't know the real estate market and doesn't know what financing is available. You need your REALTOR®'s help to get all this information together. In either case, be sure to read the offer carefully after it is completed. Be sure it says exactly what you want and every necessary clause is included.

Preprinted Contract Forms

In some states, only an attorney may prepare a real estate contract. The real estate departments of other states have approved preprinted forms to be used for contracts between buyers and sellers. REALTORS® often use these forms; the blanks may be filled in and conditions and clauses may be added. However, the seller in any state may have an attorney prepare a contract form to be used for the seller's transactions. Owners, builders and developers who have several properties to sell often use their own preprinted contract forms. Very seldom are any of these contracts illegal. However, these contracts may not be in your best interest.

Do not assume that because the contract form is preprinted, the wording protects you, the buyer, or is in your best interest. Read the contract. Read every clause in the contract. If you don't understand every part of the contract, ask for an explanation. Arrange to have your attorney check the contract for errors and/or omissions, as well as wording that protects you, *before* you sign it. Be sure you agree to the terms of the contract *before* you sign it.

If the contract form does not have enough space for you to include all the clauses you feel are necessary, an additional sheet of paper may be used for this purpose. It can be titled "Addendum to Contract" or

"Additional Provisions to the Contract" or "Exhibit I to the Contract."
A sample form is shown in Figure 36.1.

Figure 36.1

ADDENDUM TO CONTRACT

RE: Contract dated _____, 19 ___

between _____ , as purchaser(s)

and _____ _____ , as seller(s)

relating to the sale and purchase of the property known as:

Address _____

Legal description _____

_____

1.

2.

3.

4.

5.

Dated this _____ day of _____ , 19 ___.

_____   _____
Purchaser   Seller

_____   _____
Purchaser   Seller

How Should Title Be Taken?

Use your full, legal name when taking title to real estate. The documents are recorded and become part of the public record. Some potential problems may be avoided later if you use your full legal name.

If one person is to be the owner of the property, title is taken as an individual or title in severalty. If two or more individuals are to be the joint owners, title may be taken in one of several different ways.

Most homes purchased by a husband and wife are owned in **joint tenancy** with rights of survivorship. With joint tenancy, each owner has an equal, undivided interest in the property. If one owner should die, the property automatically belongs to the surviving owner or owners. **Tenancy in common**, on the other hand, does not have rights of survivorship. Joint owners, who take title in tenancy in common, have an undivided interest in the property that may or may not be equal. Each owner has the right to sell, trade, give away or will his or her interest independently of the other owner(s), even though this is not always practical. If one of the owners should die, his or her interest in the property passes to his or her estate.

Partnership ownership is useful in certain situations, such as when one owner is an investor. The title is in the name of the partnership instead of the individuals. Consult with your attorney to draw up the partnership agreement.

How you take title to real property has far-reaching legal and tax implications. Discuss this with your attorney and tax accountant.

What about the Earnest Money Deposit?

Earnest money or "good faith money" accompanies the offer when it is made to the seller. *This money should never be given directly to the seller or the seller's attorney.* It is best to provide the earnest money in the form of a check or money order made out to the listing real estate company. The offer should state the exact amount of the earnest money, who is providing the earnest money, the form in which it is being given (check, money order, etc.), to whom it is being given (the name of the real estate broker or the real estate company) and how the money may be used (usually as partial payment for the property).

It is also important that the offer state exactly what happens to the earnest money. For example, if the offer is not finalized into a contract by the buyer and seller, the earnest money is returned immediately to the purchaser. If the contract is successfully negotiated between the buyer and seller, the real estate broker deposits the earnest money in his or her trust account and handles the money in strict accordance with the instructions in the contract. The language of the contract is important.

Beware of contract forms used by builders. Sometimes the contract provides for the earnest money to be placed in the builder's general operating fund, giving the builder the use of your money until closing. If the builder should declare bankruptcy, you could lose your earnest money.

For the buyer's protection, the contract should state that the earnest money will be returned to the buyer if any contingency in the contract is not met.

Put the Financing Arrangements in the Offer

In addition to the sale price, the offer should state exactly how you intend to pay for the property. If you intend to pay cash, this fact should be stated. If you intend to assume an existing loan, the down payment and the details of the loan to be assumed should be included so there are no misunderstandings. These details include lender and loan number, remaining balance, remaining term, interest rate, monthly principal and interest (PI) payment and assumption fee. If you intend to obtain a new loan, either from an institutional lender or the seller, the type of loan, loan amount, the interest rate, term and all terms and conditions of the new loan should be clearly stated.

Whatever the financial arrangements, they should be included in the offer and become part of the contract. It is in your best interest to make the contract contingent upon the buyer being able to obtain the desired financing.

Inclusions and Exclusions May Cause Problems

The offer should state exactly what is included in the offering price. One definition of real estate is "land, including the buildings and/or improvements on it and its natural assets, as minerals, water, etc." Therefore, everything attached to the property is often presumed to be part of it. This is not necessarily so. It is up to the buyer and the seller to decide what is included or excluded in the sale price.

The contract should also state that all inclusions are the ones presently in the property (the seller cannot replace the lighting fixtures, refrigerator, draperies, etc.) and are to be paid for in full and are to be in their present working condition when they are transferred to the buyer. A description of the water rights and mineral rights should be given if they are included. Take time and make the effort to have specific language in this part of the contract. It may save a lot of misunderstanding, inconvenience and frustration later.

Illegal Side Agreements Are Not Allowed

Sometimes the seller wants more money for his or her property than he or she may get under ordinary circumstances. For instance, the buyer wants a VA loan but because of points that cannot be paid by the borrower, the seller will not actually receive as much as he or she wants from the sale. So the seller suggests that the borrower buy the refrigerator or lawn mower or something else for a very high price—much more than the item is worth—to compensate for the points.

These "under the table" arrangements are illegal in all VA and FHA contracts, and, in most states, they are illegal for all contracts. All agreements between the buyer and seller should be made part of the contract and be out in the open. Do not be a party to an illegal side agreement.

Who Pays for Which Closing Costs?

The contract should state which party pays for which closing costs and the amounts. The contract should state specifically who pays for points and the appraisal.

Evidence of Title Is Important

The buyer has the right to expect the seller to furnish proof of ownership. The contract should state what evidence of title, either a title insurance policy or an abstract of title, will be provided to the purchaser and who will pay for the title work. (See Chapter 41.)

The Deed Transfers Ownership

Title to the property is transferred by deed, the legal document with which the seller gives up his or her claim to the property in favor of the buyer. There are two basic types of deeds: the warranty deed and the quitclaim deed.

With a warranty deed, the seller gives the purchaser certain legal, binding assurances as to the condition of the title of the property being sold. The quitclaim deed gives the buyer whatever interest the seller may have in the property, but with no warranty as to his or her interest or title. A warranty deed is preferred. Ask for it in the offer.

Taxes, Liens, Rents, Insurance, Etc.

The contract should state exactly how taxes, existing liens, water and sewer charges, rents, insurance premiums, propane, fuel oil, firewood, etc., are to be handled.

Taxes for the year in which you close may be paid either by the seller or the buyer, but are most often prorated to the day of the closing. The contract should call for all back taxes to be paid by the seller.

Rental income is usually prorated to the day of the closing. However, the buyer and seller may agree to handle this in a different manner.

Hazard insurance may sometimes be transferred to the new buyer. It can be prorated or included in the sale price. If the policy is to be transferred to the new buyer, notify the insurance company in plenty of time so you have a *written* statement before closing, stating that the insurance company accepts the new purchaser and that the insurance will remain in full effect. Usually it is in the buyer's best interest to purchase a new homeowner's policy before closing. Make the new insurance policy effective the date title is transferred.

Mortgage insurance is usually prorated to the day of closing for both FHA loans and conventional loans that are being assumed.

Utilities are most often handled between the buyer and seller according to the date of possession; often the charges are prorated. In some areas, unpaid utility bills (most often for water and/or sewer services) may become a lien against the property. If this is the case in your area, money should be collected from the seller before or at closing and the final utility bill should be paid by the closing agent doing the disbursements.

Liens and **encumbrances** should also be covered. The contract should state that *all* liens and encumbrances (or all except the loan you are assuming) are to be paid in full and releases obtained before closing, or at the time of closing, using the proceeds of the sale.

When Will the Closing Be?

The contract should state the date of delivery of deed—the date when the purchaser will actually become the owner of the property. Closing or delivery of deed may take place sooner if it is acceptable to the buyer and seller. Closing may also be postponed if it is agreed upon by both parties; however, a written extension agreement *must* be used if it is necessary to delay closing. Word the extension agreement so that it becomes part of the contract.

The Hour and the Place of Closing

It is better if someone other than the buyer or seller determines the time and place of closing. Usually it is the lender if a new loan is involved, or the listing real estate broker. With so many people involved it may be impossible to pick a time that pleases everyone. The lender, the real estate broker and the title company should be given first consideration in this instance. Your real estate transaction is important and you should be willing to take time off work or otherwise be inconvenienced to help the closing go smoothly.

Don't Let Possession Be a Hassle

The contract should state a definite date and time when the new owners will actually take possession of the property. This does not always happen on the day of closing; often the seller will need a few days to pack up and move. Any length of time is permissible as long as the buyer and seller agree. Often the contract wording will read "on or before *(a date)* at *(a time)*." The seller may then give possession sooner if he or she is able to move out earlier.

It should be noted if the property is being occupied by renters who have tenancy rights. It is the seller's responsibility to give possession as stated in the contract, even if the property is rented.

It is to the buyer's advantage to have a penalty clause in the contract to encourage the seller to perform according to the contract and give possession as stated. The penalty clause should give the purchaser the right to evict the seller and charge the seller a daily rental fee if possession is not given. This daily rental fee *should be excessive*. It is intended to be a penalty, and $200 a day is not unusual. It should be more if the seller has a large family. If the daily penalty fee is only $25 or $50, and the seller is having a problem with the place to which he or she is moving, the seller may choose to stay in your new home rather than pay a large motel bill.

What Happens if the Property Should Be Damaged?

A clause should be included in the contract that states the condition in which the property is to be delivered. The rights and responsibilities of both parties should be clearly stated in case the property is damaged by fire or in any other manner before the closing date.

Defaults—More Problems?

The rights and responsibilities of each party should be clearly stated in case either the buyer or the seller defaults and does not perform in accordance with the contract.

Protect Yourself with Inspections

Every inspection that is required by law or wanted by the buyer should be stipulated in the contract. The wording should clearly state the exact purpose of each inspection, who is to do the inspection (registered engineer, licensed or certified inspector or a named individual or company), who is to order and pay for the inspection, when the inspection is to be completed and how the results of the inspection will affect the contract.

It is not enough just to state that the well is to be inspected. Is it to be a health department inspection (all you want to know is if the water is safe to drink)? Or is it to be a complete water analysis? Do you want to know the depth and capacity of the well, the condition of the pump, the size of the storage tank? If you are not satisfied with the results of the inspection, what happens? Does the seller agree to make the necessary repairs? Do you have the right to void the contract and have your earnest money returned to you? Or do you have to go ahead and buy a property that has an inadequate well? If the contract is contingent upon "a satisfactory inspection," who determines whether it is satisfactory? How and when is the contingency to be removed? As you can see, the wording of the contract is extremely important.

It's also a good idea to provide for a final inspection of the property by the buyer a couple of days before closing. If you wait until the day of closing for a final walk-through and there is a problem, it may be difficult to take care of it before closing.

Take Extra Care with New Construction

If the home is not completed at the time you offer to purchase it, extra care should be taken to specifically describe the home's features. Blueprints, specifications, types of materials, brand names and style numbers of the furnace, air conditioner, hot water heater, appliances, etc., quality of fixtures, paneling, carpeting, countertops, other floor coverings—all of this information should be made part of the contract.

A final inspection is always needed for new construction.

You Don't Need a Trash Problem

If the property has junk or trash you want removed, request it in the contract, and include a penalty in case the trash is not removed. A certain amount of the seller's proceeds may be withheld by the title company, escrow company or some other third party. Then if all trash is not removed by a certain date, a commercial trash hauler will be hired and paid with this money.

Additions and Repairs? Protect Yourself

If the seller tells you he or she will make additions, do certain repairs, redecorate or do anything else to the property, get this statement in writing.

The contract should state that the work is to be completed by a certain date—at least two or three days before closing. If the work is not completed, money can be escrowed at closing or the buyer can be given the money to complete the work. The wording in the contract should be very specific so the buyer is protected. Sometimes it is better if the new purchaser is given a repair or fix-up allowance at closing and makes the arrangements to do the work after she or he takes title to the property. Work out the situation to your satisfaction, and then clearly state the agreement in the contract.

All Contingencies Should Be Clearly Stated

If the contract depends on you selling and/or closing another property, arranging bridge financing, finalizing a transfer, getting Aunt Beverly's estate settlement or any other reason, be sure to put the contingency in writing in the contract. Also include dates, the way in which notice is to be given if the contingency cannot be met and that the earnest money will be returned to the purchaser if the contract is voided.

VI
FROM CONTRACT TO CLOSING

37. Handle Your Real Estate Transaction in a Businesslike Manner

Your home will be one of the largest purchases you will ever make. It will also be the most complicated. Many people will be involved for many different reasons. Plan now to handle the entire real estate transaction in a competent, organized, businesslike manner.

The purchase offer that you make to the seller will be the first or one of the first documents you will sign. By the time you take title to your new home you will have signed many documents. You should receive a copy of each document. Be sure each copy is legible. If you receive the fourth or fifth carbon copy and it cannot be read, ask for a copy of the original made on a copy machine.

You must set up a system so you can keep track of the entire home-buying process. A simple system will work best. Obtain a large manila envelope and put *every* document you receive into it. But before you put each document in, write on it the date and the name of the person you received it from.

Use the outside of the envelope to keep a written diary of your home-buying experience. Every time anything happens concerning your home, record it on the outside of the envelope. Each entry should include the date, the approximate time and a brief description. If the item is a telephone call (there will be many), include the name of the person you talked to and the topic of conversation. Ask for last names of secretaries, title and lender personnel, etc., if necessary. For longer conversations, such as shopping for your loan, use a separate sheet of paper and then put it inside the envelope. Also, make notes of when your REALTOR® stops by to see you, appointments you have with the lender, title company, attorney, etc., and things you receive in the mail.

Jot down questions you want to ask your REALTOR®, attorney, loan officer, etc., on scratch paper and paper clip them to the outside of the envelope so you won't forget them. Date and keep all informal notes and messages concerning your home.

Keep the envelope near the phone so it will be handy to use.

It is extremely important to set up and follow through with a system such as this. It will help you in many ways:

- By knowing you are organized, you will be more confident and have a feeling of being in charge of your own real estate transaction.

- Because you are paying attention, important items and details will not be overlooked. Potential problems may be avoided.

- If a problem should arise, you will recognize it earlier. The documents and an accurate running account of the transaction will be a help in solving the problem.

- Many decisions will have to be made between the time the offer is written and the closing. You will feel less intimidated and be able to make decisions that are in your best interest.

- You will better understand and enjoy the entire home-buying procedure.

Remember, your real estate transaction is more important to you, the home-buyer, than to anyone else.

38. Prepare for an Around-the-Table Closing

As soon as the contract on the home you are buying has been finalized, preparations begin for a successful closing and settlement. Even though the laws, regulations and customs vary from state to state and from one locality to another, all real estate closings accomplish these four things:

1. Transfer title from the seller to the purchaser.
2. Complete the financial arrangements.
3. Give an accounting of all monies involved in the transaction.
4. Disburse the monies in a correct and proper manner.

Real estate closings are handled in one of two very different ways—either an around-the-table closing or an escrow closing—and each may have variations. This chapter will help you prepare for an around-the-table closing. Chapter 39 discusses the escrow closing. Your REALTOR® can tell you which type of closing will be used for your real estate transaction. In most states where around-the-table closings are used, the listing real estate broker is responsible for closing the transaction. Your REALTOR® continues to represent you and works with the listing broker to see that everything is handled correctly.

As soon as your purchase contract is finalized, the listing broker will open a file that will eventually contain all the documents necessary for your transaction. Your contract will be the first and most important document in the file; *the contract is the controlling document in an around-the-table closing.* This is why it is so important that the contract clearly states all the items agreed to by the buyer and seller. The contract, in turn, calls for many other documents, such as inspection reports, tax certificates and the title commitment. Still more documents are necessary, depending on the financing arrangements. Federal, state and local laws require other documents.

If you are a cash buyer using your own available assets to purchase your home, your REALTOR® or attorney and/or the listing broker will order all documents necessary for closing.

If you are assuming a loan and are required to qualify, you will need to set an appointment with the lender and provide the necessary information. The listing broker or your REALTOR® or attorney will obtain a copy of the original mortgage or deed of trust (it's best if you have it before writing the offer) and order the assumption statement and other documents.

If you have obtained private financing, your attorney, with the approval of the attorney of the seller or other private investor, will usually draw up the new loan documents. Your REALTOR®, attorney and/or the listing broker will order and obtain all necessary documents.

If your home is to be financed with a new loan from an institutional lender, your REALTOR® will help you shop for a lender and make arrangements for a loan application. Your REALTOR® and the listing broker will work closely with the loan officer to order all documents.

Your REALTOR® will stay in contact with you during this period to answer questions and let you know how everything is progressing. The results of various inspections will be given to you as they become available. You will be notified when the appraisal is completed and be given the conditions, if any, and the appraised value. Your REALTOR® will discuss the title commitment or title binder with you. If you are using an abstract, your attorney will need to discuss it with you.

The biggest moment before the actual closing is when you are notified that your loan has been approved (if there is to be a new loan). When all contingencies have been removed and all information and documents are available, the time and place for the closing will be set according to the contract.

If you and/or your attorney want to see any of the paperwork before the closing, now is the time to ask your REALTOR® to make the arrangements. There have been closings where the typing of loan papers, settlement statements and other documents was completed only minutes before the closing started.

A day or so before the closing, you will be notified of the exact amount of money you will need; you will need to visit your bank and get a certified check or cashier's check for this exact amount. (Personal checks are almost never accepted at closings.) Have this check made out to you at the time it is issued, unless your REALTOR® tells you otherwise. During the closing you can endorse the check over to whomever is disbursing the funds.

At the appointed time and place, the purchaser and seller, along with their REALTORS® and attorneys, gather around the table for the closing. In most states, the listing broker is responsible for conducting the closing, but he or she may employ an agent, such as a title company, to handle the closing. In some states, only a lawyer may handle a real estate closing.

At all closings, the buyer and seller receive separate settlement statements that give an exact accounting of the expenses and credits for each party. These statements are reviewed, each item is explained and all copies are signed and handed out to those who require them.

Financing arrangements are also completed. A representative of the lender usually conducts this part of the closing if there is a new loan from an institutional lender. Otherwise, the listing broker or an attorney will present, explain and ask you to sign the loan papers and supporting documents. Sometime during the closing, you will be asked for the cashier's or certified check; you may endorse it over to the proper person or company at that time.

The big moment comes when the seller signs the deed and presents it to you, the new owner. The deed is the instrument that officially transfers title.

Most around-the-table closings are happy, friendly affairs. Usually the buyer and seller work out their own arrangements to transfer utilities, obtain keys and even meet the neighbors.

After the buyer and seller have left the closing, the lender, title representatives, REALTORS® and attorneys follow through and take care of other details. Liens are paid off, releases obtained, documents recorded and the title insurance policy issued.

39. Opening an Escrow and the Full Escrow Closing

Full escrow closings are required by law in some states and used because of preference in others. The escrow closing will accomplish the same four things as an around-the-table closing—transfer title from the seller to the purchaser, complete the financial arrangements, give an accounting of all monies involved in the transaction and disburse the monies in a correct and proper manner—but in an entirely different way. Your REALTOR® will tell you whether yours will be an escrow closing.

Escrow closings are not social events, as are many around-the-table closings; usually the buyer and seller never see each other. The entire procedure is handled by an escrow holder, a neutral third party who holds all funds and documents, takes care of all clerical details and disburses all funds.

Shortly after the contract to buy your home is finalized, and either before or after you make application for a loan (if necessary), you will need to open an escrow. The buyer ordinarily has the opportunity to choose the company that will be the escrow holder. Both title companies and private escrow companies provide full escrow services. Because escrow fees vary considerably, as do the competency and professionalism of the different companies, shop carefully for an escrow holder and let your REALTOR® advise you.

An escrow is opened by giving the escrow officer the information concerning your transaction and a copy of the contract. Additional information will be obtained from a title commitment and from the lender. You also may be required to deposit a sum of money at this time. It is not unusual for the earnest money to be held by the escrow holder rather than in the listing broker's trustee account.

The escrow officer will have detailed escrow instructions typed for the buyer, seller and lender. Escrow instructions should cover everything concerning the transaction. Go over each point in the contract to see that it is included in the escrow instructions; the wording should clearly state what you intend. *When you sign the escrow instructions you invalidate your contract; the escrow instructions replace your contract and become the controlling document.*

Most companies handling escrows will not accept responsibility for the transfer of personal property items and matters of agreement such as possession, property maintenance until closing, etc. If the contract is to be invalidated by the signing of the escrow instructions, these things must be handled in some other way. Your attorney may draw up an additional document that will provide for these items. Otherwise a clause, such as stated below, should be inserted in the escrow instructions so that part of the purchase contract remains in effect.

These escrow instructions do not supersede, modify or cancel the terms of the purchase contract dated _____
between _____ , purchaser(s)
and _____ , seller(s)
for the property known as:
address: _____
legal description: _____
in so far as the purchase contract relates to matters not actually pertinent to the escrow instructions, such as, but not limited to, personal property items, inspections, repairs, warranties or possession.

Contingencies are another problem area in escrow closings. All contingencies should be removed in a positive manner; escrow instructions should read that a contingency will be removed when an appropriate statement is signed by the proper party. Avoid the use of "buyer's silence" or "seller's silence" as an automatic waiver of a contingency.

Escrow instructions should clearly state which documents must be provided by the seller, which party pays for each item, what things will be prorated and how the prorations will be made, and the date or dates when additional money must be deposited with the escrow holder. Use extra care in examining the part of your escrow instructions where costs are listed. You do not want to agree to pay for an inspection or some other item that would not otherwise be your responsibility.

Take your time and review your escrow instructions very carefully with your REALTOR® and your attorney *before* you sign them. When the instructions are signed by all parties and returned, the escrow officer may begin to accumulate all the information and documents for your closing. If there will be a new loan, he or she will work closely with the loan officer. Check periodically with the escrow and loan officers to see that everything is going smoothly.

Your escrow is said to be "in perfection" or a "perfect escrow" when all financing and title requirements are met and all instructions may be carried out. A "perfect escrow" may be closed.

The lender will make arrangements for you to sign all the necessary loan papers and close the loan. Separate settlement statements that give a complete accounting of all monies involved in the transaction will be prepared for the buyer and seller. After the settlement statements are explained, approved and signed, all the necessary documents are recorded and the title policy is issued. The final disbursement of funds is usually made only after all documents are recorded.

40. Shop for a Lender and Prepare for the Loan Application

If you plan to get a new loan from an institutional lender, you must make a formal loan application soon after your purchase contract is finalized. Since each loan is made for a specific borrower on a specific property, it is necessary to wait until you have a firm contract before you make the loan application, or at least complete the loan application.

If your loan will be a VA loan, your REALTOR® has an obligation to get the lowest points for the seller, all other things being equal. Points for FHA loans may be paid by either the buyer or the seller. However, consider using a VA or FHA lender who may make and approve your loan without first sending all the paperwork to the VA or FHA office. It may save you several weeks' time. Even if your loan cannot be lender-approved (if you are a self-employed borrower, for instance), it's still wise to use one of these lenders. They do a greater volume of VA and FHA business and are more likely to assemble the loan package so that the VA or FHA personnel may provide faster approval.

If you need a conventional loan, shop for a lender *after* you have a finalized contract, even if you have talked to a lender previously. Every lender knows that a finalized contract means a loan is going to be placed. Remember, lending is a competitive business. You may be able to negotiate a lower interest rate, lower up-front costs or maybe a loan with better terms and conditions. One of the services most REALTOR® organizations provide to their members is an up-to-date listing of lenders and the types of loans they are making. Usually the listing includes information on the loan to value ratios, the interest rates, terms, discount points, origination fees, etc. Let your REALTOR® help you shop for a loan.

Be concerned about all the terms, requirements and costs of the loans you are considering. You have the right to know everything about the loan you will be responsible for repaying. For every financing plan you are considering, prepare a complete Loan Profile. (See Chapter 10.) With this information, you can compare the various loans and choose the financing plan that is best for your own special situation.

Loan Profile

Here are some of the questions you will want to ask the lender for the Loan Profile for each financing plan. Get very specific answers.

1. *Down payment.* What down payment will be required for the home you are buying? Would it be possible to make a smaller down payment with the use of private mortgage insurance? Will a larger down payment enable you to obtain a lower interest rate?

2. *Interest rate.* What rate of interest will you pay on the money you borrow? Will the interest rate remain the same for the term of the loan? If not, how often and to what extent may the interest rate be changed?

3. *Interest in arrears or interest in advance.* Will the interest be paid in arrears or in advance?

4. *The term.* What is the term of the loan? Is a longer term loan available? Will the interest rate and/or up-front costs be lower for a shorter term, such as a 15-year loan or 20-year loan?

5. *Balloon payment.* Does the loan have a balloon payment? When is it due? Will the lender guarantee to refinance the loan at the time the balloon is due? What will the new terms, conditions and loan costs be at the time the loan is refinanced? (Get all this in writing.)

6. *Mortgage insurance.* If your loan is a high ratio loan, will private mortgage insurance be required? How will you pay for the mortgage insurance and what will it cost? Is the mortgage insurance included in the interest rate already quoted or will it be added to that rate? Will you be able to stop paying for the mortgage insurance when the principal amount of the loan becomes less than 80 percent or 75 percent of the value of the property? Will an appraisal be required at that time?

7. *Up-front loan costs.* What fees is the lender charging to make the loan? What are these fees for? Loan origination fee? Mortgage insurance? Discount points (prepaid interest)? Does the borrower or the seller pay these fees? What other costs must be paid to obtain the loan? What is the estimated amount of money needed for the entire initial investment in your home? This includes the down payment, all closing costs and all other expenses that must be paid before or at closing.

8. *Loan repayment schedule.* What will your monthly principal and interest (PI) payment be? Will money for taxes and insurance be

escrowed or may you pay these yourself? What will your total monthly payment include and how much will it be? Will the monthly PI payment increase? When? How much? How often can it be changed? What will the changes be based on? Are there any maximum or minimum levels? What is the largest amount your PI payment can be? How soon can this amount be charged? Can the loan have negative amortization?

9. *Assumption clause.* When it is time to sell your home, may the loan be assumed by the new purchaser? Will the interest rate remain the same? Will the new purchaser be required to qualify? What assumption fees will be charged?

10. *Due on sale clause.* Will the loan documents contain a due on sale clause?

11. *Prepayment privilege or penalty.* Are there any restrictions or costs if you wish to prepay any or all of the loan at any time?

12. *Late payment penalty.* Can the monthly payment be made to a local institution? On what day of the month is the payment due? On what day will the payment be considered late? What penalty will be charged for a late payment?

One final step remains: check on the reputation of the lender. Some common complaints about lenders include not honoring the original information given the borrower or REALTOR®, imposing extra charges for services usually provided without additional cost, and not providing competent service in preparing the loan package—information is not sent for, files get lost, documents are not prepared properly, etc. Some borrowers also have valid complaints concerning how the loan servicing is handled after the loan is closed. Your REALTOR® is in a much better position than you to know the reputation of the lender. Be sure to let your REALTOR® help you with this.

The Loan Application

The loan application is most often taken in the lender's office. However, it is not unusual for the loan officer to take an application in your REALTOR®'s office or in your home. Always set an appointment ahead of time. Filling out loan applications may require an hour or more, so allow yourself enough time.

If applying for a loan is a new experience for you, you will probably find it interesting. If you are married, it is to your advantage for both you and your spouse to be present. If the coborrowers are not married, each must complete an individual application.

Remember, the loan officer is working for you to help you obtain the loan. He or she must ask very specific questions about your financial situation. Your complete cooperation is required. Also, you should take this opportunity to ask any and all questions you have concerning the financing plan and your future obligations. The loan officer may make suggestions that will help you meet the lender's guidelines.

Information required for the loan application may be divided into four areas.

Income. Income from all sources by all borrowers may be considered. However, the receipt of alimony, separate maintenance or child support money need not be disclosed if the applicant does not wish to use this source of income for qualifying purposes.

Assets. Information on all your assets is necessary to establish your net worth.

Debts and Obligations. All debts, loans and other financial obligations must be revealed including alimony, separate maintenance and child support payments.

Credit References. Information concerning debts that have been paid plus other good credit references are necessary.

You can expedite the loan processing if you have the following information available at your appointment:

- Full name, address including zip code, phone number and social security number of each borrower

- Names and addresses, including zip codes, of all employers of each applicant during the last four years. You will also need dates of employment and rates of pay.

- Self-employed applicants or those working on a commission basis will need tax returns for the last four years. Profit and loss statements should be included when appropriate.

- Names, addresses including zip codes, account numbers and current balances of all checking and savings accounts in financial institutions

- Complete information on all stocks, bonds, mutual funds and other securities you own

- Information on life insurance policies, including face amount, monthly premium and cash value. If the cash value is to be used as part of the initial investment, include the complete address of the company. The present cash value must be verified.

- Information on all automobiles, recreational vehicles, etc. Include the make, model, year, estimated value, present loan balance and monthly payment.

- Information on all real estate you own. Include the complete address, estimated present value, mortgage loan balance, monthly payments, lender, loan number and net rental income, if applicable.

- Information concerning other assets. Estimate the value of jewelry, silverware, furniture, clothing, other household items, collections and all other possessions.

- Names of credit card companies and other creditors, addresses including zip codes, account numbers, payment schedules and outstanding balances of all debts. Be sure to include doctor, dentist and hospital bills.

- All information concerning alimony, separate maintenance and child support payments that you are obligated to make

- You will be asked for good credit references. Have information available concerning consumer loans that have been repaid and other good credit references.

- If you are applying for a VA loan, you will need your certificate of eligibility, if one has been issued, or form DD214 (separation papers) and a VA form 1880. If you have had a prior VA loan, supply as much information as possible on that property: the complete address, the date the property was sold, the name of the person to whom the property was sold, the lender's name and address, the loan number and the VA case number.

The loan officer will appreciate your help in providing this information for the loan application. Usually you are expected to pay for the credit report and appraisal at the time of the loan application. When you set the appointment you can ask how much money you will need. Again, customs vary.

Lender Responsibilities

The lender is required by law to comply with certain rules, regulations and procedures when accepting a loan application. The Equal Credit Opportunity Act protects the loan applicant from discriminatory practices by the lender. The lender must treat all applicants fairly and may not discriminate because of race, color, religion, national origin, sex, marital status or age. If you feel you have been discriminated against by a lender, you may contact the regional office of the Federal Reserve Bank concerning your rights under this act.

The Fair Credit Reporting Act gives you certain access rights to your credit report. You are entitled to a summary of the credit report showing the nature, substance and sources of the information it contains. If you feel your ability to obtain financing has been adversely affected by a credit report, you have the right to inspect a summary of that report free of charge. You may wish to challenge the accuracy of the report and require that corrections be made.

The Real Estate Settlement Procedures Act, known as RESPA, requires that the lender give you a HUD-approved booklet about settlement costs. The lender also must give you a good-faith estimate of the itemized settlement or closing costs you are likely to incur. The booklet and the cost estimates may be given to you at the time the loan application is taken or they may be mailed to you by the lender within three days.

If the borrower is inquiring about adjustable rate mortgages (ARMs), Regulation Z (the truth-in-lending regulation) requires the lender to make available the following:

1. The educational brochure about ARMs called the *Consumer Handbook on Adjustable Rate Mortgages* or a suitable substitute

2. Complete disclosure of all the terms and conditions of each adjustable rate program

3. An explanation of how to calculate payment amounts for the loan and an example showing how payments on a $10,000 loan would have changed in response to actual historical data on the index to be applied

4. A statement showing the initial and maximum interest rates and payments for a $10,000 loan originated at the most recent rate in the historical example

The lender is also required to provide a truth-in-lending statement that discloses the annual percentage rate (APR) or effective interest rate of your loan. This rate is usually higher than the contract interest rate because the APR includes additional charges, such as discount points, fees and certain other charges made by the lender. Any additional charges that may be made for the early prepayment of the loan must also be disclosed in the truth-in-lending statement. The lender is not required to provide the truth-in-lending statement until the final loan papers are to be signed. However, you have a right to request and receive information concerning *all* aspects of the loan you are applying for at the time of application.

At the time of application for a loan, the lender does not have to promise or guarantee in any way that you will be given a loan. However, if the lender does promise or indicate directly to you, the loan applicant, that the loan will be made if certain conditions are met, then the lender is obligated to make the loan to you if those conditions are met.

Soon after your application has been taken, the loan officer will open a file, often called a loan package, for you. The loan officer and a loan processor, working as a team, will begin to accumulate all the necessary information about you and the property. Credit reports, employment and account verifications, title work, the appraisal, the survey, inspection reports, tax certificates, payoff statements for liens that must be removed and all other required documents will be ordered by the loan officer, your REALTOR® or attorney, the listing broker or the escrow officer, depending upon your special situation and the custom in your area.

When all the necessary information and documents have been obtained, your loan package will be submitted for approval. If your loan is a VA or FHA loan and you are using a direct endorsement lender, your loan may be approved quickly. Otherwise, your loan package may have to go to the appropriate government agency. It will take from a few days to several weeks to get loan approval. Conventional loans are often approved in a few days.

Your REALTOR® or loan officer will notify you of loan approval. As an added precaution, after your loan is approved and before the actual closing takes place, ask your REALTOR® and/or attorney to read the mortgage or deed of trust and promissory note that you will be asked to sign. Check to see that the terms and conditions of the approved loan are the same as they were when you shopped for the loan. Also recheck the loan costs. Be sure the points, interest rate or anything else has not been changed to make your loan more expensive.

41. Title Insurance Is a Must

You become the owner of your home when the deed, the legal document used to transfer title, is properly prepared, signed by the seller (if the property is owned by more than one person, each owner must sign the deed) and given to you. It is extremely important to know that the title you will receive is a "good" title—that the seller is actually the owner of the property and has a right to transfer title, and that there are no claims that might seriously diminish your rights to the property.

A title search is *always* necessary before you close your real estate transaction. The title search is made by a title insurance company, an abstract company or by your attorney.

The title search is a thorough examination of all recorded documents that affect the property. It begins with the early history of the land and follows the "chain of title" as the property was passed from one owner to the next. It is important that each transfer was handled correctly so that each owner had a valid title. The title search will show who owns the property and how title is held. It will also show all liens, encumbrances, restrictions, easements, covenants, judgments and anything else that may cloud the title and diminish your rights to the property you are purchasing.

If you are obtaining a new loan from an institutional lender, the lender will require a title search to protect his or her interest in the property. A title search is *still* necessary if you are assuming existing financing, obtaining a private loan or paying cash for your home.

Abstract of Title: A History of the Property

A few areas of the country still use abstracts of title quite extensively. The abstract is a written history of the property with the recorded instruments and opinions of the lawyers being added from time to time as necessary. An abstract often becomes a good-sized book, depending on how often title to the property is transferred and other documents concerning the property are recorded.

If an abstract is to be used as evidence of title, an abstract company or a lawyer will do the title search and bring the abstract up to date.

Your attorney will then give his or her written opinion as to the status of the title. After closing, the new documents created by this real estate transaction will be recorded and added to the abstract.

If you have a competent attorney and all the documents are properly executed and recorded, the use of an abstract is safe and should present no problems. However, if a problem should arise, an abstract gives you no guarantees and no insurance against a claim to your title; you will have to work out any problems through your attorney.

Title Insurance Gives Better Protection

A title insurance policy is the most widely used evidence of title. The title insurance company will do a complete title search and issue a title commitment (sometimes called a binder or preliminary title report) for the title insurance policy. This commitment is usually divided into three parts.

Part 1. The first part contains the following general information:

- The effective date of the title commitment. Nothing recorded after this date will be shown so it will be necessary to have the commitment updated just before closing.

- The legal description of the property

- The name(s) of the present owner(s) and the manner in which title is held

- The name(s) of the purchaser(s) and how title is to be taken

- The amount of insurance coverage provided, which should be the same as the contract price

- The cost of the insurance premium for an owner's policy, a one-time charge that will insure against claims to your title as long as you own the property

Read this part of the commitment carefully to make sure that all the information is correct. Check to be sure the legal description is the same as that on the contract, that all persons presently in title have signed the contract as sellers, and that the insurance coverage is the same as the contract price. See that the name of each purchaser is spelled correctly. It is suggested that each purchaser spell out his or her full name rather than using initials.

Part 2. In many states this part of the commitment gives the requirements that must be met before the title insurance policy will be issued. These requirements include such things as:

- furnishing the proper legal documents to create the estate or interest to be insured;

- releasing of specific liens and encumbrances now on the property if called for in the contract;

- providing a certificate of satisfaction for any judgments against any parties to the real estate transaction;

- furnishing proof of payment of all bills for labor and materials furnished or to be furnished in connection with the improvements erected or to be erected;

- furnishing a survey showing the property to be free of discrepancies, conflicts in boundary lines, shortages in areas, encroachments and any other surveying facts not disclosed by public records;

- furnishing inspection reports as called for in the contract or required by law;

- paying all back taxes and assessments on the property;

- recording documents as specified; and

- anything else that the title company feels is necessary to properly insure your interest in the property.

Title commitments for some properties have a great many requirements; others have only a few. The lender, your REALTOR®, your attorney and/or the escrow officer will take care of most of the paperwork for you. But don't wait until the last minute. Be sure these requirements are satisfied. It takes time to obtain inspection reports, payoffs and releases.

Part 3. The exceptions are given in the third part of the title commitment. These are items that *will not* be insured against. Read the exceptions very carefully and be sure you understand them.

A common exception is the rights or claims of parties in possession not recorded in the public record. If the property is rented, the tenants may have rights that will prevent you from moving into your new home when you take title (see Chapter 36).

Other exceptions have to do with taxes not yet due and with other claims not shown on the public record. Sometimes exceptions have to do with a part of the property you are buying or with access to the property. If any part of the property or any easement or right of way giving you access is shown as an exception, you should be concerned. Also, be concerned if water rights or mineral rights show up in the exception portion of the commitment.

Discuss each exception and the consequences that it might have with your REALTOR® and/or your attorney. Additional title work may be necessary, or the title company may be able to insure against a potential problem for an additional premium. Ask for buyer's lien protection if it has not been included; this should be provided at no additional cost.

Additional pages may be attached to the title commitment. If there are protective covenants on the property, a copy of these should be provided. If the home is a condominium, a copy of the declaration, the bylaws and other recorded documents may be provided by the title company if you have not already received them.

The above information pertains to the title commitment. The actual owner's title insurance policy will be issued after closing when all requirements are complied with and *the premium has been paid*. (The lender usually requires a mortgagee's title policy to protect his or her interest in the property. A mortgagee's policy does not protect the owner against claims. You need an owner's title insurance policy.) There have been instances when the proper documents were not recorded or the premium was not paid and, consequently, the title policy was never issued. Don't let this happen to you. Be sure your real estate transaction is handled properly.

In almost every instance, it is in the buyer's best interest to insist on an owner's title insurance policy rather than an abstract. The policies are issued by large ongoing companies who guarantee the accuracy of their title searches. If a claim against your title should arise, the company will pay for the defense and just compensation for any errors.

Often old abstracts are destroyed when title insurance is first placed on a property. You may want to make arrangements with both the seller and the title company to keep the old abstract of your property for its historical and sentimental value.

42. Comments on the Property Appraisal

An appraisal is an estimate of value. Real estate appraisals are made to estimate the value of a property for several reasons: for tax purposes, for a divorce settlement, for a company buyout plan, for estate taxes, for insurance purposes, for use of the property as security for a loan as well as to estimate value in the sale of a property. Who does the appraisal, how it is done and the reason for the appraisal all affect the estimated value.

Many magazine and newspaper articles and real estate books suggest that the buyer or seller order an appraisal to determine the market value and sale price of a property. By definition, however, market value is the highest price a willing and able buyer would pay and a seller would accept, both being fully informed and not under undue pressure, after the property has been exposed to the marketplace for a reasonable period of time. Therefore, *an appraisal cannot determine market value.*

The sale price (and the market value) should be determined only through negotiations between the buyer and the seller. Even the most qualified appraiser using the best information available cannot evaluate a property from the same perspective as the buyer. Only the buyer knows his or her own wants and needs and the value of the special features of a property.

If you, the buyer, feel you need the help of an appraisal, hire a qualified appraiser who is very familiar with the area where the home is located. Pay the appraiser yourself so the appraisal report is yours. Study the appraisal report carefully and use it to help determine your offering price. Do not consider the value placed on the property in the appraisal report to be the market value until you have negotiated with the seller.

For the purposes of this book, there are two times when a property appraisal is necessary: for **ad valorem** property taxes and for a new mortgage loan.

Institutional lenders usually require a property appraisal for a new mortgage loan. Most appraisals for loan purposes are made *after* the contract has been negotiated and finalized and market value has been established. It is important to note that these appraisals are made for loan purposes, to justify the contract price. The appraiser is given the contract price when he or she is given other information on the property.

Lenders decide which appraisers may do their appraisals. If a recent appraisal is available for the property, the lender may or may not accept it. Appraisals for VA and FHA loan purposes must be done by government-approved appraisers.

The appraisal, the estimating of the value of a property, is approached in three ways: the replacement cost of the property, the income available from the property and the price comparison of similar properties that have been sold recently.

The replacement cost of the property using today's land and building costs often gives all but the most recently constructed homes a higher than contract value. The income approach usually gives a home a lower value because rents have not been able to keep pace with the rising price of homes. The price comparison of similar recently sold properties is the most valid approach to appraising homes in today's market. Because supply and demand determine value, the important question is: What are similar homes selling for?

If the buyer shops carefully and negotiates the best price possible for the home that fits his or her needs, there should not be a problem concerning contract price and appraised value. If the appraisal shows a lower value than the price you negotiated, *and* this lower value will prevent you from obtaining the loan you want, you should make some effort to find out why the appraisal is low. Any one of several reasons may be the cause:

1. There is the possibility that you have agreed to pay too much for the property. This could happen if you were under pressure to buy and did not take the time or make the effort to shop the market yourself. If you think this is the reason for the low appraisal, take the time to look at more homes and determine value for yourself.

2. The appraiser may have overlooked a major feature, such as a garage, a fireplace, an extra room, etc.

3. The appraiser may not have used the most recent comparables. In a rising market, it is sometimes difficult for an appraiser to keep his or her records up to date.

4. If the lender does not have the funds, or for some other reason chooses not to make the loan after taking the loan application, he or she may use a low appraisal to get out of making the loan.

5. An unscrupulous lender may use a low appraisal to his or her own advantage. When the loan application is taken, the lender

may learn that the borrower has additional cash assets that may be invested in the property. With a low appraisal, the lender can require a larger down payment and make a lower loan to value ratio loan.

If you have paid for the appraisal or are expected to pay for it, you have the right to see the actual appraisal report. This will show you all the figures used by the appraiser and how the estimate of value was determined. Look it over carefully with the help of your REALTOR®. If you find a mistake or feel better comparables are available, ask for a reconsideration. Your REALTOR® and the lender will know how to prepare the request for a reconsideration.

An FHA appraisal differs from others because of the strict FHA property requirements. A narrow lot, an outdated floor plan, an unacceptable (to FHA) location or some other feature that is impossible to change often prevents a property from being considered for an FHA loan. An FHA appraiser may also require that certain repairs or improvements be made before the loan is approved. If such conditions are required in the appraisal, the necessary repairs must be made and the property reinspected by the FHA appraiser or the lender.

Sometimes the buyer mistakenly believes that a low appraisal is to his or her advantage—that a seller must sell the property for the lower appraised value. This is not true unless a clause to this effect was written into the contract. If you have asked for a reconsideration and the appraised value is still less than the contract price, one of five things may happen:

1. The seller may lower the sale price to the appraised value.

2. The buyer may make a larger down payment and buy the property at the contract price.

3. The seller and buyer may compromise and agree to a new price somewhere in between.

4. The seller and buyer may agree to extend the contract date, if necessary, and the buyer may go to another lender, order a new appraisal and try to get the desired loan. This often works when the buyer wants a conventional loan. It usually won't work for a VA or FHA loan.

5. The contract may be voided. The earnest money will be returned to the buyer if the contract was contingent upon obtaining a particular loan and a good-faith effort was made.

Note: The property appraisal we have just discussed is to be used for loan purposes—the property will be used as security for a mortgage loan. Do not read more than this into the appraisal. The appraisal *does not:* (1) determine market value; (2) include a thorough inspection of the property; (3) guarantee in any way the condition of the property; or (4) give any warranties or protections as to the condition of the property or any component of the property.

The property taxes you pay are based on the appraisal value of your home as determined by the tax assessor. It is wise to determine whether your taxes are approximately the same as similar homes in your area. If you suspect your taxes are higher than necessary, you may ask to see the assessor's records. Read the property report to determine if any mistakes have been made. The tax assessor's office can tell you what steps to take to ask for a tax adjustment.

43. Tax Certificate, Survey and Inspection Reports

Many documents will give additional information concerning the property you wish to buy. Often these documents are required by the lender before a new loan will be approved. Whether or not you are getting a new loan, it is in your best interest to request a tax certificate, a survey and the inspection reports you feel are necessary. They should be ordered soon after the contract is finalized; they must be available before closing.

You Always Need a Tax Certificate

A tax certificate should be obtained before *every* closing for the buyer's protection. The tax certificate will show the property's legal description, address and the amount of property tax, if any, that is owed. If taxes for prior years have not been paid, they should be paid before or at closing according to the terms of the contract. In most areas the tax certificate is your guarantee that you will not be responsible for back taxes that do not show on the certificate.

Sometimes special assessments and/or taxes for streets, sewer systems, parks, schools, etc., do not show up on the same tax certificate. It may be necessary to obtain tax certificates from more than one taxing authority. Ask your REALTOR® and/or attorney for help in locating all the information and documents you need.

Many real estate contracts require taxes to be apportioned to the day of closing based on information on the tax certificate. The amount will be either debited or credited on the settlement statements, depending on whether taxes are paid in advance or arrears in your area. A final tax agreement is usually signed at closing.

The Survey Answers Questions about Boundaries

A recent survey is usually required when an institutional lender is providing new financing, unless the property is part of a condominium or townhouse complex. Often the title company will require a survey. Even when a survey is not specifically required, it is usually in the buyer's best interest to obtain one. The survey should always be made by an established company with a good reputation that will guarantee the accuracy of its work.

A complete survey is necessary when a parcel of land is being divided or if there is any question concerning the boundary markers. The surveyor will set pins on all corners of the property.

A less expensive improvement survey may be sufficient to protect the interest of the buyer if the property is a part of a subdivision. The surveyor uses the recorded plat map and other recorded documents that show utility and drainage easements. He or she then checks to be sure there are no encroachments on the property, that no improvements are improperly placed over easements, and that improvements do not violate covenants, zoning laws or building regulations.

Use Inspection Reports to Avoid Potential Problems

Each inspection report should be ordered soon after the contract is finalized. Use only established, reputable companies who will guarantee the accuracy of the information in their inspection reports. If work is required, make arrangements to have it completed, inspected and accepted before closing. If the seller is to pay for the work, be sure the bills are paid before or at closing or require that the seller escrow enough money to cover the cost of the work.

44. Understand Each Closing Document Before You Sign It

Many documents will be presented to you at the closing. However, each closing is unique and only the documents required for your specific transaction will be necessary. Ask your attorney and/or REALTOR® to check each document to see that it is prepared properly. Read each document carefully and be sure you understand it before you accept and sign it.

Settlement Statements

Settlement statements, prepared for every closing, give an accounting of all monies involved in the real estate transaction. Separate statements are prepared for the buyer and seller. Each statement gives the name(s) of the buyer(s) and seller(s), the property's legal description and address, the settlement date and the date of proration. All debits and credits are itemized and the exact balance due to or from the buyer or seller is shown at the bottom of the statement. The buyer and seller each approve and sign their own statement.

The Deed

The deed transfers title to the new owner. It is the legal instrument that conveys fee simple title of real property from the seller to the buyer. Usually only one page in length, the deed is the most important document and should be checked very carefully for errors. Be sure all names are spelled correctly and that the legal description is correct. The deed includes the following:

- The name(s) of the seller(s) as it(they) appeared in the public record at the time title was taken, as well as the present name if there has been a change (such as a new marital name)
- The full, legal name(s) of the purchaser(s)
- The manner in which the purchasers wish to take title (joint tenancy, tenancy in common, etc.)
- The legal description of the property and the address, including zip code

- The consideration paid for the property—usually the sale price, but in some instances a much smaller sum

- The correct wording by which the property is conveyed to the purchaser(s) and by which the seller(s) gives up all rights and claims to the property in favor of the purchaser(s)

Different types of deeds may be used. A warranty deed will state the condition of the title, the warranties that go with the title and any exceptions to a clear and absolute title. A quitclaim deed only transfers the interest that the grantor may have, but without any warranty of a valid title or interest in the property.

The deed is signed by the seller(s) and dated, and the signature(s) is (are) notarized. Delivering the deed to the buyer(s) completes the legal transfer of title. The deed should then be recorded to become part of the public record, even though this step is not always required for the deed to be legally valid.

The Mortgage and the Deed of Trust

If new financing is placed on the property, either a mortgage or a deed of trust (trust deed) may be used. These are the legal instruments that pledge the property as security for the loan. It is not uncommon for more than one mortgage or deed of trust to be placed on the property at a closing.

The mortgage contains the legal description and address of the property, the name(s) of the borrower(s), also known as the mortgagor(s), the lender or mortgagee and the terms and conditions of the loan. The amount of the payments, how, when and to whom they are to be made, as well as information concerning possible penalties and foreclosure, are included in the mortgage document.

The same types of information are in the deed of trust. However, the deed of trust differs from a mortgage in that there are three parties instead of two. The borrower, called a trustor, gives the deed of trust to a neutral third party, called a trustee. In the event of a default, the trustee may sell the property and transfer the money to the lender, called the beneficiary, as payment for the debt.

In both the mortgage and the deed of trust, the rights and obligations of the borrower and lender may vary; each document should be considered unique. Read the document carefully and ask questions, if necessary, so you understand all your rights and obligations before you sign it.

The Promissory Note

The promissory note is your personal promise to repay the loan. A promissory note is often used as a companion document to a mortgage or deed of trust. By signing this instrument the borrower acknowledges his or her debt, assumes personal liability and promises repayment according to the terms of the note. The borrower also may give the note holder rights to the property if the note is not repaid as promised.

The Assumption Statement

An assumption statement is necessary when existing financing is to be assumed. The assumption statement is ordered from the lender. This document states that the lender approves the new borrower, if necessary, and gives the current status of the loan. The present loan balance, the remaining term, the interest rate (the new interest rate if it is being increased), the monthly principal and interest (PI) payment, the total monthly payment (including the escrow amount for taxes and insurance) and the balance in the escrow account (for taxes and insurance) are all given. The new purchaser ordinarily "buys" the seller's escrow account at closing and continues to make the monthly payment (or the adjusted larger payment) in the same manner as the previous borrower. By signing the assumption statement, the new borrower accepts the assumption statement as accurate and assumes the loan and its terms and conditions.

Releases

The title commitment will show the liens, judgments, etc., that must be paid off or satisfied by the seller before or at the time of closing. The release is the document that shows the debt has been paid. All paperwork should be ordered far enough in advance so that it is available at closing. Releases must be signed and recorded before the title insurance policy will be issued. Ask your REALTOR® and/or attorney to be sure that the releases are obtained.

The Bill of Sale

The bill of sale or chattel mortgage transfers ownership of personal property from the seller to the buyer and states that the items are owned unencumbered by the seller. The document is signed by the seller and given to the buyer. Depending on the laws and customs in your area, notarization of the signature(s) on the bill of sale may or may not be required and it may or may not be necessary to record this document. Ask your REALTOR® or attorney.

The Lien Waiver

The lien waiver protects the investor-lender. Sometimes the buyer or seller, anticipating the move into the new home, will order carpet, a new fence or other improvements before closing on the property. To protect themselves, lenders providing new financing often require the buyer and seller to sign a lien waiver. This document states that the parties have not contracted for, or ordered any items or in any other way caused a lien to be placed against the property.

Agreements

The real estate tax agreement shows how the property taxes are adjusted or prorated and the responsibilities of the buyer and the seller. The tax agreement is signed by both parties.

Other statements of agreement between seller and buyer are often presented and signed by both parties at closing. These agreements may concern such things as possession, rent backs, proration of utility expenses, monies escrowed for repairs or improvements, etc.

Truth-in-Lending Disclosure Statement

Institutional lenders are required to provide a truth-in-lending disclosure statement for borrowers who obtain a new first mortgage on an owner-occupied residence. The following information is given in the statement:

- The name and address of the lender

- The principal amount of the loan, the interest rate, the amount of the PI payment, the mortgage insurance premium, if applicable, the number of installments, and the first payment due date

- The prepaid finance charges paid by both the seller and buyer

- Loan costs that are not finance charges (these are itemized)

- The total finance charges for the loan if it is held until maturity

- The total of all scheduled PI payments if the loan is held until maturity

- The late charge amount and when it may be assessed

- The conditions under which a prepayment penalty may be charged and the penalty amount

- The annual percentage rate (APR) of the loan using certain finance charges and rounded up to the nearest 0.25 percent

If the new loan is an adjustable rate mortgage, the lender is required to provide the borrower with certain additional disclosures: (1) that the transaction contains an adjustable rate feature and (2) a statement that the adjustable rate disclosures have been provided earlier. (Further information must be furnished to the borrower throughout the term of an adjustable rate mortgage. Notice must be given to the borrower of an adjusted payment amount, the interest rate, index rate and loan balance once during any year when there is a rate adjustment, whether or not there is a payment change. The notice must be mailed not less than 25 days or more than 120 days before the new payment is due and must give the current and previous interest rates and the index values upon which the current and prior interest rates are based. The disclosure must also indicate the extent to which any increase in the interest rate has not been fully implemented.)

RESPA Form

The Real Estate Settlement Procedures Act (RESPA) requires that a HUD-approved form be given to all borrowers who obtain a new loan on their home from an institutional lender. All transaction costs for both the buyer and seller are itemized and the amounts due to or from both the buyer and seller are shown. The figures used on this form should be the same as those found on the settlement statements, but may be grouped and arranged differently.

FHA Side Agreement Statement

The Federal Housing Administration requires the buyer and seller to sign a form stating that there are no side agreements between the buyer and seller other than those which are part of the contract. This statement is necessary for a new FHA loan.

VII
MOVING AND SETTLING IN

45. Moving Can Be Easier

As soon as you know you will be moving into a new home, begin planning for your new life-style. The small things you do now will help you feel comfortable and enjoy your new home immediately.

Any move to an area you are unfamiliar with, whether it is in the same state or across the country, may be considered a long-distance move. It isn't unusual to feel uneasy and more than a little skeptical about moving to an unknown place.

Information about the New Area

As you begin to familiarize yourself with the new city or part of town, your anxieties will lessen and you will look forward to living in your new home. Community-oriented information is available from many different sources. For example, you may write to the local chamber of commerce or the visitor's bureau. Begin reading the newspaper from the new city if you are not already doing so. You may subscribe and have it sent to your current home, or the paper may be available at a local newstand.

Many large companies provide special services for their transferred employees. Besides all the general information about the new area, often special assistance is given on an individual basis to families with special needs. In addition, most of the large interstate moving companies have information available. While it may be too early to actually get a moving estimate, you may call and request that an information packet about the new community be sent to you. Also, most REALTORS® can put you in touch with a real estate company in the new area through a referral service. The REALTOR® in the new area can provide information and answer questions.

If you have school-age children, gathering information is an important part of their move. The more children know about their new home the easier it will be for them to adjust. They will be able to look forward to new and exciting places to visit and interesting things to do.

Encourage and help your children to send for the information themselves. They may ask for maps and information on recreational facilities, athletic events and schools. Also, request information on activities of special interest to each family member.

Timing Your Move

Some thought should be given to when you will move. Some companies expect their employees to be able to relocate with very little notice. However, most people being transferred or moving on their own have some time to plan the move. Of course, major consideration should be given to purchasing a new home and selling the present one, as well as when the new job begins.

Many parents try to postpone their move to keep their children in school until the end of the term. Often these parents do not realize how difficult this may make the move for children in grade school and junior high school. If you wait until school is out and then move, your children will have a long summer without their former friends; even the most self-confident child may worry about the new school, new friends and new activities.

If you are going to move to another city, consider moving as soon as possible, even if it is in the middle of the school year. The sooner children are in their new schools, the better. Schedule a conference with your children's teachers within a couple weeks to help you spot and solve any problems that may arise and insure that your children are receiving the special help they may need. The sooner your children make new friends and become involved in new activities, the more they will like their new home. Encourage your children to continue old friendships. Perhaps they could invite their friends for a visit to the new home.

There is an exception to these comments. Sometimes it is important for high-school-age children to complete the school term because good grades in certain classes may be necessary to get into college. Also, it may be more difficult for an older child to leave a team-sport activity before the season ends.

The move will be more pleasant if the needs and desires of all family members are given consideration. Usually a satisfactory compromise can be found.

Short Distance Moves

Most moves are to new homes in the same community, often within the same neighborhood. If your children will change schools, it is sometimes wise to drive them to their present schools until the end of the school term or wait until the end of the term to move. However, children should visit their new schools and meet their teachers before classes end for the summer. Soon after moving to the new home, involve your children in activities that will help them make new friends and keep their old friends.

Sorting Out and Throwing Out

Think of the move as a new beginning. This is a good time to throw out what you no longer need or want. It is never too soon to start this process. Getting rid of all the things you don't want will make packing and unpacking much easier.

Mentally survey your present home and count up the number of drawers, closets, cupboards, cabinets and other cubbyholes that now hold your things. Go through each one before it's time to do the actual packing. Tackle one drawer or cupboard at a time, leaving only those items you want to keep. If you are selling your present home, you might want to start with the closets. An uncluttered look, particularly in the closets, will help your home show better. Immediately box and label the items you want to keep but won't be needing right away.

Before you move your discard pile to the curb for the trash pickup, consider having a garage or yard sale. It's kind of fun to see your junk become someone else's new-found treasure, and it can be profitable, too! Try to hold your sale at least three to four weeks before your actual moving date. If you can interest your neighbors in participating, so much the better. Besides the fun of doing it together and sharing the work, you will be able to attract more customers with a larger sale. If you have never been involved in a garage or yard sale you might use your library's *Reader's Guide to Periodical Literature* to locate magazine articles on the "how-tos" of garage sales.

Also, charitable organizations are usually happy to receive discards. If you call early, they will often come and pick up the items. Be sure to ask for a receipt for income tax purposes because the fair market value of your contributions is a tax deduction.

Other Concerns after Home Hunting

Once you have found the right home, finalized the contract, arranged for financing and opened escrow, if necessary, most of your attention can be focused on other important matters. Many details not directly related to the real estate transaction must also be settled. A little extra planning now will help everyone in the family feel comfortable and be happy in their new home.

If this is a long-distance move and you are not likely to visit the area again until closing or moving day, there are a few things that should be taken care of before you return to your present home. Even in short moves, these things should not be left until the last minute.

Arrange for property insurance while you are in the new community rather than doing it with long-distance telephone calls. You will probably want a homeowner's policy with broad coverage and possibly extra protection for certain valuables. Some lenders and real estate companies have insurance departments; however, you are never obligated to buy insurance from them. Feel free to shop around. The cost for the same coverage may vary. If you wish, call two or three agents and ask that quotes be sent to your present address so you can compare prices. When you have all the information, let your loan officer or your REALTOR® know your final decision so the first year's insurance premium can be paid at the time of closing and the policy becomes effective as soon as the title is given to you.

Your present insurance agent(s) needs to know about your move. Your homeowner's or renter's policy should not be cancelled until your present home is sold and closed and the last piece of your furniture is moved out. Your address must be changed on your car insurance policy. If you are moving to another state, the policy may need to be adjusted or rewritten. Life insurance and medical insurance companies will also want your new address. If you are leaving one job and taking another, try to extend the coverage you have until a new policy takes effect.

Whether the move is across town or across the country, try to arrange activities for all family members as soon as the new home is selected. It's important for everyone to make new friends and social contacts as soon as possible. Often you must register weeks in advance for swimming lessons, a bowling league or a soccer team. Also, make arrangements to transfer into another scout troop or 4-H club. It's difficult to get involved in many activities without advance planning.

You should also visit the schools your children will attend soon after you have selected your new home. Find out which records the schools will need and anything else that will help to make the move as pleasant and easy as possible for your children. The new schools will need to send for your children's records. You will need the names and addresses, including zip codes, of the schools your children have been attending.

You may need birth certificates, immunization records, etc., when you register your children for school or sign them up for other activities. Put these records in a place where they will be available or carry them with you on a long-distance move.

Call the telephone company well in advance of your move to request service. In some areas, there is a waiting period either to obtain service or for a credit check so you won't have to pay a deposit. Also, you may want to buy your own phones. The additional time will allow you to shop for them. Ask to have your new telephone number assigned as soon as possible, even before your service is started.

Select a bank near your new home and make arrangements to open new accounts. The availability of a guaranteed check card will be a great asset when you are cashing checks before you get your resident driver's license. When you get your new telephone number, have the bank print your new checks. All banks, savings and loan associations and investment companies need to be notified of your address change. If you are moving out of the area, your money may be transferred automatically to the new bank if you wish.

Once you are back at your present home, there are many other things that must be done. Magazine companies, book clubs, etc., need at least four weeks' notice to assure that you will receive the publications at your new address. All creditors and credit card companies must be notified of your move and given your new address.

Your doctors may be able to refer you to health care professionals in the community where you are moving. You will probably not be allowed to hand carry your medical and dental records, so be sure you have all the correct names and addresses, including zip codes, so your new doctors may send for them.

Getting all the facts and figures for tax returns may be difficult later. For medical tax deductions get the names, addresses and telephone numbers of all doctors, dentists and hospitals. If you don't have statements showing payments, call and ask for copies. Insurance payments, the cost of medicines and such expenses as glasses are deductible if you can verify the amounts. Transportation expenses for medical reasons are another deductible item. You may wish to check the mileage and estimate the number of trips. Also total up your charitable deductions (the fair market value of donated items as well as monetary contributions).

Finally, it's a good idea to pack a telephone book from your current community when you move to a new area. It will be a handy reference tool when you need to look up other addresses.

Planning the Actual Move

Begin making final arrangements for the actual move about two months before your moving date. You may use an approximate date until you have loan approval and/or a very strong indication that you will be able to close and take possession of your new home as stated in the contract.

There are three basic types of moves, each with many variations. The one you choose will depend on your own special situation: how much furniture and other possessions you have to move, how far you are moving and how much the move will cost. Be sure to keep an itemized list and receipts of all expenses pertaining to the move. Many of these items may be tax deductible.

The Do-It-Yourself Move. Many people moving a short distance pack and move themselves. If you have a truck or trailer, or can borrow one and can talk several strong friends into helping, you're all set. Trucks and trailers may also be rented for short-distance and long-distance, do-it-yourself moves. Look into the total overall costs, including renting the dolly, padding and trailer hitch, if necessary, and paying for gas and mileage. Be sure there are advantages to moving this way.

The Intrastate Move. Most people use at least some professional services, even when making short-distance moves. Companies operating within the state usually offer a variety of services and may charge a flat rate or an hourly fee. Often the hourly rate is quoted for two men and a van. Usually the hourly rate for three men and a van is only a little more. Sometimes a moving company representative will give you a flat rate for the entire job.

Your local or intrastate move may include all the packing and un-packing, and the loading and unloading, of all your household goods. Or you may choose to use only some of the company's available services.

If you are going to hire someone to move your appliances, piano and heavy furniture, consider also letting that company move the smaller pieces and all your boxes. It will probably not cost much more if you are paying by the hour.

The Interstate Move. Moves across state lines come under the jurisdiction of the Interstate Commerce Commission (ICC). In the past, the cost of these moves was always determined by the ICC; rates were strictly regulated based on distance and weight. This situation no longer exists. Recently, the trucking industry has been somewhat deregulated, and moving companies are now free to offer discounts. There is now competition in the marketplace, which benefits consumers.

Moving companies offer a wide range of services (for additional costs, of course), including packing/unpacking, storage, a choice of insurance coverage, etc. They also give a great deal of free help in the form of pamphlets and booklets covering everything from how to hold garage sales to how to move pets and plants. Many of the larger companies provide free change of address cards, sticky labels for packing boxes and even maps, information and entertainment guides to your new community.

Check on the reputation of the moving companies you are considering. Ask friends and associates about the quality of the service, reliability of moving dates, and follow-up procedures on any problems or claims. Call only the highly recommended companies for estimates. Here are some things to keep in mind:

1. Moving costs are based on the distance and the actual weight of your possessions. Be aware that the moving companies' representatives give you only nonbinding estimates of weight. Watch out for low-ball weight estimates.

2. Moving costs may be negotiated. When a moving representative calls on you, you may ask for a discount. If you are able to move during the less busy months, or even during the middle of the month, you will be in a better bargaining position.

3. Pickup and delivery dates may be guaranteed. Ask the moving representative for an explanation of his or her company's policies concerning firm moving dates. At least one company will pay a rebate if it is not able to meet the guaranteed dates.

4. Moving companies may now offer written binding contracts stating the services that will be rendered and the costs. Both the client being moved and the moving company must honor the terms of the contract.

5. Additional insurance coverage is recommended. The standard insurance usually included in the cost of interstate moves is only 60¢ a pound. This means if an article weighing two pounds is broken, you would receive $1.20, regardless of the article's value. Most moving companies offer a choice of two additional types of coverage: depreciated value coverage and full replacement value coverage. Ask the moving company representative for details. Also, ask if the insurance still applies if you pack and unpack yourself.

6. If your company is paying for your move, find out exactly what your company policy is and what services will be covered. Even if your company will not pay for additional insurance coverage, it is a good idea to have the extra protection.

7. Find out how the moving company expects to be paid. Both intrastate and interstate movers customarily require cash or certified funds (not a personal check) at the time the van arrives and before your furniture is unloaded. Some companies will accept credit cards. Movers will bill your company for the move *only* if arrangements have been made in advance. Many companies expect their employees to pay for the move and submit the bill for reimbursement at a later date.

Packing and Unpacking

Packing up and leaving one home and getting unpacked and settled into another is never easy. Even the "all expenses paid" moves have their bad, sometimes disastrous moments. But moving does not have to be a major hassle. Plan ahead and try to foresee possible problems and pitfalls so that things go smoother and much of the hassle is avoided.

Even if the movers are going to do all your packing and unpacking, you will want to supervise. Letting the mover-packers/unpackers do their thing in their own way can be disastrous.

Here are some practical packing and unpacking suggestions:

1. Make it clear to the packers how *you* want the packing done—all the good china packed together, all the everyday dishes packed together, the frequently used pots and pans packed together, etc.

2. Insist that each box be labeled clearly and specifically the contents, the room it is to be placed in and whether it will be needed immediately. Don't let any box be marked "miscellaneous."

3. If you are going to do any or all of the packing yourself, collect a supply of sturdy cartons and the other things you will need well ahead of time. Boxes discarded by liquor stores are excellent because of their strength and small size. You also might follow moving vans and ask the people moving in if you can have the cartons and packing materials they will be discarding. Your REALTOR® might be able to help you locate people moving into a new home. Boxes and other packing materials may also be purchased from moving companies.

   Besides boxes, you will need a supply of paper towels, facial tissue, paper napkins and/or plain newsprint and newspapers. Nothing should be wrapped directly in printed newspaper because the ink can rub off and leave permanent stains. However, newspaper may be used to pad and cushion articles.

4. If you are going to do a lot of the packing yourself, get started on it a week or two before moving day. Try not to stay up packing most of the night before moving day. Try to leave some time the last few days to visit with friends and do some fun activities.

5. If you have children, let them help pack their own toys and games, even if you are paying for packing services. Helping with the packing will make the move seem more real to them.

6. Consider doing some or all of the unpacking yourself, even if the unpacking cost is included in the packing/unpacking service. If you supervise the packing, you can stack boxes of things you do not need immediately and unpack them when and as you want.

7. Pack the mattress pad, clean sheets and pillowcases, blanket, pillows and bedspread all together for each bed. Clearly label the box.

8. Pack a small chest of drawers with all the things you will need the day your furniture arrives. Some things you may want to include are:

cleaning compounds	pan or tea kettle	scissors
clean rags	paper and pencil	sharp knife
cookies or crackers	paper cups	shelf paper
instant coffee	paper plates	silverware
instant fruit drink	paper towels	toilet tissue
Kleenex	ruler	transparent tape

If you have children, you will want to include a couple of favorite toys or games in the chest. Ask the movers to place this chest of drawers on the van last so it will be one of the first things moved into your new home.

9. If you have a baby or toddler, ask to have the baby bed loaded last so it will be one of the first things taken off the van. Put clean baby bed sheets and changes of clothing in the chest of drawers along with other essential items.

10. Have the movers load the vacuum cleaner last so it can be unloaded first. If you have it handy, you may not need it.

46. Good Records Will Save Tax Dollars

One of the many benefits of owning a home is the tax savings you can realize. By setting up a simple bookkeeping system now to keep accurate records and receipts, you will save tax dollars both this year and in the future. The record keeping chores are not difficult or time-consuming. However, it is important that some matters be taken care of in the first three or four weeks after you have closed on your home.

The first priority should be to rework your budget using your new housing expenses. Be sure to allow some money each month for savings and investments. Consider having a certain amount automatically transferred each month into a special savings account. Also, you may want to increase your tax exemptions so a smaller portion is withheld from your paychecks.

Then you need to set up a simple filing system to keep all your household records in order—your budget, tax records, the basis of your home (see page 213), and so forth. You need some type of filing cabinet. A sturdy metal filing cabinet with hanging folders is a good investment, but you can also purchase a heavy cardboard file box or fashion one out of a moving carton. Even a desk or dresser drawer will work if it allows you enough room. You will also need a supply of folders or heavy manila envelopes. (Throwing receipts into a shoe box is the least satisfactory type of filing system.)

The first section of your file should be for your monthly budget. Use a simple system that fits your situation. Information in Chapter 3 may be helpful. The second and third sections should be used to keep track of income tax deductions and the basis of your home. A filing cabinet, if large enough, may also be used to hold insurance policies; operating instructions and warranty information for kitchen appliances, the TV, the stereo, etc.; investment information; personal and medical records; closing documents from your real estate transaction; tax returns; and other important documents.

Costs and Expenses

There are many costs and expenses (along with the benefits) associated with buying, owning and selling your home. Some of these costs and expenses have immediate tax consequences in the form of deductions and credits. The tax consequences of other costs and expenses are long-range, but still important. Taking advantage of all tax savings to which you are entitled will be easier if you understand how the IRS categorizes the various costs and expenses for federal income tax purposes.

Equity Payments. The down payment you make at the time you purchase your home and the principal payment you make each month are equity payments. This is money spent to buy your home. For our purposes, equity payments have no tax consequences; that is, they are not deductible.

Tax Deductible Expenses. Taxes and interest expenses are deductible for the year in which they are paid. Some costs shown on your settlement statements when you buy your home and sell your previous home may be deductible. Many other expenses, such as fees charged by attorneys, accountants and other professionals, as well as certain house hunting and moving expenses, may be deductible depending on the circumstances. Check with your accountant.

Personal Expenses. The IRS defines the many costs associated with keeping your home in good condition as personal expenses. These include homeowner's insurance, decorating expenses, such as painting a room, and repair expenses, such as replacing a broken window or fixing a leaky faucet. Because we are discussing your home, these expenses are not deductible.

Home-Buying Expenses. Expenses related to your real estate transaction that are not immediately deductible and are not personal expenses may be considered home-buying expenses. Home-buying expenses increase the basis of your home.

Capital Improvements. The IRS says a capital improvement must add value to your home, prolong the life of your home or adapt your home to a new use. Installing a fence, building a patio, converting the basement into a recreation room and redoing the plumbing or wiring are examples of capital improvements.

Sometimes deciding whether a particular cost is a personal expense or an improvement may be difficult. Since it is a judgment call, even IRS agents do not always agree. For example, installing a sprinkler system and lawn are capital improvements. Buying the fertilizer and paying the water bill are personal expenses. Trees are improvements. But what about the tulips, raspberry bushes and strawberry plants? Since they are going to grow year after year and add to the value of your home, could they be capital improvements?

Home-Selling Expenses. Expenses relating to the real estate transaction when you sell your home that are not tax deductible are considered selling expenses and will be used in figuring the capital basis on your home. The IRS will also let you include in the selling expenses the cost of all decorating, fixing up and repairing of your home that is (1) done during the 89 days before the day you sign the contract to sell and (2) paid for no later than 30 days after the sale.

Tax Deductions for Form 1040

Tax deductions for Schedule A of Federal Income Tax Form 1040 are divided into five categories: medical and dental expenses, taxes, interest expenses, contributions and miscellaneous. Your filing system should have a folder for each. A sixth folder is needed for tax credits. List the tax deductible items and their amounts on individual sheets that are kept in each folder.

Taxes. Property taxes for the time you actually own the home are deductible by you, whether they are paid by you or were paid in advance by the seller. Paying money into a tax escrow account is not considered to be the same as paying taxes. Either the actual tax bill or a statement from the lender will show the exact amount of taxes you pay for the year. Other taxes paid at the time of settlement may be deductible. Check with your accountant.

Interest Expenses. The interest portion of each monthly payment is deductible. Prepaid interest or interest paid by the seller that paid the interest on your mortgage from the day you took title until the first payment was due is deductible by you, whether or not it is shown on the settlement statement.

Points (prepaid interest) that you paid to obtain the loan as the borrower are deductible. Points paid by you so the buyer of your previous home could obtain a loan may be deductible. Some accountants suggest both the borrower and the seller pay for points at closing with a separate check. If you paid a prepayment penalty (an interest payment) when you repaid the loan on the home you sold, it is deductible, too.

Contributions. The fair market value of all items you gave to a charitable organization when you moved (and any other time) may be deductible provided you have receipts.

Miscellaneous. The amount you paid for this book is deductible, as is the cost of setting up your filing system—the filing cabinet, folders, paper, etc. The amount you paid for the credit report and other expenses related to qualifying you (as opposed to the property) to invest in your home is probably deductible. Check with your accountant.

The amount you paid experts to give you advice about your home investment, provided the information was not required by law or the lender, is probably deductible. In some states these expenses may include attorney and accountant fees and some inspection reports. Check with your accountant.

Certain expenses associated with job hunting and moving to a new location may also be deductible, depending on the circumstances. Again, check with your accountant.

Tax Credits

A tax credit offsets your tax bill dollar for dollar, making it more valuable than a tax deduction. In the past, tax credits have been used to encourage home improvements that result in energy conservation. At this time there is talk of using a tax credit to help the first-time buyer purchase a home. If tax credits become available, your REALTOR® can give you the details.

Tracking the Basis

The IRS uses a basis system to determine the capital gains on your home and the tax due. Actually there can be no capital gains until your home is sold and a profit is realized. Also, the tax on the capital gains may be postponed indefinitely and possibly forgiven entirely if you follow certain IRS guidelines.

Even though you have just purchased your home, it is important to understand the IRS basis system. By keeping complete and accurate records, you will lessen any tax that may be due in the future. Take all tax credits and tax deductions to which you are entitled before you consider adjustments to the basis of your home.

The basis and capital gains form shown in Figure 46.1 at the end of this chapter provides an easy way for you to track the basis of your home and figure the capital gains when the home is sold. You will need three folders in this part of your filing system. The first one is for the basis and capital gains form.

The second folder is for keeping track of all capital improvements. You could keep a numbered, running list showing the item, the date purchased and the amount paid. Whatever the number on the list, put the same number on the receipt. If the receipt does not show the date, the company, the item or service that was performed and the cost, write it on the receipt before putting it in the folder. It is amazing how fast the cost of towel rods, wall shelves and rose bushes adds up, along with more major improvements. The cost of energy-related improvements, minus the tax credit, if available, may also be added to your list of capital improvements. Assessments or special charges made by your municipal or county government for new streets, sidewalks, parks, etc., or repairs to these facilities that are not immediately deductible on your tax return may be added to your list of capital improvements.

The list in the third folder shows every item that decreases the value of your property, both in actuality and for tax purposes. The amount of depreciation claimed if part of your home is used for business purposes, etc., should be on the list. Casualty losses must also be subtracted from the basis. If you sell or give away any part of your property (this includes easements and rights-of-way), your basis is reduced by the fair market value.

By keeping records of these items, it is easy to figure the basis of your home. It is the original cost (contract price plus buying expenses) minus deferred capital gains from the previous home(s) you have owned. Of course, there has been no profit if you have just bought your first home. Each capital improvement increases the basis of your home. Depreciation and casualty losses decrease the basis. The basis is also decreased when any part of the property is sold or given away.

Postponing Capital Gains Taxes

The tax the IRS would like to collect on the capital gains you realize when you sell your home may be postponed if you meet both of these IRS requirements:

- You purchase another principal residence within 24 months before or after the date you sell your previous principal residence; *and*

- The cost of the new principal residence (contract price plus buying expenses), plus capital improvements made within the 24-month period, is greater than the adjusted sale price (selling price minus selling expenses) of your previous principal residence.

Usually you may defer capital gains from only one home that is bought and sold within 24 months. Ask your accountant for details.

If your new home is less expensive than the home you are selling, only a portion of the capital gains may be taxed. However, even this tax burden may be lessened, depending on the way your home is sold. Ask your REALTOR® for help.

The Once-in-a-Lifetime $125,000
Capital Gains Exclusion

Up to $125,000 of capital gains may never be taxed if certain IRS guidelines are met. If you are at least 55 years old, you have owned your present home for three years and have lived in it for three of the last five years, you may be able to use the once-in-a-lifetime $125,000 exclusion. Up to $125,000 of capital gains will not be taxed—ever. (See Chapter 24.)

Figure 46.1

Basis and Capital Gains Form

Home #1 Address _____

Date purchased _____ Date sold _____

Buying: Contract price $_____

Add buying expenses   + _____

Subtract deferred capital gains   – ══════

Basis of Home #1 $_____

Selling: Selling price $_____

Subtract selling expenses   – _____

Subtract improvements during ownership   – _____

Add depreciation, etc., during ownership   + _____

Subtract basis of Home #1   – ══════

Capital gains $_____

. . . .

Home #2 Address _____

Date purchased _____ Date sold _____

Buying: Contract price $_____

Add buying expenses   + _____

Subtract deferred capital gains   – ══════

Basis of Home #2 $_____

Selling: Selling price $_____

Subtract selling expenses   – _____

Subtract improvements during ownership   – _____

Add depreciation, etc., during ownership   + _____

Subtract Basis of Home #2   – ══════

Capital gains $_____

47. Relax and Enjoy

Finding your new home, closing the real estate transaction, moving out of the old place and into the new and getting involved in new activities are enormous undertakings. Sometimes the task of getting settled seems to go on and on—getting the appliances hooked up, unpacking the boxes, putting up the curtains and draperies, hanging the pictures, etc. If you work out a plan and take it a little at a time, it won't be long before your new home is really yours—the way you want it to be.

However, there are a few other details that must be attended to soon after you purchase your home. These things should *not* be put off. They need to be taken care of in the first couple of weeks, at least within the first month, after you move into your new home.

Review Your Move

Were all the boxes and pieces of furniture delivered? Was anything broken or damaged? If anything is missing or damaged, act immediately. Put in a claim to the moving company.

Examine New Construction

If your home is newly constructed and you notice any problems, contact the builder immediately. Sometimes a problem involves the work of a subcontractor and the builder must get the subcontractor to fix it. However, all your complaints should go directly to the builder. The sooner you bring a problem to the builder's attention, the better the chance of getting it fixed.

Look Over Warranties and Service Policies

Even if your home is not newly constructed, there may be a warranty for a recently replaced range, dishwasher, hot water heater, etc. Sometimes the seller or real estate company provides a special home warranty or insurance policy. Be aware of the date that the warranty or service policy expires. Make a note of this date on your calendar so you can check the product before that date and put in a claim if necessary.

Give Your New Home a Safety Checkup

Do all the doors and windows lock properly? Is there a security lock for the patio door? Is there a wide-angle peephole in the front door, or should one be installed? Does your new home have smoke detectors? If not, they should be installed immediately.

Send Change of Address Cards

Notify everyone with whom you do business of your move. See Chapter 45.

Apply for a New Driver's License

If you have moved to a new state, you must apply for a new driver's license. If you have moved within the same state, you need a driver's license with your new address on it.

Register To Vote

Register now so that when there is an election you will be eligible to vote.

Update and Maintain Your Budget and Filing System

These items also need to be taken care of now. (See Chapter 46.) These follow-up chores are not as difficult or as time-consuming as they seem. Getting them taken care of will give you great peace of mind.

Finally, it's time to enjoy—to live the new life-style you have worked so hard to get. Give your home the attention and loving care such a prized possession deserves and it will serve you well and give you happiness now and in the future.

Appendix: Amortization Factors

To determine the monthly PI (principal and interest) payment:
1. Locate the factor for the desired interest rate and term.
2. Multiply this rate/term factor by the loan amount.

To determine the principal amount of the loan:
1. Locate the factor for the desired interest rate and term.
2. Divide the monthly PI (principal and interest) payment by this rate/term factor.

Term in Years	INTEREST RATE					
	4%	4¼%	4½%	4¾%	5%	5¼%
5	.0184165	.0185296	.0186430	.0187569	.0188712	.0189860
8	.0121893	.0123059	.0124232	.0125412	.0126599	.0127793
10	.0101245	.0102438	.0103638	.0104848	.0106066	.0107292
12	.0087553	.0088772	.0090001	.0091240	.0092489	.0093748
15	.0073969	.0075228	.0076499	.0077783	.0079079	.0080388
18	.0065020	.0066319	.0067632	.0068961	.0070303	.0071660
20	.0060598	.0061923	.0063265	.0064622	.0065996	.0067384
25	.0052784	.0054174	.0055583	.0057012	.0058459	.0059925
30	.0047742	.0049194	.0050669	.0052165	.0053682	.0055220
35	.0044277	.0045789	.0047326	.0048886	.0050469	.0052074
40	.0041794	.0043362	.0044956	.0046576	.0048220	.0049887

Term in Years	INTEREST RATE					
	5½%	5¾%	6%	6¼%	6½%	6¾%
5	.0191012	.0192168	.0193328	.0194490	.0195661	.0196835
8	.0128993	.0130200	.0131414	.0132640	.0133862	.0135096
10	.0108526	.0109769	.0111021	.0112280	.0113548	.0114824
12	.0095017	.0096296	.0097585	.0098880	.0100192	.0101510
15	.0081708	.0083041	.0084386	.0085740	.0087111	.0088491
18	.0073032	.0074417	.0075816	.0077230	.0078656	.0080096
20	.0068789	.0070208	.0071643	.0073093	.0074557	.0076036
25	.0061409	.0062911	.0064430	.0065970	.0067521	.0069091
30	.0056779	.0058357	.0059955	.0061570	.0063207	.0064860
35	.0053702	.0055350	.0057019	.0058710	.0060415	.0062142
40	.0051577	.0053289	.0055021	.0056770	.0058546	.0060336

Term in Years	INTEREST RATE					
	7%	7¼%	7½%	7¾%	8%	8¼%
5	.0198012	.0199193	.0200379	.0201570	.0202764	.0203963
8	.0136337	.0137585	.0138838	.0140099	.0141367	.0142640
10	.0116108	.0117401	.0118702	.0120010	.0121328	.0122653
12	.0102838	.0104176	.0105523	.0106879	.0108245	.0109620
15	.0089883	.0091286	.0092701	.0094128	.0095565	.0097014
18	.0081550	.0083017	.0084497	.0085990	.0087496	.0089015
20	.0077530	.0079038	.0080593	.0082095	.0083644	.0085207
25	.0070680	.0072281	.0073899	.0075533	.0077182	.0078845
30	.0066530	.0068218	.0069921	.0071641	.0073376	.0075127
35	.0063886	.0065647	.0067424	.0069218	.0071026	.0072849
40	.0062143	.0063967	.0065807	.0067662	.0069531	.0071414
50	.0060169	.0062089	.0064023	.0065970	.0067927	.0069896

Term in Years	INTEREST RATE					
	8½%	8¾%	9%	9¼%	9½%	9¾%
5	.0205165	.0206372	.0207584	.0208799	.0210019	.0211243
8	.0143921	.0145208	.0146502	.0147802	.0149109	.0150423
10	.0123986	.0125327	.0126676	.0128033	.0129398	.0130771
12	.0111006	.0112400	.0113803	.0115216	.0116637	.0118069
15	.0098479	.0099949	.0101427	.0102919	.0104422	.0105937
18	.0090546	.0092089	.0093644	.0095212	.0096791	.0098382
20	.0086782	.0088371	.0089972	.0091587	.0093213	.0094852
25	.0080523	.0082214	.0083920	.0085638	.0087370	.0089114
30	.0076891	.0078670	.0080462	.0082268	.0084085	.0085916
35	.0074686	.0076536	.0078399	.0080274	.0082161	.0084059
40	.0073309	.0075217	.0077136	.0079066	.0081006	.0082956
50	.0071874	.0073861	.0075857	.0077860	.0079871	.0081888

Term in Years	INTEREST RATE					
	10%	10¼%	10½%	10¾%	11%	11¼%
5	.0212471	.0213703	.0214940	.0216180	.0217425	.0218674
8	.0151742	.0153068	.0154401	.0155740	.0157085	.0158436
10	.0132151	.0133540	.0134935	.0136339	.0137751	.0139169
12	.0119508	.0120957	.0122415	.0123881	.0125356	.0126840
15	.0107461	.0108996	.0110540	.0112095	.0113660	.0115235
18	.0099984	.0101598	.0103223	.0104859	.0106505	.0108162
20	.0096503	.0098165	.0099838	.0101523	.0103219	.0104926
25	.0090871	.0092639	.0094419	.0096210	.0098012	.0099824
30	.0087758	.0089611	.0091474	.0093349	.0095233	.0097127
35	.0085967	.0087886	.0089813	.0091750	.0093696	.0095649
40	.0084916	.0086882	.0088857	.0090840	.0092829	.0094826
50	.0083911	.0085939	.0087972	.0090010	.0092052	.0094098

Term in Years	INTEREST RATE					
	11½%	11¾%	12%	12¼%	12½%	12¾%
5	.0219927	.0221184	.0222445	.0223710	.0224980	.0226254
8	.0159794	.0161158	.0162529	.0163906	.0165289	.0166678
10	.0140596	.0142030	.0143471	.0144920	.0146377	.0147840
12	.0128332	.0129833	.0131342	.0132860	.0134386	.0135921
15	.0116819	.0118414	.0120017	.0121630	.0123253	.0124884
18	.0109830	.0111507	.0113195	.0114892	.0116600	.0118317
20	.0106643	.0108371	.0110109	.0111857	.0113615	.0115382
25	.0101647	.0103480	.0105323	.0107175	.0109036	.0110906
30	.0099030	.0100941	.0102862	.0104790	.0106726	.0108670
35	.0097611	.0099579	.0101555	.0103537	.0105525	.0107519
40	.0096828	.0098836	.0100850	.0102869	.0104892	.0106919
50	.0096148	.0098200	.0100256	.0102314	.0104375	.0106438

Term in Years	INTEREST RATE					
	13%	13¼%	13½%	13¾%	14%	14¼%
5	.0227531	.0228813	.0230099	.0231389	.0232683	.0233981
8	.0168073	.0169475	.0170882	.0172296	.0173716	.0175141
10	.0149311	.0150789	.0152275	.0153767	.0155267	.0156774
12	.0137463	.0139014	.0140572	.0142139	.0143713	.0145295
15	.0126525	.0128174	.0129832	.0131499	.0133175	.0134858
18	.0120043	.0121779	.0123523	.0125276	.0127038	.0128809
20	.0117158	.0118944	.0120738	.0122541	.0124353	.0126172
25	.0112784	.0114671	.0116565	.0118467	.0120377	.0122293
30	.0110620	.0112578	.0114542	.0116512	.0118486	.0120469
35	.0109520	.0111524	.0113534	.0115548	.0117567	.0119590
40	.0108951	.0110987	.0113026	.0115069	.0117114	.0119162
50	.0108502	.0110569	.0112637	.0114707	.0116778	.0118850

Term in Years	INTEREST RATE					
	14½%	14¾%	15%	15¼%	15½%	15¾%
5	.0235283	.0236590	.0237900	.0239241	.0240532	.0241855
8	.0176573	.0178011	.0179455	.0180904	.0182360	.0183821
10	.0158287	.0159808	.0161335	.0162870	.0164411	.0165959
12	.0146885	.0148483	.0150088	.0151701	.0153321	.0154948
15	.0136551	.0138251	.0139959	.0141675	.0143400	.0145131
18	.0130587	.0132374	.0134169	.0135972	.0137782	.0139600
20	.0128000	.0129836	.0131679	.0133530	.0135389	.0137254
25	.0124217	.0126147	.0128084	.0130026	.0131975	.0133929
30	.0122456	.0124448	.0126445	.0128446	.0130452	.0132462
35	.0121617	.0123647	.0125681	.0127718	.0129758	.0131801
40	.0121213	.0123267	.0125322	.0127380	.0129440	.0131502
50	.0120930	.0122973	.0125072	.0127148	.0129225	.0131303

Term in Years	INTEREST RATE					
	16%	16¼%	16½%	16¾%	17%	17¼%
5	.0243181	.0244511	.0245846	.0247184	.0248526	.0249872
8	.0185288	.0186761	.0188240	.0189725	.0191215	.0192710
10	.0167514	.0169075	.0170643	.0172217	.0173798	.0175385
12	.0156583	.0158225	.0159874	.0161530	.0163193	.0164862
15	.0146871	.0148617	.0150371	.0152133	.0153901	.0155676
18	.0141425	.0143257	.0145096	.0146942	.0148795	.0150654
20	.0139126	.0141005	.0142891	.0144782	.0146681	.0148584
25	.0135889	.0137855	.0139825	.0141800	.0143780	.0145764
30	.0134476	.0136494	.0138515	.0140540	.0142568	.0144599
35	.0133847	.0135895	.0137945	.0139998	.0142053	.0144109
40	.0133565	.0135630	.0137696	.0139764	.0141832	.0143902
50	.0133381	.0135459	.0137538	.0139617	.0141697	.0143777

Term in Years	INTEREST RATE					
	17½%	17¾%	18%	18¼%	18½%	18¾%
5	.0251222	.0252576	.0253935	.0255296	.0256662	.0258032
8	.0194212	.0195719	.0197233	.0198751	.0200274	.0201804
10	.0176979	.0178579	.0180186	.0181798	.0183417	.0185041
12	.0166539	.0168222	.0169912	.0171608	.0173311	.0175021
15	.0157458	.0159247	.0161043	.0162844	.0164652	.0166467
18	.0152519	.0154391	.0156269	.0158153	.0160042	.0161938
20	.0150494	.0152410	.0154332	.0156258	.0158190	.0160127
25	.0147753	.0149746	.0151743	.0153744	.0155748	.0157757
30	.0146633	.0148669	.0150709	.0152750	.0154794	.0156841
35	.0146168	.0148228	.0150289	.0152352	.0154417	.0156483
40	.0145973	.0148045	.0150118	.0152192	.0154266	.0156342
50	.0145858	.0147939	.0150020	.0152101	.0154183	.0156264

Glossary

absolute fee simple title—Unqualified title; the best title one can have. The owner has unlimited control and may sell, trade, give away or dispose of property in any way he or she chooses.

abstract of title—A history of all the recorded documents dealing with the title to a property.

accelerated depreciation—Any method of depreciation providing for faster write-off than straight line depreciation.

acceleration clause—A clause in a mortgage or deed of trust that gives the lender the right to demand payment in full on a certain date (see **balloon clause**) or upon the happening of a certain event, such as when the home is sold (see **due-on-sale clause**), not making a payment when due, or transfer of ownership without the lender's consent.

acceptance—Voluntarily agreeing to the price and terms of an offer. A contract is created by offer and acceptance.

acquisition costs—1. In some Federal Housing Administration loan programs the FHA maximum loan amounts are based on acquisition costs; that is, the purchase price or appraised value (whichever is less) plus allowable closing costs.   2. The purchase price plus all other costs of acquiring a property.

act of God—Damage caused by nature rather than destruction by man.

addendum—A change or addition to correct an error or alter a part of a contract without changing the principal intent of the contract.

adjustable rate mortgage (ARM)—A loan with an interest rate that can be adjusted up or down according to the terms of the mortgage or deed of trust.

ad valorem—"According to value." A method of taxation using value to determine the amount of the tax.

agency—Any relationship in which one party acts for another.

agreement of sale—Depending on local interpretation, it could mean a purchase agreement, a contract or a conditional sales contract.

air space—The individual owner's estate in condominium ownership.

alienation—The transfer of property from one owner to another.

alienation clause—See **due-on-sale clause**.

ALTA—American Land Title Association. An organization of title insurance companies that has adopted certain standardized insurance policy forms to be used nationally.

alternative mortgage instrument (AMI)—Any conventional mortgage made by an institutional lender that is *not* the ordinary, level-payment, long-term loan.

amendment—See **addendum.**

amenities—Any additional things that increase the desirability or enjoyment of a property. These can be part of the property, such as a swimming pool, club room, etc., or they can be nearby facilities, such as a lake, shopping center, golf course, etc.

AMI—See **alternative mortgage instrument.**

American Society of Home Inspectors (ASHI)—A national organization that requires experience, training and adherence to a rigid code of ethics of its member home inspectors.

amortization—Repayment of a loan in regular equal installments that pay both the principal and interest (PI).

amortization factor—A number for a given interest rate and term that when multiplied by the principal amount of the loan will give the monthly principal and interest (PI) payment. By dividing the monthly PI payment by the amortization rate/term factor, the principal amount of the loan can be obtained.

amortization schedule—A printout showing each payment for a certain loan. The exact principal amount, interest amount and the remaining principal balance are shown for each payment.

amortization tables—Tables showing the principal and interest (PI) payment for a particular loan. If any three of the following four factors are given—interest rate, term of the loan, principal amount of the loan or PI payment—the fourth factor can be determined by using the tables.

amortized loan—A loan that will be completely repaid in equal installments that are part principal and part interest. Most mortgage loans are amortized loans.

annual—By the year; yearly.

annual percentage rate (APR)—A federal truth-in-lending requirement. Supposedly the actual rate of interest to be paid, figured by using the contract interest rate, certain finance charges and the time the borrower has the use of the money borrowed.

annum—Year.

appraisal—An estimate of value. The reason for the appraisal, the factual data used and the qualifications of the appraiser should all be considered when judging the worth of the appraisal.

appraisal report—A written report by an appraiser giving all the factual data that supports the opinion of value, such as the sale price of comparable properties, appraisal formulas and qualifications of the appraiser.

appraiser—A person qualified by education and experience to estimate the value of a property.

appreciation—An increase in value of a property due to improvements, economic conditions or the elimination of negative factors.

APR—See **annual percentage rate.**

ARM—See **adjustable rate mortgage.**

arrears—1. A payment made after it is due is made in arrears. 2. Interest is paid in arrears when it is paid at the end of the interest period. For example, if the April 1 payment pays the interest for March, interest is paid in arrears. If the April 1 payment pays the interest for April, interest is paid in advance.

ASHI—See **American Society of Home Inspectors.**

"as is" condition—The existing condition of the property at the time of the sale with no representation by the seller as to the quality or condition.

asking price—The price put on the property by the owner/seller.

assessed value—The value given a property as a basis for taxation.

assessment—1. The amount of the tax levied. 2. See **maintenance fee.**

assets—Everything owned by a person that has exchange value.

assumption clause—A clause written into the mortgage or deed of trust stating the terms and conditions by which the loan can be assumed.

assumption fee—A charge made by a lender for processing records, doing paperwork, etc., when an existing loan is assumed.

assumption of mortgage or deed of trust—An agreement by a purchaser taking title to a property to also assume the liability for the existing mortgage or deed of trust.

attorney in fact—One who is authorized to perform certain acts for another under power of attorney; a legal agent.

balloon clause—A clause in a mortgage or deed of trust that requires the entire remaining principal balance of the loan (the balloon payment) to be paid on or before a certain date. The balloon payment is due before the loan is completely amortized.

balloon loan—A loan that is repaid by a series of equal principal and interest payments and then one large (balloon) payment that pays the entire remaining balance of the loan.

basis—The book value of a property. The value of a property used when figuring depreciation, capital gains, taxes, etc.

beneficiary—When a deed of trust is used the lender is called the beneficiary.

bid—A term used to describe an offer to purchase real property.

bill of sale—An instrument used to transfer personal property.

binder—1. A report issued by a title insurance company stating the condition of title and the terms under which an insurance policy will be issued. 2. In a few states, a preliminary agreement between the buyer and seller of a property that is used until a formal contract is finalized.

blueprint—A detailed building plan used by the construction workmen.

bond—1. An instrument used to finance long-term debt. 2. An insurance agreement, such as a performance bond, that guarantees that a thing will be done or completed as stated or the party suffering the loss will receive compensation.

breach of contract—Failure to perform a contract without legal justification.

bridge financing—Usually a loan that allows a seller to buy a new home before his or her present home is sold. The bridge loan is secured by the equity in the home being sold.

broker, real estate—A person licensed by the state to carry on real estate business and receive a fee for his or her part in bringing together the buyer and seller.

budget—A plan for spending money. Budgets include an estimate of expenses for a certain period of time and the amount of income needed to pay the expenses.

built-ins—Cabinets, shelving, appliances, etc., framed into the building construction and not movable.

buydown loans—Loans that have a lower interest rate for the first year or the first few years because the seller has prepaid some of the interest costs.

buyer's agent—A real estate sales agent acting as the exclusive agent for a buyer. The use of a buyer's agent must be disclosed in the contract.

buyer's market—Conditions favoring the buyer. In real estate, this occurs when more homes are for sale than there are willing and able buyers.

buyer's silence—The taking of no positive action by the buyer. In some circumstances buyer's silence can be deemed a waiver of a contingency.

bylaws—Rules and regulations that provide for the administration and maintenance of the condominium or townhouse complex.

call clause—See **acceleration clause.**

capital gains—Profit from the sale of an asset. Capital gains from the sale of a principal residence may receive favorable tax treatment.

capital improvements—Expenditures on a home that are more than ordinary repairs; expenditures that extend the useful life of a property, add value, make the property more useable or adapt the property to a new use.

cash—Ready money, including currency, checks, bank notes, travelers checks, etc.

cash flow—The money received from income property after all expenses are paid.

cashier's check—A check drawn by a bank on its own account rather than the account of a depositor. A cashier's check is acceptable at closing.

caveat emptor—"Let the buyer beware." It is the buyer's responsibility to carefully inspect a property and judge its quality and condition.

CC&Rs—See **declaration.**

certificate of eligibility—Issued by the Department of Veterans Affairs, it states the entitlement (eligibility) that a veteran has for a VA loan.

certificate of occupancy (CO)—Issued by the local building department, it states the property is in proper condition to be occupied. One usually cannot move into a newly constructed home without a CO.

certificate of reasonable value (CRV)—The name given to a Department of Veterans Affairs (VA) appraisal report.

certified check—A personal check drawn on an individual account certified as good by the bank. A certified check is usually acceptable at closing.

chain of title—A history of property ownership dating back as far as records are available.

chattel—Personal property.

closing—See **settlement.**

closing costs—See **settlement costs.**

closing statement—See **settlement statement.**

cloud on a title—An invalid claim on a property that, if valid, would affect the rights of the owner. A cloud can be removed by a quitclaim deed or court action.

CO—See **certificate of occupancy.**

coborrower—A borrower acting jointly with one or more others.

collateral security—Property pledged as security for repayment of a loan.

commission—Compensation paid to a real estate broker for services.

commitment—1. A written promise to make a loan for a certain amount and with specific terms. 2. The preliminary report issued by a title insurance company stating the terms on which it will issue a title insurance policy.

common areas or common elements—Those parts of a condominium or townhouse complex that are owned jointly by all unit owners.

comparables—Recently sold properties used as comparisons to help determine the value of another property.

conditional sale contract—Sale in which the title to the property does not pass to the buyer until certain conditions are met. Also called a land contract, an installment land contract or a contract for deed.

condominium—1. Individual fee ownership of an air space living unit along with an undivided interest in the common areas in a multiunit complex. 2. One living unit in a condominium complex.

condominium conversion—The act of changing ownership of an apartment complex from a single owner (an individual, partnership or corporation) to individual fee ownership of each unit.

condominium fee—See **maintenance fee.**

condominium map—A recorded map showing condominium units and common areas using both vertical and horizontal measurements.

consideration—Anything that has value and induces one to enter into a contract. It may be money, personal service or even love and affection.

construction loan—Usually a short-term loan to be used to pay for materials and labor as the home is being built. When the home is completed this loan is repaid with a long-term mortgage loan.

contingency—In a real estate contract, the dependence upon something happening or not happening to make the contract binding.

contract—A written agreement, enforceable by law.

contract for deed—See **conditional sale contract.**

contractual lien—A voluntary lien, such as a mortgage or deed of trust.

conventional loan—A mortgage loan made by an institutional lender and not insured or guaranteed by the government.

conveyance—Another name for an instrument by which an interest in real property is created, transferred, mortgaged or assigned.

cooperative apartment—An apartment in a complex in which the right to occupy a living unit is obtained by the purchase of stock in the corporation that owns the complex. This is not the same as individual fee ownership of a condominium.

cosigner—One who signs a promissory note in addition to the maker. A cosigner is responsible for the obligation only if the maker defaults.

cost recovery—The IRS term for depreciation.

counteroffer—An offer made in response to an offer.

covenant—A recorded agreement promising the performance or nonperformance of certain acts, or stipulating certain uses or nonuses of the property.

crawl space—The space within the foundation walls and beneath the flooring in a home without a basement.

credit rating—The evaluation of a person's financial situation and credit worthiness based on past credit history.

credit report—A statement provided by a credit bureau used to help determine a borrower's credit worthiness.

CRV—See **certificate of reasonable value.**

cul-de-sac—A street with only one outlet; also called a dead-end street.

debt—Money owed to another.

debt service—1. The amount of financing on a property. 2. The total amount of money needed by a person to make payments as agreed on his or her debts.

declaration—The most important condominium or townhouse complex document. The legal instrument that creates the condominium or townhouse ownership, fully describes the complex and each unit in it, provides for the homeowners' association and sets forth the rules, regulations and restrictions as to the use of all areas of the complex. The declaration is also called the "decs," the declaration of codes, covenants and restrictions (CC&Rs) or the master deed.

deed—A written instrument or document that conveys or transfers title when properly executed and delivered.

deed of trust—An instrument by which real estate is pledged as security for the payment of a debt. In many states a deed of trust is used instead of a mortgage. The deed of trust transfers title to the property to a third party (the trustee), who holds title until the loan is paid in full. If the borrower defaults the trustee may sell the property at a public sale to pay off the loan. Also called a trust deed.

deed restrictions—Limitations on the use of the property placed in the deed and binding on all future owners.

default—The nonperformance of an obligation.

deferred maintenance—Repairs necessary to put the property in ordinary, good condition.

depreciation—1. Actual decrease in value caused by age, deterioration, obsolescence or economic conditions. 2. An accounting procedure that allows a deduction for income tax purposes.

direct endorsement lender—A lender who is approved to originate and close certain FHA and VA loans without first submitting all paperwork to the government agencies.

discount—An amount of money needed to increase the yield of a loan.

document—See **instrument**.

documentary fee—A state tax on the sale of real property that can range from a few dollars to hundreds of dollars, depending on the laws of the state in which the property is located. Also called a transfer tax.

domicile—The legal term for the place where a person lives; the home, the principal residence.

double—One building with two living units. Also called a duplex.

down payment—That part of the purchase price paid from a buyer's own funds, as opposed to the part that is financed.

due-on-sale clause—A clause in a mortgage or deed of trust that causes the entire debt to become immediately due and payable upon transfer of ownership of the secured property.

duplex—One building with two living units.

earnest money—A good-faith deposit given by a purchaser at the time an offer is made. This money should be handled according to instructions in the contract.

easement—A right that the public, a company or an individual may have to use or cross over the property of another.

effective interest rate—See **annual percentage rate**.

encroachment—Usually a wall, fence or part of a building constructed on or over the property of another.

encumbrance—A claim on a property, such as a lien, a mortgage, an easement, etc.

entitlement—The amount of eligibility a veteran has for a VA loan.

Equal Credit Opportunity Act—A federal law that requires lenders to make loans based only on the credit worthiness of applicants. Discrimination based on race, color, age, sex, national origin, religion or life-style is strictly prohibited.

equity—The owner's interest in the property. Usually the market value of a property less the amount of the mortgage(s) and/or other encumbrances against it.

escape clause—A required clause in VA and FHA contracts that states that a buyer will not lose his or her earnest money if a contract is defeated because the appraisal is less than the contract price.

escrow—1. An account set up by the lender for the borrower into which regular payments are made for future taxes and/or insurance premiums. The lender then pays the taxes and/or insurance premiums when due from the account.
2. Closing procedure whereby a third party handles all money and documents in strict accordance with instructions signed by both buyer and seller.

escrow agent or officer—The third party responsible to both the buyer and seller or lender and borrower for carrying out the signed escrow instructions.

escrow instructions—Detailed instructions signed by both the buyer and seller or the lender and borrower that enable the escrow agent to carry out the closing procedures.

estate—1. The rights and interests one has in the ownership of real property.
2. A large park-like property with an expensive home.

execute—To complete, perform, fulfill or make valid. The carrying out of the terms of a contract; the signing, sealing and delivering of a document.

extension—A continuance under the same conditions. An extension agreement usually gives the parties more time to perform the same contract.

Fair Credit Reporting Act—A federal law giving one the right to see his or her credit report.

Fannie Mae—See **Federal National Mortgage Association**.

Farmers Home Administration (FmHA)—An agency of the Department of Agriculture that offers loan programs for borrowers living in small towns and rural areas.

Federal Home Loan Mortgage Corporation (FHLMC)—A secondary marketing organization primarily used by savings and loan associations; nicknamed "Freddie Mac."

Federal Housing Administration (FHA)—An agency of the Department of Housing and Urban Development that insures mortgage loans made by institutional lenders against default.

Federal National Mortgage Association (FNMA)—A marketing organization that buys mortgage loans in the secondary market; nicknamed "Fannie Mae."

fee, fee simple, absolute fee simple ownership—Usually all mean the same thing. Absolute and unqualified title. The owner has unlimited control and may sell, trade, give away or dispose of the property in any way he or she chooses.

FHA loans—Mortgage loans made by institutional lenders and insured by the Federal Housing Administration. The borrower pays for the insurance.

FHA-Vet loans—FHA loans with a special provision for veterans that decreases the amount of down payment needed.

fiduciary—A person in a position of trust and confidence.

first mortgage or first deed of trust—A loan secured by real property having first claim over and before all other voluntary liens if there is a foreclosure.

FmHA—See **Farmers Home Administration**.

foreclosure—A legal procedure by which property is sold to pay a debt on which the borrower has defaulted.

forfeiture—The loss of money or anything of value because of failure to perform.

fourplex—One building with four living units.

Freddie Mac—See **Federal Home Loan Mortgage Corporation.**

free and clear—Property that is completely paid for; there are no loans or other liens against the property.

full disclosure—The revealing of all known facts that may affect the decision of the buyer or the seller.

garden level—Often the lowest living unit(s) in a condominium complex; the floor of which is sometimes three to five feet below ground level.

GEM—See **growing equity mortgage.**

gift—The voluntary transfer of money or property to another with no material consideration.

GI loan—See **VA loans.**

Ginnie Mae—See **Government National Mortgage Association.**

Government National Mortgage Association (GNMA)—A marketing organization involved in buying government guaranteed or insured loans in the secondary market; nicknamed "Ginnie Mae."

graduated payment mortgage (GPM)—A loan with a graduated payment schedule and negative amortization. The payments during the first few years do not cover the entire interest expense so the loan balance increases each month. The loan payments increase each year until at some point the payments level off and the loan is amortized over the remaining term.

grantee—The person who receives title in a deed; usually the purchaser.

grantor—The person who gives up title in a deed; usually the seller.

gross income—Total income before any expenses or deductions.

growing equity mortgage (GEM)—A loan in which the principal payments are increased according to a predetermined schedule.

guaranty—An agreement to pay a debt or perform an obligation of another, but only if and when the other person fails to do so.

hazard insurance—Lenders require homeowners to carry at least minimum insurance coverage for such things as fire and wind damage. Most homeowners prefer a policy that gives broader coverage and includes liability protection.

high-rise condominiums—Condominium complexes with buildings of four or more stories that require the use of elevators.

homeowners' association—1. The governing body of a condominium or townhouse complex to which all the unit owners belong. 2. An association of people who own homes in a certain area.

HUD—The Department of Housing and Urban Development.

hypothecate—To mortgage; to pledge as security without actually transferring title or possession.

improvement—Any permanent structure placed on land.

inclusions and exclusions—Items, often of a personal property nature, that are to be included or excluded from the sale price of the entire property.

index—A report of interest rates averaged periodically that is used to determine the rate of interest charged on an adjustable rate mortgage. There are many indexes; the loan document should specify which index is to be used.

installment land contract, installment contract—See **conditional sale contract**.

installment sale—A type of sale that may qualify the seller for more favorable tax treatment.

institutional lender—A bank, mortgage company, savings and loan association or other business that makes loans to the public as a major part of its ordinary business.

instrument—Any writing having legal form and significance. A legal document.

insurance policy—A contract, paid in advance, under which one party (the insurer) agrees to pay a certain sum to another party (the insured) if a loss should occur under a given set of circumstances. There are many types of insurance.

insurance premium—The payment made for an insurance policy.

interest—1. Money charged or received for the use of money. 2. A right or claim to a property.

interest rate—A percentage of an amount of money charged or received for its use. Unless otherwise stated, interest is figured on a yearly basis even though it is paid monthly, quarterly, etc.

investment—The use of money to make a profit.

involuntary lien—A claim or lien that attaches to a property without the consent of the owner, such as a tax lien.

joint tenancy—An equal, undivided ownership of property by two or more persons with rights of survivorship. See **unities.**

junior lien, junior mortgage—A lien that does not have the first claim on a property; a second mortgage or possibly a "third," "fourth," etc.

land contract—See **conditional sale contract.**

late payment penalty—A fee charged for failure to make an installment payment as agreed.

lease with option to purchase—A lease with a clause that gives the lessee the right to purchase the property within a given period of time. The price and terms of the purchase must be stated in order for the option to be valid.

leasehold—The legal interest a tenant holds for a specified time in a property. A leasehold interest is less than a fee interest.

legal age—The age at which a person is legally able to contract. Each state sets the legal age for its residents, usually from 18 to 21.

legal rate of interest—A rate of interest established by law rather than by contract.

lessee—The tenant; the person to whom a lease is given.

lessor—The landlord; the person who gives a lease.

level payment mortgage—A loan with the same interest rate and the same monthly principal and interest (PI) payment for the term of the loan.

leverage—The use of borrowed money, with or without a cash down payment, to purchase property.

liability—A general term that includes all types of debts and obligations.

lien—An encumbrance or claim against property for money, such as a mortgage, a tax lien or a judgment.

limited common areas—Those parts of a condominium complex that are jointly owned by all but may be used by only one or a few owners. Limited common areas might include stairways, balconies, patios, etc.

liquid assets—Cash or assets that can be converted to cash immediately.

lis pendens—A legal notice recorded to show a suit or other legal action is pending concerning the property.

listing—A contract between the owner of real estate and a licensed real estate broker that enables the broker to secure a buyer for the property at a certain price and terms and to be paid a fee (commission) for services.

listing agent—The real estate broker who has a listing contract with the owner of the property.

loan package—The file of all documents and other items concerning both the purchaser and the property that the lender needs in order to decide to make or not make the loan.

loan profile—A complete listing of all the features, terms and conditions of a particular loan.

loan to value ratio—The percentage of the sale price or appraised value (whichever is less) that the lender will loan.

lot—A general term referring to a parcel of real property.

low-rise condominiums—Condominiums in buildings of no more than three stories that usually do not require elevators.

LPM—See **level payment mortgage.**

LTV—See **loan to value ratio.**

magic loans—Loans with high loan to value ratios that are insured with private mortgage insurance. The Mortgage Guaranty Insurance Corporation (MGIC) was one of the first companies to offer this insurance.

maintenance fee—The amount charged each condominium or townhouse owner to pay for certain services, maintain the common areas and pay the expenses of the homeowners' association.

maker—The borrower; the person who signs a note and promises to make payments as agreed.

manufactured housing—Housing units that are built or partially built in a factory and moved to the site.

margin—The amount added to the index interest rate to determine the rate of interest the borrower is to pay for an adjustable rate mortgage. The margin is usually from 1 percent to 4 percent and stays the same for the term of the loan. Also called a markup.

marketable title—Title that a responsible, prudent purchaser would consider buying.

market value—The contract price agreed on by a buyer and seller when both are informed and not under undue pressure to buy or sell.

markup—See **margin.**

master deed—See **declaration.**

material fact—A fact that could affect the decision or judgment of a person entering into a contract.

mechanic's lien—A legal claim for payment for the cost of labor and materials used in construction.

merchantable—See **marketable title.**

mill—One-tenth of one cent. Used in expressing a tax rate.

mineral rights—See **subsurface rights.**

MIP—See **mortgage insurance premium.**

mobile home—A home constructed on a trailer-type base with axle and wheels that is towed to the site, as opposed to a home that is constructed on-site.

mobile home park—A park-like area especially constructed for mobile homes with utilities and other amenities available. For a monthly fee a person may place his or her mobile home in a designated space.

mortgage—1. To pledge real property as security for the payment of a debt without giving up title to the property. 2. The instrument or document by which real estate is pledged as security for the loan. 3. A general term for any loan for buying real property whereby the property becomes security for the loan. 4. A term used for the loan documents—the mortgage or deed of trust and the promissory note.

mortgage insurance—See **private mortgage insurance** and/or **mortgage insurance premium.**

mortgage insurance premium (MIP)—Required for FHA loans to insure against default. The borrower pays for the insurance.

mortgagee—The party lending the money for the loan and receiving the mortgage.

mortgagor—The party who borrows the money and gives the mortgage, usually the purchaser.

multiple listing—A property listed by one real estate broker but available to other brokers so that each may have the opportunity to sell the property.

National Association of REALTORS® (NAR)—A professional organization of men and women engaged in the real estate business. It currently has more than 500,000 members.

negative amortization—Repayment of a loan with scheduled payments that do not pay the entire interest expense. The unpaid interest is added to the loan principal so that the loan balance increases each month.

negative amortization mortgage—See **graduated payment mortgage.**

net worth—The difference between the total assets and total liabilities of a person, company, corporation, etc.

notary public—A person who is authorized by the state to attest to the authenticity of signatures.

note—A legal agreement in which the signer promises to pay the person named or the bearer a definite sum of money at a specified time (date) or on demand. A note usually provides for interest and may or may not be secured by a mortgage or deed of trust.

obsolescence—Loss in value because design and/or features become outdated or old-fashioned for today's living requirements.

offer—A proposal with a definite price and terms made with the intent of entering into a contract.

option—A written agreement that gives a potential purchaser the right to buy the property at a stated price and terms within a certain period of time.

ordinance—A law or statute, usually by a local governing body.

orientation—The placement of a building on a lot.

original cost—The purchase price paid by the present owner who may or may not be the first owner.

origination fee—A charge made by an institutional lender for the work involved in making a new loan. This fee is usually 1 percent or more of the loan amount.

owner occupied—A home that is lived in by the owner.

owner of record—The owner of property according to the recorded documents in the county.

ownership—Rights to use, enjoy and dispose of property to the exclusion of others.

paper—A general term for a mortgage, deed of trust, note or other instrument or document that is given in place of cash.

parcel—A general term for any part or portion of land.

party wall—A wall that is part of two adjoining properties that may be under different ownerships.

payoff—The complete repayment of a loan.

penthouse—A condominium or apartment on the roof or top floor of a building.

per annum—Yearly.

per diem—Daily.

per se—By itself, of itself.

personal property—Any property that is not real estate property.

PI payment—One payment that is part principal and part interest. Amortized loans are repaid with a series of equal PI payments. However, as each payment is made, the interest amount decreases and the principal amount increases as the loan is gradually repaid.

PITI—Principal, interest, taxes and insurance. The usual monthly house payment.

plat—A map of a parcel of land.

PMI—See **private mortgage insurance.**

point—A discount paid to the lender. One point is 1 percent of the loan amount.

possession—Being in physical control, whether owner or not.

power of attorney—Authority given by one person to another to act for him or her in certain circumstances.

preliminary title report—See **title commitment.**

premium—A general term for the money paid for an insurance policy.

prepaid interest—Interest paid before it is due.

prepaid items—Normal expenses of property ownership that the lender requires to be paid before or at closing, such as the hazard insurance premium and taxes.

prepayment penalty—An extra charge for repaying all or part of a loan before it is due.

prepayment privilege—The right to repay a loan in whole or in part at any time without a penalty.

price—The amount of money that is asked for a property offered for sale.

prime or prime interest rate—The most favorable interest rate commercial banks charge their best customers for short-term loans (not long-term mortgage loans).

principal—1. A party to a contract. 2. A person who gives authority to another to act as his or her agent. 3. The amount of money that is borrowed.

principal residence—Your home; the place you live. If you have more than one home your principal residence is where you are registered to vote.

priority—That which comes first in time and importance. The time of recording establishes priority for liens.

private lenders—Individuals, groups of individuals and companies who occasionally make mortgage loans; however, making loans is not a large part of their business.

private mortgage insurance (PMI)—Insurance provided by a private company, as opposed to a government agency, that insures an investor against loss. Private mortgage insurance is often necessary for loans with higher than 75 percent or 80 percent loan to value ratios or other high risk factors.

private property—Property owned by a person, group of persons or a corporation as opposed to being owned by the government.

promissory note—See **note.**

property—Anything that is owned.

property line—The boundary line of a lot.

property tax—A tax levied on real and/or personal property. A property tax is usually based on the value of the property.

prorate—To divide into proportionate amounts. Taxes, utility costs, insurance premiums, rents, etc., are often prorated so the seller and buyer each pay their share based on the actual days they own the property.

public records—Each county keeps records of all documents that are necessary to give public notice. Many documents associated with real estate transactions are recorded.

purchase agreement—A contract between the seller and buyer of real property setting forth the price and all terms and conditions on which they have agreed.

purchase money mortgage—A mortgage accepted by the seller from the buyer in order to help the buyer purchase the seller's property.

quadraplex—A building with four living units. Also called a fourplex.

quiet title suit—A court action used to determine ownership of a property or to remove a cloud on a title.

quitclaim deed—A legal instrument that transfers title or interest to a property but gives no guarantees as to what the title or interest might be. Often used as a release to give up title or interest in a property when there is no sale.

real estate—1. Land, its natural assets and all buildings and improvements on it. 2. Real estate may refer to the rights of ownership in real property as well as to the property itself.

real fixtures—Permanently attached fixtures that are considered part of the real estate.

real property—Real estate.

REALTOR®—A member of the National Association of REALTORS®.

reconveyance—An instrument used to transfer a property from a trustee to an owner upon payment in full of a deed of trust. See **release.**

recording—Filing documents in a legal manner so they become part of the public record.

Regulation Z—A regulation under the Truth-in-Lending Act that requires an institutional lender to give a borrower certain disclosure information and a written estimate of all costs associated with getting a loan.

release—A legal instrument stating that an obligation, such as a mortgage or judgment, has been paid in full. A release should be recorded.

renewable mortgage plan—See **rollover mortgage plan.**

rescind—To void a contract in such a way that it is as if it never existed.

rescission of a contract—The voiding of a contract in such a way that the parties to it are in the same position as if there had never been a contract.

reservation—A right created and retained by the grantor.

reserve(s)—Funds that have been set aside for a certain purpose.

residence—Home; the place where someone lives. See **domicile.**

RESPA—Real Estate Settlement Procedures Act. A federal law that requires full disclosure of certain costs when a residential property is being financed by an institutional lender.

restriction—A limitation on the use of a property.

revoke—To cancel, annul, void or take back.

right of first refusal—A condition sometimes found in a condominium or townhouse declaration that gives another unit owner or the association the right to buy the unit at the same price and terms offered the seller by an outside party.

right of survivorship—Upon the death of one party the ownership of the property is automatically transferred from the deceased to the survivor(s).

rights of ownership—The titled person's possession, use, control, enjoyment and disposal of property.

rollover mortgage plan—The interest rate of this mortgage plan is renegotiated at certain predetermined times.

row houses—Individual homes constructed in a row with common side walls and sometimes a common roof. Often called townhouses.

running with the land—Passing with the transfer of ownership of the land, such as covenants and easements. Sometimes water and/or mineral rights run with the land.

SAM—See **shared appreciation mortgage.**

second, second mortgage or secondary financing—A loan secured by a mortgage or deed of trust that is junior or secondary to another mortgage or deed of trust.

secondary mortgage market—The buying and selling of mortgages by banks, brokers, government agencies or companies in the private sector who act as middlemen between the lenders, who originate the loans, and investors.

seller's market—Conditions favoring the seller. In real estate this occurs when there are more willing and able buyers than there are homes for sale.

seller's silence—The taking of no positive action by a seller. In some circumstances this can be deemed a waiver of a contingency.

selling agent—The real estate agent representing the buyer of the property.

septic system—A sewage system often used where sewers have not been installed. Waste is drained through pipes into a septic tank.

septic tank—A large container buried underground into which waste is drained.

Bacterial action changes the solids into gases and liquids, which then seep into the ground.

setback—The distance from a lot line to the point where a building, fence or other improvement may be built.

settlement—The procedure in which title to real property is transferred from seller to buyer. All documents are executed, funds are disbursed and a complete accounting of all monies is made to both the buyer and the seller. Also called the closing.

settlement costs—Usually includes all the expenses over and above the price of a home that must be paid before the transfer of title.

settlement statement—A statement prepared at the time of closing giving a complete accounting of all monies involved in a real estate transaction. Separate settlement statements are prepared for the buyer and seller.

severalty—An estate in severalty is property owned by one individual.

shared appreciation mortgage—A mortgage plan in which one owner lives in a home and another owner is an investor. They agree to share the costs, responsibilities and benefits of ownership according to a predetermined plan.

single-family detached—A term used to describe a one-family house on its own lot.

site—A general term for a plot of land suitable for a specific use.

situs—Place, location.

slab—A concrete floor in a home without a basement. The concrete floor or slab is also the foundation of the building.

special assessment—1. A lien placed on real property to pay for public improvements, such as sewer systems, sidewalks or streets, that directly benefit the property. 2. A fee levied against condominium or townhouse owners to cover unexpected or new expenses.

specific performance—A clause in a contract that allows either the buyer or the seller to take legal action to force compliance with the contract by the defaulting party.

sprinkler system—1. A system of water pipes in the ceilings of high-rise buildings to be used in case of fire. 2. A system of pipes under a lawn used for watering grass, shrubbery, etc.

statute of frauds—State law requiring that certain contracts be in writing. All contracts for the sale of real estate must be in writing.

straight line depreciation—The simplest method of depreciation that reduces the basis of a property by an equal amount each year. Usually not the best method of depreciation to use for residential property.

"subject to" clause—A clause stating the new buyer acknowledges the existing mortgage or deed of trust and takes title "subject to" it. The original mortgagor remains responsible for any deficiency should there be a foreclosure of the mortgage. This differs from an assumption clause whereby the new buyer "assumes and agrees to pay" the existing mortgage.

subordination agreement—An agreement in writing that allows one lien to take a lesser position to another. A subordination agreement is often used so a construction loan can be given priority over a loan on vacant land.

subsurface rights—Rights to oil, gas or other minerals under the surface of the land. The owner of the land may or may not own subsurface rights.

sump pump—A pumping device used to remove water from around and under a basement or within a crawl space in order to keep the area dry.

survey—A document showing the boundaries of a parcel of land, its area, improvements, easements and sometimes topography.

sweat equity—A program that allows a purchaser to do work on the property in place of all or part of the down payment.

take out loan—A permanent, long-term mortgage for real estate after construction is completed.

tax base—The assessed value of real property. This figure is multiplied by the tax rate to determine the amount of tax due.

tax lien—1. A property tax lien for nonpayment of taxes attaches only to the property upon which taxes are unpaid. 2. A federal income tax lien may attach to all property owned by the person owing the taxes.

tax roll—The county list describing each parcel of property, the owner, the assessed value and the tax amount.

tax shelter—A general term referring to any income tax advantages to which the owner of property may be entitled.

tenancy in common—Undivided ownership of real property by two or more persons. Ownership rights need not be equal and there are no rights of survivorship.

tender—Money, services or something else of value offered in connection with a contract.

term—1. A period of time. 2. The length of time, usually expressed in months or years, over which a loan is amortized.

terminate—To end or stop.

termite—A small insect, similar to an ant, that eats wood and may cause substantial damage to buildings made of wood.

termite inspection—An inspection, often required by law, to determine the presence of termites and the extent of damage, if any.

terms—The considerations, other than price, in a contract, such as the way payments will be made, which items will be prorated, when possession will be given, etc.

third party—A general term referring to anyone not a party to a contract or agreement.

"time is of the essence" clause—Clause that binds each party to performance on or before the time(s) specified in the contract. If one party does not perform according to the specified time(s) the other party may consider the contract in default.

title—1. Ownership. 2. The evidence one has of rights of ownership; most often it is a title insurance policy.

title commitment—A report showing the condition of the title before a sale. The title commitment also states the terms and conditions that must be met before a title insurance policy will be issued.

title insurance—Insurance against loss resulting from claims and defects of title. Insurance is for a specifically described piece of real property.

title search—The systematic review of all recorded documents to determine the condition of title to a specific parcel of real property.

torrens title system—A title system still used in some areas. Title is registered with a registrar of land titles instead of being recorded.

townhouse—1. A legal term used to describe a type of real property. Individual fee ownership of the entire townhouse structure (there may be party walls) plus at least the land directly under it, as well as an interest in the common elements if the townhouse is part of a complex. This differs from a condominium, which is ownership of an air space living unit and an interest in the common elements. 2. A general term describing a style of home, usually an attached row house two or more stories high.

tract—A parcel of land. A subdivision.

tract house—One of many similar houses built in a subdivision using the builder's plans.

transfer tax—A state tax on the transfer of real property. It can range from a few dollars to hundreds of dollars, depending on the laws of the state in which the property is located. Also called a documentary fee.

triplex—One building that has three separate living units.

trust deed—See **deed of trust.**

trustee—One who holds the title to real property under the terms of a deed of trust.

undivided interest—Ownership of part of an entire property that cannot be divided or separated. The interest each owner holds need not be equal.

unencumbered—Free and clear ownership. There are no liens on the property.

unit—Common name given to one home or living unit in a subdivision or a condominium, townhouse or cooperative complex.

unit deed—A name sometimes given to the instrument that transfers title to a condominium.

unities—Unities of time, title, interest and possession are the necessary conditions for a valid joint tenancy. The joint tenants must acquire equal interest in the property at the same time, by the same conveyance or document, and under the same title. Also, joint tenants must have equal rights to possession.

unmarketable title—Not salable. A title with such serious defects that a prudent buyer would not purchase the property.

unrecorded instrument—A mortgage, deed, etc., that is not recorded in the office of the county recorder and not protected under recording statutes. An unrecorded instrument may be valid between the parties involved but not against innocent third parties.

usury—Charging an illegal rate of interest on a loan.

valid—Legally binding. Done in accordance with legal procedures.

VA loans—Mortgage loans made by institutional lenders and guaranteed against default by the Department of Veterans Affairs. These loans, available to eligible veterans, have favorable terms and conditions.

value—The usefulness or worth of something. The benefits the buyer will receive.

variable rate mortgage—See **adjustable rate mortgage.**

verify—To confirm or prove to be true.

vested interest—Ownership rights at the present time.

void—Not binding. Having no legal form.

voidable—Can be made void but not void in itself.

voluntary lien—A lien placed on the property by the voluntary act of the owner, such as a mortgage loan.

VRM—Variable rate mortgage. See **adjustable rate mortgage.**

waive—To knowingly and willingly give up or surrender a right, benefit or claim.

waiver—A written instrument stating that a right, benefit or claim is being surrendered voluntarily.

warrant—1. To legally guarantee that the title being transferred is of good quality. 2. To legally assure that the physical condition of a property is as represented.

warranty—A legally binding written instrument by which the seller guarantees the property is or shall be as represented.

warranty deed—The deed used in many states to transfer title to real property. The grantor guarantees the quality of the title to the grantee.

water rights—The rights of an owner of real property to the use of certain water. Water rights may run with the land or be transferred separately without land, depending on state laws.

water table—The depth below the surface of the land at which natural underground water is found.

wear and tear—The loss of value or the deterioration of a property due to normal and reasonable use.

without recourse—Wording to protect against personal liability. In the event of a default, a mortgage or deed of trust securing a note without recourse allows the investor to look only to the property for repayment.

wrap-around mortgage—A junior mortgage with a face value greater than the first mortgage (and possibly other junior mortgages) that it secures. The mortgagee under the wrap-around collects the payment, and then from this amount, makes the payment on the first mortgage or, in the case of more than one wrap, on the most previous wrap.

yield—The income earned on an investment. Yield is usually expressed as a percent: the ratio of income from an investment to the total cost of the investment.

zero lot line zoning—The authority to construct a home on a boundary line of a lot without the usual set back. This allows for better use of small lots.

zoning—Authority given a local government to control and determine the use of land.

Index